JOHN STEINBECK'S RE-VISION OF AMERICA

Louis Owens

JOHN STEINBECK'S
RE-VISION OF AMERICA

The University of Georgia Press
Athens

© 1985 by the University of Georgia Press
Athens, Georgia 30602
All rights reserved

Designed by Sandra Strother Hudson
Set in Linotron 202 Meridien and Gill Sans Bold display
The paper in this book meets the guidelines for
permanence and durability of the Committee on
Production Guidelines for Book Longevity of the
Council on Library Resources.

Printed in the United States of America
89 88 87 86 85   5 4 3 2 1

Library of Congress Cataloging in Publication Data

Owens, Louis.
John Steinbeck's re-vision of America.

Includes bibliographical references and index.
1. Steinbeck, John, 1902–1968—Criticism and
interpretation. I. Title. II. Title:
John Steinbeck's re-vision of America.
PS3537.T3234Z785 1985   813'.52   84-8609
ISBN 0-8203-0736-X (alk. paper)

Portions of this book are based on the following
previously published articles by Louis Owens:
"Steinbeck's 'Mystical Outcrying': *To a God Unknown* and
Log from the Sea of Cortez" and "*The Wayward Bus:* A
Triumph of Nature," both published in *San Jose Studies;*
and "Steinbeck's 'Flight': Into the Jaws of Death,"
"Steinbeck's 'The Murder': Illusions of Chivalry," and
"The Threshold of War: Steinbeck's Quest in *Once There
Was a War*," published in *Steinbeck Studies.*

For Polly

The new eye is being opened here in the west—
the new seeing.

JOHN STEINBECK

CONTENTS

Contents

PREFACE

John Steinbeck occupies a problematic position in American letters. One of America's and the world's most beloved and popular writers almost from the beginning of his career in the early thirties, Steinbeck has never been warmly embraced by America's critical establishment. As a recent review pointed out, seeming to damn with very faint praise, while Steinbeck's fiction is consistently taught in America's secondary schools, he has yet to penetrate the gleaming halls of academe with much success. In the politicized thirties, when his reputation was fixed, Steinbeck's critical reception undoubtedly suffered from the fact that he was too easily and often simplistically labeled "proletarian." In addition, Steinbeck's stories of migrants, fruit-tramps, and social dropouts, while reinforcing the proletarian identification, seemed too far from the mainstream of Modernism to excite many critics, critics who failed to recognize Steinbeck's debt to T. S. Eliot, Jessie Weston, and Sir James Frazer. And still today critics and academics are prone to take the facile approach to Steinbeck's fiction, parroting the familiar, and by now quite hackneyed, accusations that Steinbeck's work is naïve, sentimental, and unfortunately romantic.

The aim of this study is to suggest that we need to take another and closer look at Steinbeck's fiction, and that such a scrutiny may show Steinbeck to be a craftsman and artist of the first rank in American literature.

I have elected to focus here on Steinbeck's major works, excluding, perhaps somewhat arbitrarily, such novels as *Cup of Gold*, *Burning Bright*, *The Moon Is Down*, and *The Short Reign of*

Pippin IV, among others. These and other unmistakably minor works might well lend themselves to another study but are outside the range of this one. While my focus here is certainly upon those Steinbeck works set in California—nearly all of his best work—my rubric expands (again, perhaps somewhat arbitrarily) to include such non-California works as *The Pearl* and *The Winter of Our Discontent,* both important, if flawed, works. In keeping with the California focus of Steinbeck's thought and writing, I have departed from the usual chronological approach to examine Steinbeck's work as it falls into the topographical divisions discussed in my introduction. Through such an organization, I hope to suggest a broader unity and thematic design both within individual works and in Steinbeck's fiction as a whole, a design which has been consistently ignored or underrated by Steinbeck's critics.

I am pleased to have the opportunity here to offer thanks and acknowledgment to Jim Woodress for his unfailing insight and support, to Peter Hays and Jack Hicks for their time and invaluable perceptions, to Del Kehl for introducing me to Steinbeck studies, and especially to Tetsumaro Hayashi for his encouragement during the past several years. Finally, the ultimate acknowledgment must go to my wife, Polly, for everything.

I am grateful to the editors of the *Steinbeck Quarterly, San Jose Studies,* and the *Arizona Quarterly* for allowing me to include here versions of or excerpts from articles on "Flight," *To a God Unknown* and *The Log from the Sea of Cortez, The Wayward Bus, Tortilla Flat, The Pastures of Heaven,* "The Murder," and *Once There Was a War* which have appeared in those journals.

In addition, I would like to extend my deep appreciation to the talented and dedicated secretarial staff of the Department of English at California State University, Northridge: Mary Alvarez, Alice Allen, Lupe Bailey, Bobbie Coleman, Patti Hoffpauir, and Carol Nadler, who have seen this manuscript through numerous revisions and in the process have never lost their equanimity nor their celebrated senses of humor.

NOTE ON EDITIONS CITED

Citations of Steinbeck's works in the text refer to the following editions:

Cup of Gold. New York: Robert M. McBride, 1929.

The Pastures of Heaven. New York: Viking Press, 1932.

To a God Unknown. New York: Covici-Friede, 1933.

Tortilla Flat. New York: Grosset and Dunlap, 1935.

In Dubious Battle. New York: Viking Press, 1936.

Of Mice and Men. New York: Viking Press, 1937.

The Long Valley. New York: Viking Press, 1938.

The Grapes of Wrath. New York: Viking Press, 1939.

Cannery Row. New York: Viking Press, 1945.

The Pearl. New York: Viking Press, 1945.

The Wayward Bus. New York: Viking Press, 1947.

The Log from the Sea of Cortez. New York: Viking Press, 1951.

East of Eden. New York: Viking Press, 1952.

Sweet Thursday. New York: Viking Press, 1954.

The Winter of Our Discontent. New York: Viking Press, 1961.

Journal of a Novel. New York: Viking Press, 1969.

Steinbeck: A Life in Letters. Edited by Elaine Steinbeck and Robert Wallsten. New York: Viking Press, 1975.

INTRODUCTION

Monterey County in northern California is Steinbeck Country, a region dominated by the long sweep of the Salinas Valley with its subterranean river and opposing ranges of mountains—the rolling Gabilans to the east and the darker, rugged Santa Lucias to the west. To the east Steinbeck Country extends across the Gabilans into the Great Central Valley, and in the west it drops from the flanks of the Santa Lucias into the Pacific Ocean. From this intricately textured landscape came the settings, the themes, the symbols of Steinbeck's greatest fiction. In this part of California, Steinbeck found the resources necessary for a life's work; when he left this country, as critics have often noted, he left behind not only these resources but his greatest work as well.

In a ledger note in 1929, as he was deeply involved in the creation of what would eventually be *To a God Unknown*, Steinbeck wrote, "The new eye is being opened here in the west— the new seeing. It is probable no one will know it for two hundred years."[1] Steinbeck's California fiction—all of his finest work—represents a lifelong attempt to open this "new eye," to awaken America to the failure at the heart of the American Dream and provide an alternative to that dream. The "new seeing" Steinbeck proposed would exchange the myth of an American Eden, with its dangerous flaws, for the ideal of commitment—commitment to what Steinbeck called "the one inseparable unit man plus his environment."[2] In nearly every story or novel he wrote, Steinbeck strove to hold the failed myth up to the light of everyday reality and to stress the necessity for commitment to place and to man as a way out of the wasteland defined by writers of the twenties.

While critics have with rare exception recognized the centrality of California in Steinbeck's writing, no one has yet taken a close look at the various parts that make up so-called Steinbeck Country or examined the impact of Steinbeck's acute sense of California's position on the American continent and in the American consciousness. Richard Astro summed up this failing in Steinbeck criticism when he stated in 1977, "We have really said very little about the importance of his sense of place; certainly we have rarely moved beyond general statements about his love for the landscape and the people of his native California."[3]

When John Steinbeck wrote in 1953 that "a man has only a little to say and he says it over and over so it looks like a design" (*Life in Letters*, pp. 474–75), he spoke with great accuracy about his own writing, but critics have almost universally missed the "new eye" Steinbeck tried so determinedly to open, and they have thus missed the design—unintentional or not—of his life's work. Such a blindness has led one critic to lament that "Steinbeck fails totally to confront that Americanism to end all Jeffersonian Americanisms—the frontier thesis. . . . Steinbeck offers not the slightest recognition of the falseness of the Eldorado of the West."[4] Such a statement overlooks the crucial fact that from the youthfully awkward *To a God Unknown* to *East of Eden* two decades later, Steinbeck again and again in short story and novel held the dangers of the westering myth up to view and offered in its place an ideal of commitment. Though he follows closely in the path of Frederick Jackson Turner in his recognition of the power of the westering pattern to shape the American consciousness and American reality, unlike Turner, Steinbeck saw no cornucopia of democracy in the retreating frontier, but rather a destructive and even fatal illusion barring Americans from the realization of any profound knowledge of the continent they had crossed.

4

Frederic Carpenter and other critics have pointed convincingly to Steinbeck's place in the Jefferson-Emerson-Whitman mainstream of American thought.[5] Others, most particularly Astro, have detailed Steinbeck's debt to the ideas of his close friend the marine biologist Edward F. Ricketts and, before Ricketts, of William Emerson Ritter, as well as to the philosophies of Briffault, Boodin, and Jan Smut.[6] No one has yet recognized clearly, however, that behind Steinbeck's holistic philosophy, his "phalanx" theory, his non-teleological thinking, his agrarianism, his mixture of Christianity and paganism, lies a profound fascination with and acute sensitivity to California's place in the American consciousness—an awareness of California as the literal and symbolic terminus of the American Eden myth. Steinbeck's overriding sense of this California quality, and of marked symbolic divisions within the landscape he wrote of, was of central importance in shaping the themes and providing the symbols and imagery of his fiction.

California in the work of John Steinbeck looms large as the final barrier to the Great Migration, the archetypal American quest which began beyond the Atlantic and ended only at the edge of the Pacific. In Steinbeck's fiction, the American myth, with its Old Testament reverberations, and the Quest of the Arthurian legends with which he had a lifelong fascination become one impulse pushing toward the Garden of the West. Poised on the edge of the continent, at the end of what had for centuries seemed an endless unraveling of new world, Steinbeck undertakes a careful, painstaking examination of the land that constitutes this supposed Eden, of the land's effects on those who inhabit it, and of the myth that Americans have pursued across a continent. Involved in this examination is the most scrupulous study offered in American literature of the values imparted by the quest for an illusory Promised Land—what Annette Kolodny has aptly termed the "stylized sequences of recurrent movements westward once the initial idyll has been . . . disrupted"[7]—and of the religious impulses underlying that quest. Beginning with *To a God Unknown* in 1933, Steinbeck rejects the Eden myth and the formal religion upon which it is based, offering in its place an ideal of commitment to "the whole thing," to "all reality, known and unknowable" (*The Log from the Sea of Cortez*, pp. 216–17). His study of man's religious impulses takes him, in *To a God Unknown*, to the very beginnings of Western religion as they are outlined in Sir James Frazer's *The Golden Bough*, and it leads him to reject repeatedly the American vision of California as Promised Land.

What is commonly called Steinbeck Country divides into four closely related and interdependent yet distinct realms with differing thematic and symbolic significance in Steinbeck's writing. These realms are the valleys, large and small, such as the great Central Valley, the Salinas Valley, the Jolon Valley (Nuestra Señora in *To a God Unknown*), and the Corral de Tierra (the Pastures of Heaven); the gentle hills called the Gabilans, which border the eastern edge of the Salinas Valley; the Santa Lucias, which cut the valley off from the sea; and, finally, the Pacific Ocean, which cuts at the edge of Steinbeck Country and marks the boundary of the westering experience. The eastern hills are closely identified in Steinbeck's writing with a strong life-force, while the western mountains are heavily symbolic of death and the unknown. Valleys in Steinbeck's fiction are invariably fallen Edens where the myth of the American Eden is treated with heavy irony. The key to these valleys is the word *timshel* of *East of Eden:* "thou mayest."

While Steinbeck's interest in marine biology and his relationship with Ricketts have been thoroughly examined, particularly in Astro's *John Steinbeck and Edward F. Ricketts: The Shaping of a Novelist*, attention has been focused almost exclusively on the influence of the sea on Steinbeck's holistic and biological view of man and his environment. Though this holistic philosophy, and the non-teleological thinking that Steinbeck and Ricketts associated with it, is of great importance to the overall thematic scope of Steinbeck's work and to his "religion" of commitment, equally important in Steinbeck's fiction is the idea of the sea as both a symbol of the unconscious and the realm just outside the so-called American Eden, the cut-off point of known experience and the final barrier to the questing or westering impulse. Jody Tiflin's grandfather sums up this aspect of the ocean in Steinbeck's fiction when, in "The Leader of the People," he says, "There's no place to go. There's the ocean to stop you. There's a line of old men along the shore hating the ocean because it stopped them" (in *The Long Valley,* p. 303). Those characters who live close to the sea, on Cannery Row or Tortilla Flat, are touched by it; living on the edge of the continent, they are marginal Americans. They exist on the edge of an ironic Eden and they repudiate the American Dream.

Richard Slotkin has pointed out that "within the body of European myths about America were two antagonistic pre-Columbian conceptions of the West: the primitive belief in the West as the land of sea, the sunset, death, darkness, passion, and dreams; and the counterbelief in the West as the Blessed Isles, the land of life's renewal, of rebirth, or reason and a higher reality."[8] Within Steinbeck's fiction these two conceptions, or myths, find their embodiment in the western mountains and sea—realms of death, the unknown, the unconscious—and in the valleys—the lodging place of the American Eden. At the same time, this opposition within Steinbeck's symbolic topography evokes another, closely related, tension deeply embedded in the American heritage: what Kolodny has recognized as the unresolvable conflict between America's yearning for a pastoral New World paradise and the increasing awareness throughout American history that violation and despoliation are an "inevitable consequence of human habitation."[9] Kolodny's perception of the opposed metaphorical male/female principles in this pastoral paradox (the land as mother/virgin, man as sheltered son and violator) casts valuable light on the opposition within Steinbeck's fiction of the intensely feminine and fecund eastern hills with the monolithic and masculine "stone mountains" of the west. In keeping with his rejection of the desired directionality of the American Dream, Steinbeck's landscape reverses the directionality of this metaphor: in his fiction west represents not unending pastoral possibilities of land as mother/virgin-bride, but rather terminus and death. It is to the east that we must turn in Steinbeck's writing, to the feminine and sensual eastern hills, in order to discover a strong life-force and the promise of life. In the tension between these opposed realms, Steinbeck's California fiction encapsulates the central historical tension within the American psyche, recognizes the irreconcilable quality of this tension, and offers a solution, a way out. Though he did not always achieve the artistic craftsmanship of *The Grapes of Wrath* or the clarity of the shorter novels (*In Dubious Battle, Tortilla Flat, Of Mice and Men, Cannery Row*), Steinbeck's entire body of fiction nonetheless represents a single-minded attempt to come to grips with the idea of America, an attempt comparable in its intensity and scope to that of such great predecessors as Melville, Hawthorne, and James.

I.

THE MOUNTAINS

John Steinbeck grew up between the Gabilan Mountains on the eastern edge of the Salinas Valley and the austere Santa Lucias to the west. In the opening pages of *East of Eden*, Steinbeck explained his childhood reaction to these two ranges of mountains, a reaction that would have a powerful effect on much of Steinbeck's writing:

> I remember that the Gabilan Mountains to the east of the valley were light gay mountains full of sun and loveliness and a kind of invitation, so that you wanted to climb into their warm foothills almost as you want to climb into the lap of a beloved mother. They were beckoning mountains with a brown grass love. The Santa Lucias stood up against the sky to the west and kept the valley from the open sea, and they were dark and brooding—unfriendly and dangerous. I always found in myself a dread of west and a love of east. Where I ever got such an idea I cannot say, unless it could be that the morning came over the peaks of the Gabilans and the night drifted back from the ridges of the Santa Lucias. It may be that the birth and death of the day had some part in my feeling about the two ranges of mountains. (p. 1)

As this statement makes obvious, the eastern mountains in Steinbeck's fiction represent the known, safe world, while the western mountains are a land of death. To enter the Santa Lucias is to confront death in one form or another—there is no exception to this in Steinbeck's fiction. Death in these mountains, however, is not simply an end; it is a transcendent experience in which one may achieve a new world-vision and become recognizably and even consciously a part of the "whole" which is unknowable except by "being it, by living into it" (*Log*, p. 148).

To a God Unknown: Steinbeck's "Mystical Outcrying"

In *To a God Unknown* (1933), we encounter Steinbeck Country for the first time. Steinbeck's first novel, *Cup of Gold* (1929), had traced an exotic, fictionalized account of the life of the buccaneer Henry Morgan from Wales to Panama. *To a God Unknown*, Steinbeck's second novel, documents Joseph Wayne's doomed struggle to establish a dynasty on the flanks of the California coast range, the Santa Lucias. In the course of this novel Joseph, in an action prefiguring "Flight," *The Red Pony*, and *The Pearl*, will climb into the heart of these mountains to die.

Perhaps derived originally from *The Green Lady*, an unfinished play by Steinbeck's close friend Webster Street,[1] *To a God Unknown* is set in the valley of Nuestra Señora, a valley nearly enveloped by the western mountains: "Two flanks of the coast range held the valley of Nuestra Señora close, on one side guarding it against the sea, and on the other against the blasting winds of the Salinas Valley" (p. 4). The product of a writer still attempting to find his voice and master his tools, *To a God Unknown* is a difficult and admittedly awkward novel, and it is at the same time indispensable to an understanding of Steinbeck's work as a whole. In this remarkably complex novel, Steinbeck's obsession with Arthurian and Judeo-Christian materials, his fascination with non-teleological thinking, and his acute sense of California as place become welded into an intricate religious statement, one that stresses commitment and points directly toward such a major later work as *The Grapes of Wrath*.

Though published in 1933, after *The Pastures of Heaven*, *To a God Unknown* had been in progress for approximately five years.[2] At first glance, this novel seems a confused mixture of pagan nature worship, Christianity, Grail Quest, and non-teleological thinking—that philosophy which would replace an interest in final causes with an acceptance of what simply "is." Joseph Wayne, the protagonist, appears at various times to be an awkward blend of Christ and fisher-king, teleological savior and non-teleological visionary. The result of this seeming uncertainty on Steinbeck's part has been that *To a God Unknown* is consistently the least understood of Steinbeck's novels and one of the most consistently maligned by critics. However, once Steinbeck's central point and complex method have been recognized in this novel, the seeming confusion disappears and the often-criticized disjuncture between theme and structure becomes insignificant. What has been termed "an impossible series of checks and balances"[3] displays, on the contrary, a remarkable unity.

At the beginning of *To a God Unknown,* Joseph yearns to become part of the westering movement, to join the trek from east to west. He tells his father, "I have a hunger for land of my own, sir. I have been reading about the West and the good cheap land there" (p. 3). In a scene reverberating with echoes of the Old Testament, Joseph receives his patriarch-father's blessing before he leaves:

"Come to me, Joseph. Put your hand here—no, here. My father did it this way. A custom so old cannot be wrong. Now, leave your hand there!" He bowed his white head, "May the blessing of God and my blessing rest on this child. May he live in the light of the Face. May he love his life." He paused for a moment. "Now, Joseph, you may go to the West. You are finished here with me." (p. 3)

Soon after Joseph makes the archetypal American journey, migrating from Vermont to the valley of Nuestra Señora, his father dies and his three brothers, with their families, join him on the new ranch. At first the ranch appears to fulfill the promises of Eden and flourishes in the small valley and the foothills of the coast range, but within a short time Joseph is forced to watch helplessly as a powerful drought reduces his animals and land to dry bones and dust. His dream of a dynasty withers, one brother is killed, Joseph's wife dies, and everyone but Joseph leaves the ranch and valley. Alone at the end, Joseph cuts his wrists and dies. Most of the novel is the story of Joseph's fierce but blind attempts to break the strength of the drought and save the wasted land.

Woven through the plot of Joseph's ill-fated attempt to settle in the coast range is a close scrutiny of man's religious impulses. As his name and novel's plot suggest, Joseph is easily identified with Joseph of Genesis, who preceded his people into Egypt. At the same time, Joseph may be identified with Joseph of Arimathea, recipient of the Grail and relative of the fisher-king of Frazer's *The Golden Bough* and Jessie Weston's *From Ritual to Romance*.[4] Christian and pagan allusions and symbols are carefully fused in *To a God Unknown* and woven into a single fabric. The most obvious example of this fusion would seem to be the novel's title, which alludes to the version of Rig-Veda 10:21 which Steinbeck chose for the book's epigraph and which asks, "Who is he to whom we shall offer our sacrifice?" In underscoring the novel's parallel Christian and pagan symbolism, critics have suggested further that the title might be intended to remind readers of the altar to the Unknown God which Paul found in Athens (Acts 17:23).[5] While such twin sources would underscore nicely the novel's Christian-pagan fusion, Steinbeck was unusually careful to distinguish his source. Writing to his publisher, Robert O. Ballou, he noted that the title "is taken from the Vedic hymns" and added, "I want no confusion with the unknown God of St. Paul" (*Life in Letters,* p. 66).

In spite of Steinbeck's careful distinction here between Christian and pagan sources, Joseph Wayne is closely identified throughout the novel with both Christ and the fisher-king. The central element in the fisher-king myths discussed by both Frazer and Weston is the belief that the well-being of the land is inextricably related to that of the fisher-king. Early in the novel Joseph Wayne accepts his own similar role and custodianship of the land, declaring, "It's mine . . . and I must take care of it" (p. 12), and later we find that "all things about him, the soil, the cattle and the people were fertile, and Joseph was the source, the root of their fertility" (p. 42). When the land appears to be dying, Joseph says, "I was appointed to care for the land, and I have failed" (p. 275). At the same time, Joseph is unmistakably associated with Christ. During their wedding Joseph's wife Elizabeth tries to envision Christ, and she finds that "He had the face, the youthful beard, the piercing puzzled eyes of Joseph" (p. 88). Still later, Joseph's hired hand, Juanito, looks at Joseph and sees "the crucified Christ hanging on His cross, dead and stained with blood" (p. 303). Joseph's role as Christ and his ultimate sacrifice are foreshadowed early in the novel: "Joseph moved into a shaft of light and spread his arms for a moment. A red rooster on the top of a manure pile outside the window looked in at Joseph, then squawked and retreated, flapping, and raucously warned the hens that something terrible would probably happen" (p. 47). Like the rooster that crows in the final section of *The Waste Land,* this is an allusion to the betrayal and Crucifixion, the ultimate symbol of Christian commitment. Finally, near the end of the novel, Father Angelo, the Catholic priest of the valley's mission, exclaims, "Thank God he [Joseph] has no will to be remembered, to be believed in . . . else there might be a new Christ here in the West" (p. 310).

The valley that Joseph inhabits is the haunt of Dionysus and perhaps even older vegetation deities. Originally a tree-god, according to Frazer, Dionysus might also be represented "sometimes as a goat and sometimes as a bull."[6] Thus, at one point Joseph sees a black cloud shaped like a goat's head emerging from beyond the western mountains, and responds by swearing, "I must maintain to myself that it was the goat. I must never betray the goat by disbelieving it" (p. 105); and later we learn that the father of Juanito's wife "had seen a fiery goat

15

crossing the Carmel Valley one night at dusk" (p. 140). In a mysterious grove above the ranch, Joseph discovers a strange altarlike rock. When Joseph first enters the sacred grove, he sees a "great black bull," one which is "hornless with shining black ringlets on his forehead," and a "long, black swinging scrotum" (p. 55). The goat and bull symbols represent not only Dionysus, god of vegetation and fertility, but an older deity which Weston calls the *Eniautos Daimon,* or "Luck of the Year," a being which "might assume the form of a bull, a goat, or a snake."[7]

Amidst this blending of Christian and pagan symbols, the chief symbol of Joseph's growing natural religion comes to be a great oak that shelters his house. After his father dies, Joseph comes quickly to believe that his father's spirit has begun to reside in the oak. He worships the tree and offers sacrifices to it throughout much of the book, until it is girdled and killed by his rigidly Christian brother, Burton. Before the oak is killed, Joseph believes that "his father's strong and simple being . . . had entered the tree" (p. 31). In worshipping the oak, Joseph is identifying his dead father with the ancient tree-spirits discussed in *The Golden Bough,* and he is moving back to the roots of Western religion, for, according to Frazer, "a god of the oak, the thunder, and the rain was worshipped of old by all the main branches of the Aryan stock in Europe, and was indeed the chief deity of their pantheon" (*The Golden Bough,* p. 184). At the same time, the oak can be identified with Zeus, a divinity of sky, rain, and thunder (p. 184), and with the Teutonic god of oak, who "was regarded as the great fertilising power, who sent rain and caused the earth to bear fruit" (p. 186).

Steinbeck skillfully introduces throughout the novel a complex of religious symbols and references, carefully blurring the distinctions between Christian and pagan because he is interested in working toward an isolation of the crucial impulse within man that underlies formal religions. His method is to set Joseph and all of his religious groping against a philosophical background of non-teleological thinking.

Steinbeck acquired his ideas concerning non-teleological thinking from Ed Ricketts. Steinbeck met Ricketts in 1930, while the extensive task of writing and revising *To a God Unknown* was in progress, and in 1940 the two men journeyed together on a zoological collecting trip to the Sea of Cortez. The results of this trip were published in 1941 as a collaboration by the two entitled *Sea of Cortez: A Leisurely Journal of Travel and Research*. A great deal of the philosophy found in the narrative portion of this book undoubtedly originated in the thoughts and notebooks of Ed Ricketts. There can be no doubt that Steinbeck was strongly influenced by Ricketts's thinking, however, and that, as far as *To a God Unknown* is concerned, Steinbeck identified with and assimilated much of Ricketts's non-teleological philosophy. Richard Astro suggests that

> in . . . *To a God Unknown* . . . the impact of the marine biologist's ideas on the novelist's fiction becomes apparent for the first time. And a careful examination of the facts concerning the composition of *To a God Unknown* suggests that by 1932 Steinbeck was already vitally interested in Ricketts' world-view—so much so, in fact, that he altered the entire thematic structure in revised versions of this philosophically crucial novel in accordance with the kind of thinking he and Ricketts were doing.[8]

Perhaps the greatest insight into what Steinbeck is attempting in *To a God Unknown* is contained in the definition of religion offered in the *Log*:

> And it is a strange thing that most of the feelings we call religious, most of the mystical outcrying which is one of the most prized and used and desired reactions of our species, is really the understanding and the attempt to say that man is related to the whole thing, known and unknowable. (pp. 216–17)

To a God Unknown is designed to demonstrate this belief, to show that underlying all religious symbols and all forms of religion is this one element: the attempt to say that man is a part of the "whole." The common element in all of the religious symbols and references that run through the book is sacrifice, finally self-sacrifice, for in sacrifice is found the ultimate statement of commitment to the earth and to man, to "all reality, known and unknowable."

The Log from the Sea of Cortez states: "Anything less than the whole forms part of the picture only, and the infinite whole is unknowable except by *being* it, by living into it" (p. 148). Throughout the novel, Joseph Wayne is seeing only parts of the picture, only fragments; his offerings hung on the oak or spilled on the earth, his sacrifice of a starving calf, even his own self-sacrifice are all only parts of an overall picture he is in the process of living into. Formal religion, whether it be Christianity or the primitive nature worship Joseph becomes increasingly involved in, represents something that must be transcended in *To a God Unknown*, and the key to this transcendence is commitment to the larger picture, to the "whole."

The Log from the Sea of Cortez also provides this definition of teleological thinking:

> What we personally conceive by the term "teleological thinking" . . . is most frequently associated with the evaluation of causes and effects, the purposiveness of events. . . . In their sometimes intolerant refusal to face the facts as they are, teleological notions may substitute a fierce but ineffectual attempt to change conditions which are assumed to be undesirable, in place of the understanding-acceptance which would pave the way for a more sensible attempt at any change which might still be indicated. (pp. 134–35)

It is clear that Joseph's actions throughout the novel represent precisely such "a fierce but ineffectual attempt to change conditions," conditions that he does not understand. In his fierce struggle to break the drought through his nature worship, Joseph is clearly acting in a teleological manner.

At the end of the novel, Joseph Wayne will sacrifice himself in order (as he mistakenly believes) to save the land, and in the final moments he will exclaim, "I should have known. . . . I am the rain" (p. 322). The picture in the *Log* of the "natural" men of northern Mexico throws an interesting light on Joseph's final moments:

> They [the Indians] seem to live on remembered things, to be so related to the seashore and the rocky hills and the loneliness that they are these things. To ask about the country is like asking about themselves. "How many toes have you?" "What toes? Let's see— of course, ten. I have known them all my life, I never thought to count them. Of course it will rain tonight, I don't know why. Something in me tells me I will rain tonight. Of course, I am the whole thing, now that I think about it. I ought to know when I will rain." (*Log*, p. 75)

This brief passage expresses the natives' intuitive awareness of their inextricable oneness with the "whole thing," their commitment to the earth and all of life, the same kind of commitment symbolized by the fisher-king. It takes Joseph Wayne a lifetime and finally a death to break through to a similar awareness.

According to Ricketts's and Steinbeck's definition, "non-teleological thinking concerns itself primarily not with what should be, or could be, or might be, but rather with what actually 'is'" (*Log*, p. 135). Teleological thinking, on the other hand, results from acting upon partial evidence, which is all we can see of the "overall pattern." It is a mistaken belief in cause-and-effect relationships, the kind of relationship that underlies all supplications to all gods, known or unknown. This is the kind of thinking which Joseph must grow out of in the course of *To a God Unknown*. In the overall pattern, "causality would be merely a name for something that exists in our partial and biased mental reconstructings. The pattern which it indexes, however, would be real, but not intellectually apperceivable because the pattern goes everywhere and is everything and cannot be encompassed by the finite mind or by anything short of life— which it is" (*Log*, p. 149). Christ dying for our sins, Adonis cast into the waves so that the earth might be renewed, Joseph cutting his wrist so that the rain will come—all of these are the result of "partial and biased mental reconstructings," a mistaken belief in causality.

Throughout the novel Steinbeck keeps his protagonist locked into a state of confused and misguided religious groping. While Joseph is attempting, in the tradition of the Vedic hymns and vegetation ceremonies, to influence the weather and break the destructive drought, Steinbeck takes pains to show that Joseph is blind to the realities of his situation. Critics have consistently misread this crucial aspect of the novel, seeing Joseph as a true "priest of nature" rather than a confused mystic. When Joseph first comes to the valley, he is told by the natives, Romas and Juanito, that the drought has come before, wasting the land and creating "hills like white ashes." This wasteland (reminiscent of that in *The Great Gatsby*) has come already "twice in the memory of the old men" (p. 23). Joseph flatly denies this cyclic reality, saying, "I don't like to think about it. It won't come again, surely" (p. 23). And later, Joseph tells his brother Thomas that he has heard about the dry years, but "something was wrong. They won't ever come again" (p. 50). Joseph's insistent denial of the realities of nature is important because it clearly undercuts the validity of his nature worship.

Early in the novel, Joseph's wife, Elizabeth, suggests the only way in which one may know the "infinite whole." As he is bringing her to the ranch for the first time, following their highly phallic entrance through the narrow cleft into the valley, Elizabeth tells Joseph, "There's a danger of being lost. . . . I thought I suddenly felt myself spreading and dissipating like a cloud, mixing with everything around me. It was a good feeling, Joseph. And then the owl went over, and I was afraid that if I mixed too much with the hills I might never be able to collapse into Elizabeth again" (p. 105). In this statement, Elizabeth foreshadows precisely what will eventually happen to Joseph. Elizabeth is afraid, but in the end it will be Joseph's ability, like the fisher-king and other vegetation deities, to sacrifice his indi-

20

vidual identity and commit himself completely to the "whole" that allows him to comprehend his unknown god.

Joseph's final transformation is foreshadowed even more explicitly in a scene following closely upon Elizabeth's death which provides an important perspective on Joseph's confused attempts to influence what he does not understand. After Elizabeth has fallen from the rock in the sacred grove and died, Joseph returns to their house and begins musing. His mind wanders in a half-sleep, and he thinks "in tones, in currents of movement, in color, in a slow plodding rhythm," until he is transformed:

> He looked down at his slouched body, at his curved arms and hands resting in his lap.
> Size changed.
> A mountain range extended in a long curve and on its end were five little ranges, stretching out with narrow valleys between them. If one looked carefully, there seemed to be towns in the valleys. The long curved range was clad in black sage, and the valleys ended on a flat of dark tillable earth, miles in length, which dropped off at last to an abyss. Good fields were there, and the houses and the people were so small they could be seen only a little. High up on a tremendous peak, towering over the ranges and the valleys, the brain of the world was set, and the eyes that looked down on the earth's body. It lay inert, knowing vaguely that it could shake off the life, the towns, the little houses of the fields with earthquake fury. . . . The world brain sorrowed a little, for it knew that some time it would have to move, and then the life would be shaken and destroyed and the long work of tillage would be gone. . . . The brain was sorry, but it could change nothing. It thought, "I will endure even a little discomfort to preserve this order which has come to exist by accident. . . ." But the towering earth was tired of sitting in one position. It moved, suddenly, and the houses crumbled, the mountains heaved horribly, and all the work of a million years was lost. (pp. 241–42)

In this complex, if somewhat clumsy, scene, Joseph has become a model of the overall pattern that "goes everywhere and is everything." The minuscule people of this dreamscape could

21

not be aware of the overall pattern called Joseph Wayne of which their little microcosm of valleys and fields is but a part, and thus they could not see the reason behind the apocalypse visited upon them. They could not see that, despite their overwhelming tragedy, the whole which is Joseph Wayne would simply go on as before. Perhaps if Joseph's reveries had continued, we might have seen survivors among the small people making sacrifices and offering prayers to an unknown god to be spared from future earthquakes. Like these little people, Joseph, as part of a greater pattern, cannot see beyond the immediate phenomenon of the drought.

As everyone is preparing to abandon the ranch and drive the remaining cattle to water outside the valley, Joseph and his brother Thomas journey over the crest of the western mountains—the Santa Lucias—for a glimpse of the sea. They meet an old man on the flanks of the coast range worshipping the setting sun and sacrificing small animals at the death of each day. The old man resembles one of the small people of Joseph's dreamscape: "The mountains sat with their feet in the sea, and the old man's house was on the knees" (p. 260). Like the little people, the old man could be shaken off his world at any moment. And like Joseph, the old man is involved in a form of nature worship, sacrificing blindly because he sees only one of the indices of the larger pattern—the setting sun. The old man has, however, gone a step farther than Joseph: he has abandoned causality. He is not attempting to appease a deity or affect the way things are; his sacrifices are simply his own intuitive "mystical outcrying," a statement of commitment. Eventually, the old man plans to sacrifice himself, and perhaps at the moment of self-sacrifice he, too, will recognize the unknown god of the novel.

Along with the mysterious old man by the sea, we encounter here our first "death by water" in this wasteland novel. Below the old man's house are "three little crosses stuck in the ground close to the cliff's edge." The old man tells Joseph that he had found three sailors, two dark and one light, washed up on the beach, and had buried them there. "The light one," he says, "wore a saint's medallion on a string around his neck" (p. 201). Nothing more is said about these drowned sailors, but in this scene Steinbeck has incorporated images of Christ and Calvary, the drowned sailor of *The Waste Land* and Frazer's drowned vegetation god, Adonis. Once again, Christianity has been carefully merged with the older vegetation ceremonies in a scene dominated by the theme of sacrifice.

Joseph fails to understand the lesson of the old man's sacrifices. He imitates the blood sacrifices when he cuts the throat of the shriveled calf, but he discovers that this has no effect on the drought. Though the old man lives in a land of perpetual moisture brought by the ocean fogs, there is no indication that his sacrifices have anything to do with this moisture. Joseph, however, in his desire to "free the waters," has been acting teleologically throughout the novel, and he misconstrues the meaning of the sacrifices here at the end. He kills the calf in the hope of bringing rain, and when this attempt apparently fails, he says, "His secret was for him. . . . It won't work for me" (p. 320). The old man's gestures were an attempt to say in ignorance that he is related to the whole, not an attempt to change or affect that whole. Joseph's misinterpretation of this fact is a sign of the confusion in which he is operating right up to the final moments of the novel.

When the death of the calf fails to bring rain, Joseph notices his own blood flowing from a scratch, and he realizes that he must give up the symbols and partial indices. He climbs to the top of the altar-rock and cuts his wrist, spreading his arms in the image of Christ. At the moment of self-sacrifice, he once again undergoes a metamorphosis echoing his earlier transformation:

> The sky was growing grey. And time passed and Joseph grew grey too. He lay on his side with his wrist outstretched and looked down the long black mountain range of his body. Then his body grew huge and light. It arose into the sky, and out of it came the streaking rain. "I should have known," he whispered. "I am the

rain." And yet he looked dully down the mountains of his body where the hills fell to an abyss. . . . He saw his hills grow dark with moisture. "I am the land," he said, "and I am the rain. The grass will grow out of me in a little while." (pp. 321–22)

Both Christ and fisher-king/vegetation god, in his moment of sacrifice Joseph has finally attained the intuitive awareness of his position in the "infinite whole" that Steinbeck attributed to the natives of northern Mexico in the *Log*. He is "spreading and dissipating like a cloud, mixing with everything" as Elizabeth unknowingly prophesied. He is *not*, however, a nature god bringing rain through self-sacrifice, as almost all critics have suggested; he is simply a man who has finally transcended his religious symbols and broken through to an apprehension of the underlying pattern in which "all things are one thing and that one thing is all things" (*Log*, p. 217). He has achieved the state which Joseph Campbell, in *The Hero with a Thousand Faces*, defines as "the hero as the incarnation of God . . . the navel of the world, the umbilical point through which the energies of eternity break into time."[9]

This final scene has created some confusion concerning *To a God Unknown*. Critics have often read Joseph's sacrifice as the cause of the rain that begins to fall and have viewed Joseph as a literal vegetation god. According to Astro, "Wayne is almost a literal Frazerian fisher-king."[10] And in a thorough Jungian reading of the novel, Robert DeMott finds that "Joseph's blood nourishes the moss at the center of the world, bringing rain that assures an end to the drought plaguing the land."[11] It is, in fact, tempting to read the novel in this way; it is even the new year, and thus the time of the dying-and-rising deity. It is important to realize, however, that Joseph's awareness that he is, ultimately, the rain, does not have to be interpreted as a belief on his part that his self-sacrifice has caused the rain. As the *Log* has informed us, causality has no place in the underlying pattern. In fact, Steinbeck has been very careful to insure that we do not see Joseph's self-sacrifice as a cause of the rain. He has with painstaking care undercut the causal relationship between the end of Joseph's life and the end of the drought. In doing this, he has denied the credibility of Joseph's nature worship.

Peter Lisca has pointed out that a pattern of "coincidences" forces the book to end ambiguously.[12] We are informed early in the novel that the drought is cyclical; therefore, the drought is to be expected and is not permanent. Joseph refuses to believe this. There have been signs of rain in the weather long before Joseph kills himself. There have been multiple sacrifices: Joseph killed the calf; Juanito has burned a candle; Father Angelo at the mission of Our Lady has prayed for rain—any of these may account for the rain in a teleological sense as easily as Joseph's death. We should also note that the bartender in town has promised to "set a barrel of whiskey in the road, free, if the rain would come tomorrow" (pp. 312–13), a powerful supplication to the unknown god.

Earlier in the novel, when Elizabeth slipped from the rock and died, a light rain began to fall. Critics have read this as a foreshadowing of the rain that falls when Joseph dies. The rain that falls upon Elizabeth's death has been carefully prepared for, however. We are told that there is a ring around the moon the night before her death, a traditional sign of coming rain; and there are clouds moving into the valley on the morning of her death, but when Elizabeth says, "Maybe there'll be rain to-night," Joseph replies, "It's only fog, Elizabeth" (p. 126). The sky has grown dark and the sun has vanished by the time Elizabeth has been "sacrificed" and the rain has come.

Signs in the weather are similar and even more abundant as Joseph's self-sacrifice draws near. Throughout the novel Joseph has refused to accept facts of nature, and here, near the end, he refuses to pay attention to the telling signs of nature all around him. When Juanito comes back to the grove before Joseph's death, Joseph asks him if he has seen any clouds and says, "It's so close to the new year, there might be clouds" (p. 299). It is the right time of the year for the rains to come, and Joseph is aware of this. On the way to visit Father Angelo, Juanito observes that "the wind is from the west." When Joseph repudiates this sign of rain (the ocean is just over the crest of the western mountains), Juanito says logically (and non-teleologically), "But sometime it must rain" (p. 306). After they have had dinner at Juanito's house, Juanito excitedly points out a ring around the moon, but Joseph refuses to accept the sign and quotes a saying, "In a dry year all signs fail" (p. 315). Joseph turns his back to the prophetic moon and rides toward the grove in the mountains. On the way back, he finds a dead cow, a symbol of the interrelatedness of life and nonlife: "Its hip was a mountain peak, and its ribs were like the long waterscars on the hillsides" (p. 317).

Joseph rides into the grove and ignores the obvious signs of approaching weather. The wind rages outside the grove as he kills the calf, and he does not even notice that "the sun [has] lost its brilliance and sheathed itself in thin clouds" (p. 320). Joseph is blinded to the immediate picture; at this point he is committed to a realization of the whole that can be attained only by total commitment, or "living into" it. Before he has climbed onto the rock and cut his wrist, the stage is set for the drought to be broken, the waters to be freed, and the wasteland of Nuestra Señora to be saved. Joseph's death has nothing to do with this phenomenon, and by introducing the unmistakable signs of changing weather, Steinbeck has asked us to view Joseph's sacrifice not as part of a cause-and-effect relationship but as the necessary culmination of the process of growing commitment that Joseph has been involved in from the beginning. When Joseph Fontenrose suggests that "we need not ask whether Joseph's rituals and sacrifices really affected the weather,"[13] he is missing the crucial meaning of the novel's climax. It is important that we realize that the sacrifices do not affect the weather, because causality has no part in the pattern Steinbeck is describing. Once the causal relationship has been denied, the

real importance of Joseph's self-sacrifice can be isolated: his sacrifice is nothing more than the ultimate statement of his commitment, the same commitment that is at the heart of all religious sacrifice, be it Christ or fisher-king, willing savior or
reluctant victim.

Richard Astro voices a common criticism of *To a God Unknown*
when he states that "Steinbeck lapses occasionally into sentimentality which results from the teleological role of savior he
assigns to a hero whose character is basically non-teleological."[14] Like Fontenrose, Astro has missed the real meaning of
Joseph's sacrifice and thus the central meaning of the novel.
Rather than lapsing into sentimentality, Steinbeck is very cal-
culating in his portrayal of Joseph as a would-be priest of nature
who fails consistently to see things as they really are. Until we
realize, in fact, that Joseph's confusion is carefully maintained
throughout the book, it is tempting to agree with Howard Levant that "the authorial indecision that presents Joseph, until
the last possible moment, as a confused mystic rather than a
convinced priest or god profoundly affects the credible presenta-
tion of nature worship." Rather than "authorial indecision,"
however, what Levant and others are reacting to is a brilliantly
sustained ambiguity that runs through the novel right up to
Joseph's final moments. In misreading this ambiguity, Levant
complains that "Steinbeck cannot resolve the structural problem presented by the fact that Joseph's self-awareness is limited
although it is the essential content of the novel."[15] Rather than
presenting a "structural problem," Joseph's "limited self-
awareness" contributes vitally to the thematic unity of this
novel. In missing this key element, critics have consistently underrated the craftsmanship of *To a God Unknown*. Despite the
obvious awkwardness and overwrought symbolism of this early
novel, within it Steinbeck has woven a tight tapestry of man's
religious history, from Christianity all the way back beyond the
legends of the Grail and fisher-king to Dionysus, Zeus, and older
deities. Joseph Wayne, who is a "repository for a little piece of

27

each man's soul, and more than that, a symbol of the earth's soul" (p. 121), moves through all of these aspects of man's religious consciousness toward an understanding of his total involvement with all of existence. In the end he achieves understanding because he is willing to make the ultimate and most elemental religious statement of all: self-sacrifice.

Though a much more ambitious and unified novel than critics have given it credit for being, *To a God Unknown* is not a great novel, nor, perhaps, a very good novel. It is a testing ground for the young novelist's strengths and weaknesses, an exploratory mission into the thematic landscape that would dominate Steinbeck's greatest fiction. Most important, out of the awkward symbolism of this novel emerged Steinbeck's great theme, the necessity for commitment—a theme that would be warped and woven through his life's work.

The failure of this first California novel—its wooden characterization and naïvely heavy-handed symbolism—is defined in Steinbeck's own description of its characters. In discussing these characters in a letter to his publisher, Robert O. Ballou, Steinbeck said, "They make no more attempt at being sincerely human than the people in the Iliad. Boileau . . . insisted that only gods, kings, and heroes were worth writing about. I firmly believe that. The detailed accounts of the lives of clerks don't interest me much, unless, of course the clerk breaks into heroism" (*Life in Letters,* p. 69). A year later, Steinbeck would write to a friend, George Albee, to say, "I am writing many stories now. Because I should like to sell some of them, I am making my characters as nearly as I can in the likeness of men. The stream underneath and the meanings I am interested in can be ignored" (*Life in Letters,* p. 94). The irony of Steinbeck's career is that he approaches greatness in his fiction only when his characters most approach a convincing "likeness of men." When the "stream underneath" flowed over the surface, he fell into the awkward symbolism and allegory that damaged and even destroyed his work, a failure we see in early and late creations like

To a God Unknown and *East of Eden.* When the stream obliterated all else, as it did in *Burning Bright,* the result was artistic disaster.

"Flight": Into the Jaws of Death

In *To a God Unknown,* Joseph Wayne's death in the western mountains led to a transcendent vision of his part in the "overall pattern" and a triumphant statement of commitment to that whole. In "Flight," a story that first appeared in *The Long Valley* (1938), Steinbeck takes us on a journey with Pepé Torres into the heart of the Santa Lucias, and we see these mountains transformed into a desolate realm where a man's ultimate triumph is to stand and accept a nameless, faceless, and inexorable death. In this story, life is at best a precarious and fleeting condition, and death is not an end but, as we saw in *To a God Unknown,* a transformation.

Critics have interpreted "Flight" as a "maturation myth,"[16] the tragedy of a Steinbeck "natural,"[17] and an allegory of man's emergence from "the primeval darkness."[18] It has been read as naturalistic[19] and as "escape from the world into primeval chaos."[20] In spite of this varied, and sometimes simplistic, critical response, however, critics have consistently ignored the meaning that the natural symbolism of the story seems to demand: that man is inextricably related to "all reality, known and unknowable." Equally central to the story is the often-overlooked emphasis that Steinbeck places on Pepé's courage in finally challenging the unknown (death) and in so doing achieving a kind of transcendence in the face of defeat.

Steinbeck introduces the idea of life's precariousness in the first sentences of the story. We are shown a picture of the Torres family farm buildings clinging to the rugged cliffs where the Santa Lucias enter the Pacific, "crouched low to the ground as though the wind might blow them into the sea" (p. 45). And we are told that Pepé's father "tripped over a stone in the field one

29

day and fell full length on a rattlesnake. When one is bitten on the chest there is not much that can be done" (p. 45). The lesson in these first few lines is that what we know as life is delicate, it can end suddenly and without warning, and the only control man can have over his death is the manner in which he accepts it. Indeed, "there is not much that can be done" except to accept death as a man. This is what Pepé must learn in the course of the story, what John Ditsky calls "the oldest of discoveries: to be a man is to know death."[21]

Pepé's flight is both away from death and toward death; it is Everyman's flight. He is forced by the death of another to flee in an attempt to save his own life, and his flight is directly toward death deep within the coast range. There is never any question that Pepé is journeying toward death. Rosy asks, "Where goes Pepé?" and Mama Torres answers, "Pepé goes on a journey. Pepé is a man now. He has a man's thing to do" (p. 53). As soon as Pepé is gone, Rosy tells Emilio, "He has gone on a journey. He will never come back." Emilio asks, cutting to the heart of the question, "Is he dead?" and Rosy answers prophetically, "He is not dead. . . . Not yet" (p. 55).

The theme of death is woven on a thread of blackness through the story. It is Pepé's black knife which initiates the cycle of death. When Pepé flees, he wears his dead father's black coat and black hat. It is the two "black ones," Rosy and Emilio, who prophesy Pepé's death. The line of gangrene running the length of Pepé's arm is black, foreshadowing his death, and it is the "dark watchers" who finally symbolize death itself. From the beginning of the story, Pepé grows increasingly dark, until in the end he will be black like the watchers.

Although Mama has warned Pepé to be wary of the "dark watchers," before he has journeyed beyond the first hill from the house Pepé has begun to resemble a dark one: "Before Pepé had gone a hundred yards, the outlines of his figure were misty; and long before he entered the canyon, he had become a gray, indefinite shadow" (p. 54). Pepé is being swallowed up by the

30

mountains (which, as we shall see, have teeth and are fully capable of devouring life): "When the gray shape of Pepé melted into the hillside and disappeared, Mama relaxed. She began the high, whining keen of the death wail" (p. 54). Mama is a non-teleological thinker; earlier she had told Pepé, "It is not good to have no medicine, for who knows when the toothache will come, or the sadness of the stomach. These things are" (p. 49), and now she has accepted Pepé's death as another thing that simply is; the death wail signifies this fact. Pepé is as good as dead once he enters the mountains, and Mama's concern is that he die like a man and not be caught "like a chicken."

As Pepé moves deeper into the mountains, the author's descriptions become increasingly surrealistic, suggesting images of desolation and death. The dry mountains become "eroding mountains" with "dead rocks and starving little black bushes" (p. 59). Upon the "waste of the mountainside . . . big outcroppings of unrotted granite" stand up "like mouldering houses" (p. 62). The coast-range landscape is beginning to resemble the "desolate cold aloneness" of the landscape within the Chinaman's eyes in *Cannery Row,* that landscape of "fantastic mountains shaped like cows' and dogs' heads and tents and mushrooms" (*Cannery Row,* p. 14). Pepé is being cut off from all humanity in the mountains. As in *Cannery Row,* the word seems to be altering the landscape, "a symbol and a delight which sucks up men and scenes, trees, plants . . . the Thing becomes the word and back to Thing again, but warped and woven into a fantastic pattern (*Cannery Row,* p. 8). Steinbeck is creating a psychic wasteland where the mountains begin to achieve a monstrous life of their own, where ridges become the "sharp backbone" of the monster, a monster with "jagged rotten teeth."

This ominous land of death is populated with the "dark watchers." John Antico suggests that these dark ones "symbolize the death that is in store for Pepé and . . . appear as premonitions of what is to come." Ditsky calls them "the walking dead of folk myth, whose company Pepé at last joins"—an interpretation difficult to support and without precedent elsewhere in Steinbeck's fiction.[22] These watchers have a more obvious though remote prototype in Steinbeck's first novel, *Cup of Gold*. In the conclusion to that fanciful novel, Steinbeck also populates the realm of death with strange figures. As Henry Morgan lies dying in the "immeasurable dark grotto" of Brother Death, he sees "strange beings, having the bodies of children, bulbous, heavy heads, but no faces. . . . Slowly the knowledge grew in him that these were his deeds and thoughts which were living with Brother Death" (pp. 266–67). The dark watchers of "Flight" are also faceless, but rather than representing Pepé's "deeds and thoughts," or being simply projections of his distressed imagination, they symbolize the pure idea of death. In *The Log from the Sea of Cortez*, Steinbeck wrote of "the low dark levels of our minds in which the dream symbols incubate and sometimes rise up to sight like the Old Man of the Sea" (p. 31). The dark watchers are "dream symbols" rising up to sight from the low dark levels of man's awareness of the death that awaits him. They are pure symbol, inhabiting the mountains that stand in Steinbeck's fiction as symbols of death and the unknown.

Steinbeck is careful to keep the posse that pursues Pepé on a nonhuman level. Throughout the story the pursuit remains faceless and nameless, represented by the neighing of a horse, the echoing thud of hooves on the trail, the whining yelp of hounds, and finally several rifle shots, one of which kills Pepé's horse, one of which wounds Pepé indirectly with a shard of granite, and one of which finally kills Pepé. It is important that the wound that Pepé first receives is inflicted by the mountains—it is a piece of the mountain that slices through Pepé's hand. The haunting death that follows Pepé remains the mysterious "unknown thing" that Jody senses in the mountains in "The Great Mountains"—the unknowable and abstract idea of death that pursues all living things. The "man's thing to do" with which Pepé is confronted from the first is the necessity of facing this unknown thing.

After Pepé is wounded, he moves under a "withered moon" deeper into the wasteland. In the process he loses his father's hat, coat, rifle, and horse; he is completely cut off from the past and cast into a state similar to that of the animals he encounters. He is so animalized that neither the wildcat nor the cougar he encounters shows any fear of him. By the end of the story Pepé is so animalized, in fact, that he has even lost the power of speech and can only make a hissing sound when he attempts to speak. John Antico sees this imagery as supporting his contention that Steinbeck is illustrating Pepé's emergence from primeval animal state into manhood in the final scene. While there can be no doubt that entering these mountains symbolizes a return from some form of civilization to a kind of primitivism, rather than emerging from the animal state, Pepé is obviously moving back into a more primitive state. He loses his possessions and becomes animalized for two less complex reasons. Steinbeck has stripped Pepé of the trappings of his father and of civilization because Pepé must face death nakedly, as man alone. In fact, Ditsky compares Pepé at this point to the near-naked Lear confronting the elements.[23] More important, however, Pepé has become like the animals because he is gradually becoming integrated into the whole that they represent; throughout the story Pepé is in the process of "dying into" nature.

From the vantage point of the "sharp backbone" of the ridge, Pepé looks across to what for him will be the final resting place, and sees that "at the top the jagged rotten teeth of the mountain showed against the sky" (p. 66). He descends to the intervening valley, and after being frightened from his muddy waterhole by the pursuit, he scrabbles desperately through the brush toward the next ridgetop. After struggling part of the night and then sleeping until dawn just one hundred feet below the summit, "in the gray light he struggled up the last slope to the ridge and crawled over and lay down behind a line of rocks" (p. 69). If we have retained the perspective Steinbeck provided of this ridgetop, we should be aware at this moment that Pepé has laid himself down behind the row of "jagged rotten teeth." And Stein-beck writes, "Below him lay a deep canyon exactly like the last. . . . And on the other side a sharp ridge stood up, thinly brushed with starving sage, littered with broken granite. Strewn over the hill there were giant outcroppings, and on the top the granite teeth stood out against the sky" (p. 69). It is plain to see at this moment that Steinbeck has led Pepé finally into the terri-ble jaws of death, surrounded by the two ridges with their op-posing rows of jagged rotten teeth. It is time for Pepé to die; he can go no farther. He will be taken back into the whole from which individual life emerges. The black buzzards, the func-tional teeth and digestive system of nature, begin to circle over-head even before Pepé is technically dead. Pepé will obviously share the fate of red pony and of Gitano and Old Easter, all of whom go into the Santa Lucias to die in *The Red Pony*—he will be devoured by the forces of death that operate in the dark mountains.

As he lies within this maw of death, Pepé undergoes an un-mistakable transcendence; Steinbeck writes: "The new day was light now. The flame of the sun came over the ridge and fell on Pepé where he lay" (p. 69). In this "new day," at the moment of death, Pepé achieves the ultimate expression of manhood by standing and facing death with what Peter Lisca calls "the calm and stoicism required by the highest conception of man-hood."[24] At this moment, he becomes a dark watcher: "He crawled slowly and mechanically to the top of a big rock on the ridge peak. Once there, he arose slowly, swaying to his feet, and stood erect. He braced his feet and stood there, black against the morning sky" (p. 70). From the "gray, indefinite shadow" that rode away from Mama Torres, Pepé has been transformed into a completely black watcher. He is dead, but he has triumphed, he has done "a man's thing." This is the triumph of which Stein-beck wrote in *East of Eden:* "Nearly all men are afraid, and they don't even know what caused their fear—shadows, perplex-ities, dangers without names or numbers, fear of a faceless death. But if you can bring yourself to face not shadows but real death, described and recognizable. . . . Then you will be a man set apart from other men. . . . Maybe this is the final purity all ringed with filth" (p. 22). This is also the triumph which will set Kino and Juana apart after their moment of truth in the dark mountains in *The Pearl.*

When Pepé is finally killed, the mountains send a small avalanche to cover his head. This avalanche has been subjected to a variety of interpretations, from a symbol of "innocence killed and buried in the moment that Man stands alone,"[25] to a merciful act on nature's part to cover up Pepé's deformed pointed head.[26] Perhaps Ditsky comes closest to Steinbeck's intention, however, when he says that "the earth, with a deliberate action . . . reclaims its own."[27] The avalanche symbolizes Pepé's return to the whole. When Pepé's face has been delicately covered by the mountain, he has ceased to be an individual; he has been accepted back into the "infinite whole," which is "unknowable except by *being* it, by living into it" (*Log,* p. 148). The living mountains and the dying Pepé are inseparable parts of this whole, reflecting the theme of man's oneness with nature that runs throughout Steinbeck's writing.

The Pearl: Shapes of Darkness

Once again, in *The Pearl,* first published in *Woman's Home Companion,* December 1945, Steinbeck takes us into a range of dark, desolate, and devouring mountains strikingly similar to those we encountered in "Flight," and once again the journey ends in an experience of death and transcendence. As it did for Joseph Wayne and for Pepé, the experience provokes a profound change, a new world-vision, and final triumph in the face of defeat.

The Pearl has generated more contradictory criticism than any other work by Steinbeck. It has been passed over lightly and

condemned as "defective" and a betrayal by such an esteemed
Steinbeck critic as Warren French; and it has been called a "triumph, a successful rendering of human experience in the
round" by another, Howard Levant.[28] As Sydney J. Krause has
pointed out in a succinct summary of *Pearl* criticism, the novel
"has been regarded on the 'black' side as defeatist, negativistic,
pessimistic, somber and pathetic, tragic, a study in futility, and a
rejection of the promise of salvation; while, on the 'white' side,
it has been taken as heroic, a rejection of naturalism, a re-estab-
lishment of the meaning of existence, a personal victory, and a
triumphant preparation for salvation."[29] The novel has been
read as a teleological parable[30] and as a non-teleological parable.[31] It has been called allegory and morality.[32]

In spite of the minor critical furor caused by this novel, critics
have paid surprisingly little attention to the key role of setting—
specifically the mountains—thematically and symbolically in
the novel.

It is likely that the mountains into which Kino and Juana flee
in *The Pearl* are modeled after a range of mountains that Steinbeck and Ricketts discovered during their expedition to the Sea
of Cortez. In *The Log from the Sea of Cortez,* Steinbeck recounts a
hunting trip for the elusive *borrego,* or bighorn sheep. Steinbeck
and Ricketts are invited by a rancher on the Mexican coast "to
go into the tremendous and desolate stone mountains to camp
and hunt" (p. 160). As they approach the rugged mountains,
they pass over a "rolling, rocky, desolate country . . . toward
the stone mountains, steep and slippery with shale" (p. 160).
The terrain leading to the base of the peaks is described as a
"fantastic" country, a term once again echoing the surreal description of the landscape within the Chinaman's eyes in *Cannery Row.* It is covered with "thorned bushes and trees" which
"crackled with heat," and "poison bushes." Once in the mountains, the party enters a "deep cleft in the granite mountains," a
cleft in which a tiny stream "fell hundreds of feet from pool to
pool" (p. 162). The resemblance between these mountains and

those in *The Pearl* is readily noted. However, these apparently real mountains quickly take on a nightmare quality beyond their natural desolation when we encounter them in the novel, and they come to represent a symbolic landscape much like that described in "Flight," a landscape within which Kino, like Pepé Torres in "Flight," must make his stand against the dark forces that pursue him. Like Pepé, Kino will make his stand within the very jaws of the mountains, and like Joseph Wayne in *To a God Unknown*, Kino will experience his rebirth of consciousness through an experience of death in a kind of *omphalos*—the stream at the heart of the world.

There are marked similarities between the stories of Pepé and Kino. Both of these characters begin their stories as "naturals"—Pepé as a bumbling child of nineteen and Kino as a naïve child of nature, completely unsophisticated—and both are closely identified with animals and undergo a process of dehumanization in the course of the stories. Both men lose the possessions of their fathers and virtually all possessions that tie them to civilization: Pepé loses his father's coat, hat, rifle, and horse, and Kino his house and, most important, his boat. Both Pepé and Kino kill a man and must flee because of this, and both kill as if by accident; Pepé's knife seemed to act of its own volition, and Kino has killed in darkness: "I was attacked in the dark . . . and in the fight I have killed a man. . . . It is all darkness—all darkness and shapes of darkness" (*The Pearl*, pp. 83–84). And, most important, though both men flee to the mountains instinctively to avoid death, it is death that they find there, and the experience makes Pepé a man and Kino, as we shall see, a man transcendent and set apart.

In "Flight" death and the impenetrable mystery of the western mountains are symbolized by the darkness that permeates the story, from Pepé's black knife to the dark watchers. In *The Pearl* darkness again symbolizes the experience of death that awaits Kino and Juana, but perhaps more significantly, darkness in this novel stands for the unknown that surrounds the

Indians, the unknown within which death is an integral factor. Our first knowledge of Kino comes in the first sentence of the novel: "Kino awakened in the near dark." In the state in which we meet him, Kino is more akin to the animal life that surrounds him than to the men who inhabit the town. His life consists of instinctive responses, responses embedded deeply within the collective unconscious of his people. He and Juana are the primal pair in the prelapsarian garden of their village, awakening to "a morning like other mornings and yet perfect among mornings" (p. 4). Though the first dawn of the story comes blindingly, Kino will soon begin a descent into darkness that will lead him ultimately into the total darkness of the climactic scene in the heart of the mountains.

Even before the pearl brings its threat into the book, darkness is an ominous force in this novel. Before Kino rises, for example, we are told that he covers his nose with his blanket to protect himself from "the dark poisonous air" of the night (p. 5). Later, we learn that Kino has his people's instinctive "fear of dark and the devils that haunt the night" (p. 90). After Kino has found the pearl, the threat of darkness grows as he sinks more deeply into his "dark night of the soul." His struggles with the evil forces all occur at night, and when his hut is burned he is forced to hide from the daylight in the darkness of Juan Tomas's house. As Kino is forced more and more to confront the unknown forces of darkness, he becomes increasingly a creature of the night. After he has killed the first "dark one," we are told that the "light made him afraid" (p. 82); and when Kino and Juana finally set off for the north, they leave "quietly in the dark." They travel at night until they are forced into the mountains, and the final scene of violence and death is acted out in darkness broken only by the rising moon.

Throughout the novel, the forces of darkness remain faceless and nameless. We are never told who or even what the shadows are that attack Kino or who has sent them, and, though we may speculate, we are not told why the dark ones pursue Kino and

Juana into the mountains. Kino's first attacker, within the hut, is described as a "dark thing" (p. 48), and when Kino is attacked the second time, we are told that "he could feel the dark creeping things waiting for him to go out into the night" (p. 72). Kino does dare to go out into the night, and when he has grappled with and killed something at last recognizably human, the body lies on the ground "with dark shiny fluid leaking from his throat" (p. 78). Joseph Fontenrose says of Kino's pursuers, "They are dark, never clearly seen, mysterious, as if Pepé's invisible pursuers in 'Flight' were one with the dark watchers."[33] In *The Pearl* the dark watchers have indeed become one with the pursuers; they represent the abstract evil that has fallen upon Kino, as if distilled from the "dark poisonous air" of the night which Kino feared from the beginning. When Kino dares to go out into the night, literally and symbolically, he is challenging the unknown, prodding dark fears into life as palpable and confrontable "things."

By dehumanizing the forces that attack Kino, Steinbeck also de-emphasizes causality and emphasizes what he and Ricketts called in the *Log* "the non-causal or non-blaming viewpoint" (p. 148). The mysterious threat that the dark figures represent from beginning to end in the novel is simply a stark fact with which Kino must come to terms once he has broken from the old order, once he has, in Juan Tomas's words, "defied not the pearl buyers, but the whole structure, the whole way of life" (p. 70). Steinbeck makes it clear that Kino has indeed isolated himself in a new realm of existence where he must face alone the forces which oppose him: "He had lost one world and had not gained another. . . . Kino had lost his old world and he must clamber on to a new one" (p. 69).

In accordance with this "non-causal or non-blaming viewpoint," Fontenrose has pointed out that "everything in *The Pearl* is in-between," that it is difficult to see only black and white, good and evil. Fontenrose suggests that "this is a non-teleological parable: This is the way things are."[34] If we try to affix the blame for Kino and Juana's situation, we find it to be very difficult. Is the threat to the family the result of the fact that Juana prayed for the pearl rather than directly for Coyotito's cure? Is it the result of the pearl buyers' attempts to cheat Kino or the fault of the unknown figure who rules these lesser men? Or is it Kino's fault for daring to defy the structure and disrupt the harmony of the "colonial animal" which is his people and village? We cannot trace a clear blame for Kino's fate to any specific cause or individual or group in the novel; the fate in store for Kino and Juana simply *is,* and Kino must grapple with it in the form of the dark pursuers. If he fails he, like Pepé, will perish; if he succeeds he will live and he will be greater than before. As it was for Pepé, Kino's struggle is the struggle of all men that Steinbeck defined in *East of Eden;* his antagonists are "shadows, perplexities, dangers without names or numbers . . . a faceless death." These shadows and perplexities, which exist in the darkness surrounding all of the Indians, become for an instant "described and recognizable" when Kino confronts them, and there can be little doubt that in the end Kino is "a man set apart from other men."

It is in the mountains that Kino must face his greatest test, and our first view of the mountains in *The Pearl* emphasizes their mystery: "A vision hung in the air to the north of the city—the vision of a mountain that was over two-hundred miles away, and the high slopes of this mountain were swaddled with pines and a great stone peak arose above the timber line" (p. 55). Like Elizabeth and Joseph in *To a God Unknown,* and like Pepé in "Flight," Kino and Juana flee instinctively toward the high place "as nearly all animals do when they are pursued" (p. 99). It is in the mountains that Kino will undergo a rebirth of consciousness precipitated by an overwhelming experience of death, and in this first view of the stone peak Steinbeck carefully juxtaposes an image of birth—"swaddled with pines"—with the image of death pervasive in his early writing, the stone mountains.

Steinbeck's description of the mountains into which Kino and Juana flee, though probably suggested by the mountains described in the *Log*, mirrors his description of the surreal coast range in "Flight." With phrases like "the naked granite mountains, rising out of the erosion rubble and standing monolithic against the sky" (p. 99), Steinbeck infuses the landscape with an atmosphere of foreboding. As in "Flight," there are "long outcroppings of granite" and "bare unmarkable stone," and, finally, there is the strong suggestion that, like Pepé, Kino and Juana and Coyotito may be devoured by the desolate mountains: "The sun moved downward toward the bare stone teeth of the mountains, and Kino set his direction for a dark and shadowy cleft in the range" (p. 102). Like Pepé, Kino is fleeing directly into the jaws of the mountains, and though Kino and Juana will survive, four lives will be left within these jaws.

The barren and ominous terrain mirrors Kino's inner desolation. Earlier, Kino has confessed that the pearl has become his soul, and in the mountains we are shown the corruption which has beset that soul:

> He looked into the pearl to find his vision. "When we sell it at last, I will have a rifle," he said, and he looked into the shining surface for his rifle, but he saw only a huddled dark body on the ground with shining blood dripping from its throat. And he said quickly, "We will be married in a great church." And in the pearl he saw Juana with her beaten face crawling home through the night. "Our son must learn to read," he said frantically. And there in the pearl Coyotito's face, thick and feverish from the medicine. (p. 94)

In this rather heavy-handed passage, the pearl reflects the real values of those things for which Kino has wished. The rifle can bring nothing but sorrow to Kino and his family—what need has a fisherman for a rifle? In the course of the novel, Kino receives a rifle and with it a crushing tragedy. Likewise, the desire for marriage in a "great church" is simply a value foisted upon the Indians by the church of the corrupt priest, a priest

41

who is an integral part of the system that oppresses and exploits the Indians without mercy. And finally, the image of Coyotito suffering from the doctor's trickery suggests that were Coyotito to become educated, he would become part of the system outside the unified whole of the village, that system represented by the corrupt priest, the doctor, and the pearl buyers.

Unfortunately, the question of Kino's desire for an education for Coyotito cannot be answered this simply, for it poses one of the central problems of the book: Is Kino justified in wanting a thing so different and so disruptive to the harmonious "whole" in which we find him in the opening pages of the novel? Or, in the end when Kino and Juana return to the village and repudiate the pearl and its values, are we to see this as a sign that Kino was wrong from the beginning? Howard Levant has suggested that Kino progresses from "personal and rather selfish desires . . . to wholly selfless, idealistic thoughts of sending Coyotito to school."[35] It is not quite so easy to distinguish between Kino's desires, however, for his desire for Coyotito's education is not completely selfless—through Coyotito's education Kino dreams of being freed from the grasp of the men in the town: "My son will read and open the books, and my son will write and will know writing. And my son will make numbers, and these things will make us free because he will know" (p. 33). Steinbeck helps his reader to resolve this dilemma, however, by making it unmistakably clear that Kino's desire to free himself and others from their entrapment is to be admired. There can be no doubt that Kino is trapped. When the doctor works his trickery on Coyotito, Kino suspects that it is a trick, but he is helpless to protect his son: "He was trapped as his people were always trapped, and would be until, as he had said, they could be sure that the things in the books were really in the books" (p. 39). And there is no doubt about Steinbeck's attitude toward Kino's challenge to the order: "For it is said that humans are never satisfied, that you give them one thing and they want something more. And this is said in disparagement, whereas it is one of the greatest talents the species has and one that has made it superior to animals that are satisfied with what they have" (p. 32). Kino's desires for a rifle and a church wedding, and even, perhaps, for his son's education, may be delusive, but the courage to have them not only forces Kino "through the horizon into a cold and lonely outside" (p. 37), but makes him superior in the end to the animals with which he and his people are identified and superior to the rest of his people who do not act upon such desires. Ironically, when Steinbeck writes that "all of the doctor's race spoke to all of Kino's race as though they were simple animals" (p. 12), the doctor's race seems fairly correct in its assessment, for the Indians' lives are much like those of animals—ruled primarily by instinct and habit. By the end of the novel, Kino and Juana will be forever risen above this level.

From the beginning of the novel, Kino struggles to escape from an entrapment that seems as inexorable as fate. Our perspective as we watch Kino is precisely the same as Kino's when, early in the novel, he watched "with the detachment of God while a dusty ant frantically tried to escape the sand trap an ant lion had dug for him" (p. 4). Throughout the novel, Kino is the ant in the trap, and the higher he climbs the more the sides of his trap close in upon him. In this respect, critics who have read *The Pearl* as naturalistic are correct.[36] From the beginning to the end, Kino, like the other Indians, is at the mercy of forces—social, economic, hereditary—which he cannot defeat. The naturalistic images and symbols of the book deny Kino the possibility of overcoming these forces—he is the ant in the trap, the small fish in the estuary preyed upon by the greater, the mouse hunted by the nighthawk. He is completely ineffectual in his attempts to protect his true pearl, Coyotito. When he sees the scorpion threatening the baby, he tries to intervene but is too late. All he can do is crush and stamp the enemy "until it was only a fragment and a moist place in the dirt" (p. 7). Similarly, he demonstrates his impotence in the face of the doctor's callousness by smashing his fist against the iron gate. And, in the end, in a scene prefigured by the scene with the scorpion, Kino leaps to prevent the rifleman from endangering the baby but is again too late and Coyotito is killed. Once again, all that Kino can do is crush the enemy just as he had crushed the scorpion— in a frenzy of killing. In a non-teleological sense, the evil forces that overpower Kino simply *are*, like the "sadness of the stomach" Pepé's mother warned of.

Kino is also trapped by shortsighted teleological thinking which assumes that the pearl will provide the ability to buy "things" that will bring greater happiness. In this thinking Kino is like the others in his village and town. The Indians, however, are especially vulnerable to this kind of thinking because they have no experience against which to judge the values suggested by the pearl. In their innocence, the Indians are non-teleological by nature; they simply accept things as they are. Kino's story is that of a man emerging from a non-teleological state of innocence (prepearl) into the teleological world of misleading values ("things" the pearl can buy), and of his final transcendence to a *conscious* recognition of non-teleological values in which the pearl loses its power. The greed and violence that Kino encounters within himself and others are based on the teleological assumption that the pearl can cause happiness. In order to be immune to the temptations of this kind of thinking, Kino must work from ignorance through experience to a conscious awakening. With the death of Coyotito, Kino awakens to the value of the true pearl he has lost, and his enslavement to the "pearl of the world" ends.

During the dark hours of his enthrallment to the pearl, Kino told Juana, "Believe me . . . I am a man," and Steinbeck had added, ironically undercutting this statement, "And his face grew crafty" (p. 74). After the loss of Coyotito and the gain of a new world-vision, Kino is more than a man just as he was less than a man before. He and Juana return to the village as transcendent beings: "The people say that the two seemed to be

44

removed from human experience; that they had gone through pain and had come out the other side; that there was almost a magical protection about them" (p. 116). The symbols of their experience of death return with them: "The sun was behind them and their long shadows stalked ahead, and they seemed to carry two towers of darkness with them. Kino had a rifle across his arm" (p. 115).

Contrary to what Warren French has suggested, Steinbeck is not simply saying here that one *can* go home again. Nor can we easily agree with Levant's assertion that, when Kino hurls the pearl back into the sea, Kino and Juana "renounce the lure of 'the world' and can reenter their former Eden, forgiven." Krause convincingly argues that "the grand gesture of a public renunciation is in itself about as forceful a demonstration of moral action as any of Steinbeck's characters ever make," but the serious import of this novel cannot be found in Krause's claim that "by this dramatic public admission of personal wrong, the man has truly reclaimed his soul." And Steinbeck is not merely telling us here, as Fontenrose suggests, that "this is the way things are."[37] When Kino and Juana return, the villagers, including Kino's brother, shrink from them in fear; they cannot "reenter their former Eden, forgiven," for they are forever set apart by their experience. Nor do they need to be forgiven, for they have been made greater than before by the knowledge they have gained. No longer will Kino and Juana be at the mercy of the pearl buyers and the corrupt town, for the values represented by the town have been discarded at the instant of Coyotito's death. Kino and Juana have been thrust into a world apart from the innocent garden of the village, and the casting away of the pearl represents not a public admission of wrong but simply the casting aside of something which no longer has any personal value.

The Pearl is a parable of man achieving greatness through the courage to challenge the unknown. Though there is never any chance that Kino will defeat the powers that oppose him, he triumphs in defeat. He illustrates Steinbeck's claim in *The Grapes of Wrath* that "man reaches, stumbles forward, painfully, mistakenly sometimes. Having stepped forward, he may slip back, but only a half step, never the full step back" (p. 154).

In *To a God Unknown* Joseph Wayne achieved his triumphant vision of his relationship with the "whole" at the moment of death. Pepé Torres, in "Flight," achieved a kind of transcendence into the "whole" represented by the mountains at the moment that he "stood up in the dark" to confront the unknown and unknowable forces pursuing him. This, too, has been Kino's triumph. Kino has gone into the night and into the dark mountains to confront the unknown, leaving the security of his known, safe world. In so doing, Kino has joined the ranks of Steinbeck's Questers, those who journey into the western mountains on a quest to know that which is unknowable except by "*being* it, by living into it." In *The Red Pony*, we shall see the most obvious of Steinbeck's questing knights, old Gitano, ride off into the Santa Lucias for a confrontation with the mystery that resides within those mountains—the mystery of his own mortality. And in this story cycle, we shall see the young boy, Jody, growing toward the same kind of courage, yearning to know, as Gitano ultimately does, what lies back within the heart of the mountains.

The Red Pony: Commitment and Quest

Like *To a God Unknown* and "Flight," the four stories that make up *The Red Pony* are set in the foothills of the Santa Lucia Mountains on the California coastline. And once again, in these stories dealing with Jody Tiflin's growing awareness of the mysteries of death, the western mountains stand out as symbols of both death and the unknown.

Of this book, Steinbeck stated:

> *The Red Pony* was written . . . when there was desolation in my
> family. The first death had occurred. And the family, which every
> child believes to be immortal, was shattered. Perhaps this is the
> first adulthood of any man or woman. The first tortured question
> of "why?" and the acceptance and the child becomes a man. *The
> Red Pony* was an attempt, an experiment if you wish, to set down
> this acceptance and growth.[38]

Critics have customarily accepted this reading of the stories in
The Red Pony, finding, with a hint from Steinbeck, that the book
is a kind of *Bildungsroman,* an initiation cycle in which Jody
Tiflin becomes increasingly aware of what Arnold L. Goldsmith
has termed "an organic theory of life ending in death which in
turn produces life." Joseph Fontenrose suggests that Jody,
through his exposure to increasing responsibilities, passes from
childhood to adulthood. Fontenrose calls the book "a story of
initiation comparable to Faulkner's 'The Bear.'" Goldsmith, in
turn, equates Jody with Hemingway's Nick Adams growing toward manhood. While Peter Lisca cautions that "it would probably be a mistake to see the whole of *The Red Pony* as illustrating
the rites of initiation step by step and in sequence," he points to
Frazer's *The Golden Bough* as a source of what he sees as "a general pattern" of ancient puberty rites in the story cycle. Robert
M. Benton claims that Lisca "stands almost alone among major
critics as one who gives serious attention to the work [*The Red
Pony*]." Benton complains rightly that "most do little more than
call the novella a *Bildungsroman*."[39]

It would be inaccurate to say that Jody Tiflin "becomes a
man" in *The Red Pony;* Jody begins the first story as "only a little
boy," and we are reminded at the beginning of each succeeding
story that Jody is still only a little boy. Jody does not grow up in
these stories morally or emotionally in any way comparable to
Ike McCaslin in "The Bear" or Nick Adams in the Hemingway
stories. The most we can find in Jody is a rather faint suggestion
of moral growth in his expanding awareness of and under-

standing of death. In fact, *The Red Pony* does not fit neatly into the category of "initiation," even though Jody does grow in these stories and death is his principal teacher. Rather than simply illustrating "the first tortured question of 'why?' and the acceptance," the four stories chronicle a different kind of growth, the growing question within Jody not of "why" but of "what"—what lies back within the mysterious dark mountains and back within the unknowable mystery of death. Developing within the boy is the courage it will take to follow in the path of old Gitano, the paisano who confronts the western mountains and death in "The Gift," the first story in *The Red Pony* cycle. This is the courage upon which any future for Jody as a "leader of people" must be founded.

The theme of death is introduced early in "The Gift." From Jody's entrance and Steinbeck's statement that "he was only a little boy," we are made vividly aware that Jody lives in a world in which death is an omnipresent reality and in which, as in "Flight," the line between life and death is very tenuous. This idea is first suggested in the "spot of blood" which Jody scrapes from his breakfast egg. "That's only a sign the rooster leaves," Billy Buck tells Jody (p. 204). It is, in fact, a sign of a chicken that will not be hatched because of Jody's breakfast. We soon learn that Billy Buck and Carl Tiflin, Jody's father, are getting ready to take some old milk cows to the butcher, and we are told incidentally that Smasher, the shepherd, has killed a coyote and lost an ear doing so. The black cypress tree where the pigs are killed makes its first appearance at this point, and, in a foreshadowing of the red pony's fate, Jody sees "two big black buzzards" circling over a nearby hill and is vaguely conscious that "some animal had died in the vicinity" (p. 206).

The opening pages of the story suggest that Jody's world is permeated by the presence of death. As yet, however, death exists for Jody as an impersonal force and even an enjoyable diversion, as his excitement over the possibility of pig killing suggests. In the course of the story, he will realize death as a personal and profound experience, and it will move from the periphery of his consciousness to implant itself deeply in his unconscious.

Once Carl and Billy have departed to sell the cows and purchase the pony (most likely with money from the slaughtered cows), references to and images of death disappear from the story as Jody becomes absorbed in the vibrant life-force of the red pony. Jody names the pony for the mountains of life, the Gabilans to the east across the Salinas Valley, and Billy Buck understands the connection: "Billy Buck knew how he felt." However, Steinbeck has insured that an awareness of death's imminence has been firmly planted in his readers' minds. And when the time comes for the pony to die, it struggles desperately away from the barn onto the slopes of the Santa Lucias, the western mountains, and, like Pepé in "Flight," falls prey to the buzzards. Thus, ironically, the power of death over life is asserted as "Gabilan Mountains" lies dying in the Santa Lucias.

What Jody has the opportunity to learn in this story is not only to accept the inevitability of death but to know death as a personal and profoundly disturbing experience. There is a suggestion that he is beginning to recognize death in a new way when, as Gabilan lies dying, he goes to the spring to meditate. While sitting at the spring, "he looked down at the dark cypress tree. The place was familiar, but curiously changed. It wasn't itself any more, but a frame for things that were happening" (p. 235). There is a suggestion that perhaps death is becoming personalized for Jody for the first time.

When Jody attacks the buzzard that has begun to feed on the dying pony, he looks as never before directly into the face of death: "His fingers found the neck of the struggling bird. The red eyes looked into his face, calm and fearless and fierce" (p. 238). And, as he batters the buzzard, we are told, "the red fearless eyes still looked at him, impersonal and unafraid and detached" (p. 238).

The gift to Jody in this first story has been much more than a pony. It has been a new awareness of the mystery and power of death. As becomes evident in the second story, "The Great Mountains," what Jody has gained has not been a new sense of the value or sacredness of life or a new sense of his responsibility to all life, but rather simply an awakened sense of wonder about the realm of death symbolized by the mountains.

The second story in *The Red Pony* begins by reminding us that we are still dealing with a young boy: "In the humming heat of a midsummer afternoon the little boy Jody listlessly looked about the ranch for something to do" (pp. 238–39). Lest we assume too much regarding the maturation that has taken place in the previous story, Steinbeck not only reminds us of Jody's immaturity, but immediately shows Jody irresponsibly destroying the swallows' "little mud houses" and cruelly tormenting "that good big dog," Doubletree Mutt. Next, Jody kills and dismembers a small bird, feeling "a little mean pain in his stomach" because he knew that the adults would disapprove of the deed.

Obviously, Gabilan's death has not taught Jody to value life or to act more responsibly toward that life. Morally, he seems not to have matured at all between the stories. However, after Jody has washed the blood from his hands in the spring, he sits and watches clouds sail over the western mountains, the "great mountains . . . growing darker and more savage until they finished with one jagged ridge, high up against the west. Curious secret mountains; he thought of the little he knew about them" (p. 241). Jody is beginning to wonder about this mysterious country. He asks his father, "Has anybody been there?" and the answer is "A few people, I guess. It's dangerous." Carl Tiflin is a shortsighted man, absorbed in the work of the ranch, a man for whom the frightening mystery of the mountains is a danger simply to be avoided. Carl is content to repeat the dubious assertion that "there's more unexplored country in the mountains of Monterey County than any other place in the

United States" (p. 241). Jody, on the contrary, shows the first promise of developing toward the future suggested in "The Leader of the People" when he says, "It would be good to go." And Steinbeck adds, "Jody knew something was there, something very wonderful because it wasn't known, something secret and mysterious" (p. 241).

The mysterious, unknown thing Jody senses in the mountains includes much to fear, for in the evening "when the sun had gone over the edge . . . and the mountains were a purple-like despair, then Jody was afraid of them; then they were so impersonal and aloof that their very imperturbability was a threat" (p. 242). This cold imperturbability is possibly so frightening to Jody because he has encountered it once before as an important element in his first direct experience of death—in the "impersonal and unafraid and detached" eyes of the buzzard.

Jody has already identified the life-force of the red pony with the Gabilan Mountains, and here he instinctively contrasts the disturbing western mountains with the eastern Gabilans: "Now he turned his head toward the mountains of the east, the Gabilans, and they were jolly mountains, with hill ranches in their creases. . . . He looked back for an instant at the Great Ones and shivered a little at the contrast" (p. 242). The two ranges of mountains stand as opposing symbols of life and death in this story, and Jody is being increasingly drawn toward the latter.

Richard F. Peterson has called this story "a strange and disturbing interlude in Steinbeck's portrait of the painful and sometimes violent education of the young boy."[40] Rather than being an interlude, however, this story illustrates the most central element in the moral awakening Jody undergoes in the course of the four stories. Here we see the blossoming of Jody's questing impulse, his desire to transcend the known and secure world of the Gabilans and the home ranch and to know what is ultimately unknowable. Already he has surpassed his father and even Billy Buck, who, like Carl, prefers not to think about the mountains. At this stage in the cycle, Steinbeck introduces Gitano, the aged Quester and bearer of the Grail, to augment this phase of Jody's education.

While it is difficult to agree completely with Peterson that Steinbeck introduces the "waste land theme" through mood and setting in this story, Peterson convincingly draws upon evidence from Weston's *From Ritual to Romance* to relate Gitano's rapier to the Grail legend. Peterson suggests that "the central event in the story which defines the roles of Gitano and Jody within the mythic pattern of the quest for the Grail is Jody's discovery of the 'lean and lovely rapier with a golden basket hilt.'" In Weston, Peterson notes evidence that "in many of the earlier forms of the Grail legend the Grail appears in juxtaposition with the Lance or Spear of Christ's passion," and suggests persuasively that Gitano's rapier may represent "this combination of Grail symbols."[41] Given Steinbeck's lifelong fascination with the Grail legend and the recurrent appearance of the quest motif in his writing, it seems likely that Peterson's interpretation is valid. However, of central importance here is not whether Gitano represents the "Maimed King" as Peterson asserts, with Jody as Quester. More important is Gitano's similarity to Joseph Wayne, Pepé Torres, and Kino. Like each of these other Steinbeck characters, Gitano represents the courage necessary to actively confront the mystery of death in the mountains. Like Joseph Wayne, Gitano expresses a deep commitment to place, returning to the place of his birth when it is time for him to die. Gitano is a version of the Grail Knight, bearing his shimmering rapier aloft as he rides off on the suggestively named horse, Old Easter, in quest of the unknowable.

Jody already has instinctively identified Gitano with the western mountains. "Did you come out of the mountains?" he asks upon first meeting the old man. And Steinbeck describes Jody's reaction to the old man: "Gitano was mysterious like the mountains. There were ranges back as far as you could see, but behind that last range against the sky there was a great unknown country. And Gitano was an old man, until you got to the dull dark eyes. And in behind them was some unknown thing" (p. 252). That unknown thing, like Hamlet's "undiscovered country," is death.

Typically, Carl Tiflin does not understand why Gitano has taken Old Easter and gone into the mountains. "I wonder what he wants back there," he says (p. 255). Jody, however, is much more sensitive to Gitano's purpose: "He looked searchingly at the mountains. . . . Jody thought of the rapier and of Gitano. And he thought of the great mountains. A longing caressed him, and it was so sharp that he wanted to cry to get it out of his breast. . . . and he was full of a nameless sorrow" (p. 256). Clifford Lawrence Lewis has suggested that Jody's "nameless sorrow" is "for the passing of a history and tradition that Gitano takes with him." Peter Lisca comes nearer the mark, however, when he asserts that Jody's sorrow comes "not from grief for Gitano or the old horse, but rather an emotional perception of that whole of which Gitano, Old Easter, the rapier, and the Great Mountains are parts, a recognition of the symbolic significance of their conjunction."[42] To be more specific, Jody's sorrow and his painful longing represent a more profound version of his earlier yearning to know what was back in the heart of the mountains. Instinctively, Jody recognizes that Gitano is riding off to meet his death and that he is not simply accepting it but actively seeking it; he is a questing knight. The emphasis is not on the simple fact that Gitano and the old horse will undoubtedly die in the mountains, but on the quest for that knowledge of man's relationship with the whole which, as it was for Joseph Wayne and Pepé Torres, is attainable in the mountains at the moment of death. We are shown here that Jody, a future "leader of the people," has a powerful questing impulse developing within him.

In contrast to the pervasive symbols of and references to death that permeate the beginning of "The Gift" and the conclusion of "The Great Mountains," "The Promise" opens in spring, the season of rebirth, or, as Steinbeck would later write in *The Wayward Bus*, of "flowering and growth." Again Jody is introduced as "the little boy, Jody," reminding us that regardless of what experiences have befallen Jody in the previous stories, he is still a child. Here, in fact, Jody seems younger than ever as he leads an imaginary army home from school and surprises his mother with a lunch pail full of smothered reptiles and insects. The spring is vibrant: "The afternoon was green and gold with spring. Underneath the spread branches of the oaks the plants grew pale and tall, and on the hills the feed was smooth and thick" (p. 256).

In this season of rebirth, Jody's father allows Jody to take the mare, Nellie, to be bred, promising that Jody may have the colt to raise when it is born. In this story Jody learns with harsh brutality the interrelatedness of life and death when Billy Buck must finally kill Nellie to save the colt and fulfill his promise to the boy. In "The Promise," Jody's vague yearning to fathom the mysteries of death represented by Gitano and the mysterious mountains is partially fulfilled. After Billy delivers the colt from the dying mare, Jody learns a new lesson: "He tried to be glad because of the colt, but the bloody face, and the haunted, tired eyes of Billy Buck hung in the air ahead of him" (p. 279). In "The Gift" Jody experienced death for the first time as a personal but uncontrollable force which must simply be accepted. In "The Great Mountains" he became aware of the courage involved in accepting one's own death and going out to confront that "unknown thing" in the mountains. In "The Promise" he watches as Billy Buck goes beyond acceptance and makes the decision as to which shall live, Nellie or the colt.

Lisca suggests that "the mare's suffering and death are the price of life and give to Jody a new sense of his responsibility to that life." Lewis states that "by compressing the time between birth and death, Steinbeck has managed to intimately connect the birth and death process."[43] While the birth of the colt certainly does provide Jody with a powerful lesson in the intimate

connection between life and death, and while he is unquestion-
ably impressed by the death of the mare, what Jody learns here
is more than "a new sense of responsibility to . . . life." Nor
does the lesson merely underscore the important theme of the
interrelatedness of life and death. Jody's real lesson is provided
by Billy Buck, by the "haunted, tired eyes" that "hung in the air
ahead of him" as he tried to think only of the new colt. Rather
than a new respect for life, Jody has a deeper understanding of
what it means to challenge death instead of merely accepting its
inevitability.

If Jody had indeed learned to value life more greatly, or to
view death more maturely as a serious and integral part of that
life which one must respect, we should expect to see a far different boy in the final story of *The Red Pony,* a boy vastly different
from the one who casually destroyed the swallows' nests or mu-
tilated the bird or exulted in the possibility of pig killing. We
should, in short, expect to meet a Jody who has a much more
mature respect for the principle of life in "The Leader of the
People."

When we do meet Jody in this final story, added to the first
three stories in the 1945 publication of *The Red Pony,* he is introduced as usual as "the little boy, Jody" (p. 283). Almost immediately, in this story, we see Jody rejoicing in the potential
slaughter of the mice: "Jody sighed with satisfaction. Those
plump, sleek, arrogant mice were doomed. For eight months
they had lived and multiplied in the haystack. They had been
immune from cats, from traps, from poison and from Jody. They
had grown smug in their security, overbearing and fat. Now the
time of disaster had come; they would not survive another day"
(p. 284). Death in this final story is once again a part of the play
world of Jody Tiflin; we get no indication of a new sense of
responsibility toward life in Jody here. When Jody tries to
please Grandfather by suggesting that there may be a pig killing,
we seem to be right back where we started in "The Gift" as far
as Jody's attitude toward death is concerned.

55

The pattern of the four stories in *The Red Pony* is to present a stark, personal encounter with death in the first story and to follow this with a more abstract experience of death in the second. The third story then introduces a second harsh, immediate experience of death, and the fourth provides another encounter with abstract values. The final story, "The Leader of the People," is about the questing impulse that is at the core of what Grandfather terms "westering"—the American migration from the Atlantic to the Pacific. Grandfather serves as a second type of Quester in the book, both similar to and very different from Gitano. Grandfather has led a wagon train to California and run into the barrier of the Pacific Ocean. He is caught up in the archetypal American westward movement, trapped in it. For Grandfather, "once made, no step could ever be retraced; once headed in a direction, the path would never bend nor the pace increase or slow" (pp. 290–91). As Jody's mother says, "If there'd been any farther west to go, he'd have gone." She adds, "He lives right by the ocean where he had to stop," and Carl Tiflin comments, "I've seen him. . . . He goes down and stares off west over the ocean" (p. 288). Grandfather is one of the pathetic old men he himself describes, lined up "along the shore hating the ocean because it stopped them" (p. 302). He encapsulates the westward movement, a microcosm of that phase of American history. "It was westering and westering," Grandfather tells Jody; "it wasn't getting here that mattered, it was movement and westering" (p. 302).

Caught up in the westering pattern, Grandfather represents one aspect of the Quester—the desire to know what is unknown, what is beyond the horizon. West is the direction of the setting sun and death, as Steinbeck suggested in *To a God Unknown*, where another old man lived right by the ocean attempting to worship that which he could not know. Grandfather is similar to Gitano in that, like the old paisano, he yearns to experience what has not been experienced, to continue the quest indefinitely. In a more important sense, however, Grandfather is involved in a much less significant and less meaningful quest than Gitano's. While Gitano demonstrated both commitment to place and the courage to explore the inner consciousness symbolized by the "unknown thing" Jody sensed within Gitano's eyes, Grandfather's quest is wholly outward and away from commitment. Grandfather is in a perpetual state of running away from commitment. When Jody suggests, "Maybe I could lead the people someday," Grandfather replies, "There's no place to go. There's the ocean to stop you." Jody says, "In boats I might, sir," and Grandfather insists, "No place to go, Jody. Every place is taken. But that's not the worst. . . . Westering has died out of the people. Westering isn't a hunger any more" (p. 303). As a serious reader of Jung, Weston, and Frazer and an acquaintance of Joseph Campbell, Steinbeck was acutely aware of the sea as a symbol of death and the unconscious—an awareness that is amply illustrated in the war dispatches he wrote in 1945, the same year as the publication of *The Red Pony* in book form.[44] The fact that it is Jody who is eager to venture into this new unknown region, whether it be the mountains or sea, suggests that he may become a greater Quester than Grandfather, that he may one day demonstrate the courage and commitment of Gitano.

Jody's sympathy for Grandfather at the end of "The Leader of the People" indicates that Jody recognizes the futility of Grandfather's predicament, that of one who cannot rest yet is confronted by a barrier he cannot surmount. Whatever promise Jody shows in this story depends upon his own incipient questing instinct, one that may allow him to move beyond the westering pattern to explore more significant territories. Jody has demonstrated no greater sensitivity to the value of life than he had in the first story; the mice may be spared for a while out of deference to Grandfather but they will most likely perish under Jody's flail another day.

Steinbeck will later recreate the westward migration in *The Grapes of Wrath,* and in so doing, he will attempt to cast off the values inherent in the westering tradition represented by Grandfather. As *To a God Unknown* demonstrated, Steinbeck's emphasis is on commitment to place and on man's understanding of his relationship to the "whole" of which he is a part. The pattern of noncommitment illustrated by the westering impulse in American history is in direct contrast to and a contradiction of the values Steinbeck asserts throughout his writing. Grandfather, unlike Gitano, is not a hero; he is simply one of the pathetic old men. He cannot and will not turn back to explore the country he has found; he will not *know* his place in the whole, for he lacks the kind of commitment demonstrated by Joseph Wayne and Gitano and suggested in Jody.

The Wayward Bus: A Triumph of Nature

In *The Wayward Bus* (1947) Steinbeck moves the terrain of his fiction across the Salinas Valley to describe an intense journey into a range of hills strikingly similar to the Gabilans. In these hills, the forces of life predominate, and the passengers of the wayward bus enter these hills to face a stark experience with these forces. When the old, battered bus named "Sweetheart" is turned aside from its everyday course by a flooding river, Juan Chicoy, "Sweetheart"'s owner and driver, guides the bus into the hills, attempting to find a way around the flood on the "old road." Once they are in the hills, it becomes clear that the key to the spiritual rejuvenation, or salvation, of Juan Chicoy's passengers lies in the ability of each to face honestly and to accept the intimate sexual, psychological, and emotional contact that life demands when the masks and façades of Hollywood-style daydreams break down.

The theme of fecund, sensual nature is introduced early in this novel, at the same time that Steinbeck brings in Juan Chicoy, the most potent, physically and spiritually, of the characters:

In the deep spring when the grass was green on fields and foothills, when the lupines and poppies made a splendid blue and gold earth, when the great trees awakened in yellow-green young leaves, then there was no more lovely place in the world. It was no beauty you could ignore by being used to it. It caught you in the throat in the morning and made a pain of pleasure in the pit of your stomach when the sun went down over it. The sweet smell of the lupines and of the grass set you breathing nervously, set you panting almost sexually. And it was in this season of flowering and growth . . . that Juan Chicoy came out to the bus. (pp. 12–13)

In this paean to the natural fertility of the environment, Juan, who will pilot the fated busload into their confrontations with themselves and with one another, is immediately and unmistakably identified with natural sexuality. Juan, "a fine, steady man . . . part Mexican and part Irish" (p. 6), believes in "the power of person as responsible and proud individual" (p. 20). Juan's religion is "practical." He is vaguely identified with Christ both by his eye-catching initials (the same as those of Jim Casy, the preacher in *The Grapes of Wrath*) and by the "dark Virgin" who "was his mother" (p. 20). In the course of the novel, Juan will face his own crisis and, like Christ, will accept responsibility for his fellow man; he will demonstrate the virtue prized by Steinbeck—commitment—and he will present his passengers with an opportunity for salvation, with an opportunity, in this vibrantly alive time of "flowering and growth," to break out of their spiritually dead lives and be reborn with the new season.

The passengers of the wayward "Sweetheart" include Pimples Carson, Juan's painfully adolescent helper in the bus driver's Rebel Corners gas station–garage, and Norma, a young ex-waitress at the Rebel Corners cafe run by Juan's wife, Alice. Norma is a willing victim of Hollywood-inspired fantasies concerning Clark Gable. Also taking part in "Sweetheart" 's journey are Ernest Horton, a cynical war veteran and hawker of deceptive and "funny" gadgets, and Van Brunt, a dying man who suffers from disturbingly uncontrollable sexual desires and a hatred of all who are not dying as he is. Making up the balance of the original passengers are Mr. and Mrs. Pritchard and their college-age daughter Mildred, all three bound for a vacation in Juan's native Mexico. Mrs. Pritchard is frigid and during a long, "successful" marriage has succeeded in suppressing most of her husband's sexual desires to the point where he does not believe such things "matter" any longer. Pritchard is a man who "had given up his freedom and then had forgotten what it was like" (p. 41). Mildred, in contrast to her parents, recognizes and enjoys her own sexuality and from the beginning is strongly attracted to Juan.

As Juan is preparing to ferry his few passengers to the small town of San Juan de la Cruz, the daily Greyhound bus deposits one final passenger at Rebel Corners. With the addition of Camille Oaks, the sexual nature of "Sweetheart"'s journey becomes intense and unmistakable. Camille, a beautiful blonde who makes a living by taking off her clothes and sitting in bowls of wine at men's club parties, has an effect on men almost identical to that of the season of "flowering and growth." Camille, who selects her name after arriving at Rebel Corners, "was the kind of girl everybody watched walk by," a girl who "put out a strong, strong feeling of sex" (p. 103). Pimples is powerfully affected by Camille; we are told that when Camille spoke, "a quick spasm kinked Pimples' stomach at the throaty tone" (p. 122). Even the worldly and mildly sinister Louie, driver of the Greyhound and exploiter of women, felt when near Camille that "his throat was closing, and a rising pressure was in his chest" (p. 114). Camille recognizes and even regrets her overwhelming sexual power, but she also accepts it: "All men wanted the same thing from her, and that was just the way it was. She took it for granted and it was true" (p. 109). John Ditsky appropriately labels Camille the "Aphrodite of California."[45] She is a personification of the potently sexual nature surrounding "Sweetheart"'s passengers on their pilgrimage. Her chosen name underscores both her identification with this nature and her important role as a goddess of natural sexuality. Her surname is the name of the dominant feature of the landscape, the oaks; her first name, Camille, translates from Latin as "a virgin of unblemished character." Camille's role in the novel is to bring the overpowering sexuality of the springtime environment into the bus, so that even during the darkest hours the passengers have no chance to forget or ignore their own sexuality with its dual potential for a natural, healthy realization or a perverse and destructive one. Acting as a catalyst, Camille causes the other characters to respond to their own sexuality.

As Ditsky has pointed out, sexuality pervades this novel and is critical in offering "whatever hope the novel presents."[46] Indeed, hope in this novel rests on man's ability to reconcile the sensual and spiritual aspects of life harmoniously, and Juan Chicoy is the priest of this reconciliation.

The palimpsest on "Sweetheart"'s front bumper emphasizes this theme of reconciliation. Still barely readable beside the name "Sweetheart" is "*el Gran Poder de Jesus.*" Rather than indicating a corruption of religious faith, or what Ditsky terms mere "gushiness,"[47] this important juxtaposition serves neatly to define Juan's natural and practical religion. "The great power of Jesus" here is the power of the life-force, that force which unites the sensual with the spiritual. For the same reason, Juan has placed a small statue of the Virgin of Guadalupe on "Sweetheart"'s dashboard, and directly above her he has hung a "little plastic kewpie doll with a cerise and green ostrich-feather headdress and a provocative sarong." This doll "was for the pleasures of the flesh and of the eye, of the nose, of the ear" (p. 20). Throughout the novel, Juan, as a "responsible and proud individual," remains firmly in control of his sexuality and firmly retains his belief in the spiritual powers of the Virgin.

Opposed to the positive sexuality of Juan and Camille is a world of superficial and corrupt sexuality, from the artificially big-busted calendar girls at Rebel Corners to the hollow viciousness of Louie, the bus driver. Through Louie, Steinbeck introduces the theme of debased sexuality: "Nearly all his waking hours Louie thought about girls. He liked to outrage them. He like to have them fall in love with him and then walk away. He called them pigs. 'I'll get a pig,' he would say, 'and you get a pig, and we'll go out on the town' " (p. 99). Edgar, the ticket clerk in the bus station, admires Louie and wishes he could be like him, but Edgar always "ended up by going down the line"—to the whorehouses (p. 106). Even the swamper and the "punk" who cleans the bus windows echo Louie's debased and unhealthy attitude toward sex.

The two bus drivers in the novel are set in deliberate contrast to one another. If Juan Chicoy, with his suggestive initials, is the potential savior of this wayward group, Louie is the sleazy Satan of his corrupt world. With his one long nail and sneering façade, the pilot of a great gleaming Greyhound, Louie epitomizes the corruption from which Juan's passengers must be delivered.

Louie tries to attract Camille and fails, but he leaves his taint behind in the form of "Mother Mahoney's Home-Baked Pies," which he delivers to Rebel Corners. The pies, subjects of much critical interest, are not even home-baked; they, too, represent the prevalent corruption of values, and the impressionable Pimples, addicted to the sweets that are the source of his nickname, is their too-willing victim. Throughout the novel Pimples's thoughts are never far from the pies, even as he is stuffing his pockets with such suggestively named candy bars as "Love Nests" and "Coconut Sweethearts."

As the passengers settle into their various roles aboard "Sweetheart," Juan attempts the journey to San Juan de la Cruz, but the bus is turned back at Breed's store by the destructive, rain-swollen San Ysidro River. Breed, guardian of the bridge and witness to the river's annual rampages, stands on the weight of his name alone as a kind of priest of this fecund valley; guardian of the threshold, he is immune to the destructive power of nature—fearless of the flooding river, but apprehensive of the arbitrary flow of civilization, which may one day build a new highway a quarter mile away and ruin his business.

Faced with the prospect of turning back, the passengers vote to attempt a detour around the flood on the back road, "a very old road, no one knew how old" (p. 216). The sexuality of the landscape becomes more pronounced: "The road ran straight toward the little foothills of the first range—rounded, woman-like hills, soft and sexual as flesh. . . . The hills were rich and lovely with water, and along the smooth and beautiful road 'Sweetheart' rolled" (p. 141). Life, rich and sensual, is the predominant force in these hills, and at this point "Sweetheart" is identified with that force. Before long, however, as Steinbeck's lumbering vehicle approaches its darkest hour, "Sweetheart" changes to reflect the moral and spiritual condition of her cargo.

The nearly explosive fertility of the foothills is framed by an austere and threatening outer landscape. The names and descriptions of landscape features underscore the ominous quality of the external world that is forcing the bus up into the hills. Unlike most of Steinbeck's works, this novel contains no authentic place names; nor is the setting easily identified with an actual place as in other Steinbeck works. Steinbeck set *The Wayward Bus* in a valley very much like the Salinas Valley and in a gentle range of hills much like the Gabilans on the eastern edge of that valley, but the valley in this novel bears the name of the patron saint of agriculture, San Juan, as is befitting such a fertile region, and it winds toward the sea rather than north–south like the Salinas Valley. The river that has formed this valley is not the Salinas but the San Ysidro, which "runs through the San Juan Valley, turning and twisting until it discharges sluggishly into Black Rock Bay under the protection of Bat Point" (p. 161). The travelers' destination, San Juan de la Cruz, may be intended to remind us of the mysticism of the author of *The Dark Night of the Soul*, but it may also have been suggested to Steinbeck by the actual coastal town of Santa Cruz near Monterey, where the Salinas River empties into the Pacific. By wrenching the setting in this way from the solid anchoring of real places and names, Steinbeck universalizes this pilgrimage and underscores the allegorical quality of the story. At the same time, the portentous names amplify the suggestion of malevolence in the river. The river symbolizes the destructive processes operating in the world, which have maimed the passengers spiritually and physically, and at one instance it becomes a serpent, threatening this gardenlike valley, "casting its coils against the mountain on the eastern edge and moving away to cross the fields and farmlands" (p. 162). The river seems to threaten not only wayfaring pilgrims but the very fertility of the land as it rips away at the earth and crashes toward the sea at floodstage, carrying prize cattle and barns in its current. At one point, a great black bull, sexual symbol of mythology and reminder of the mysterious black bull of *To a God Unknown*, tumbles past Breed's store in the midst of the current, sacrificed to the flood.

"Sweetheart" moves into the hills seeking high ground and safe passage, and the ominous rains, threatening destruction for the sinners, are swept in over the coast range. Even before the bus has left Rebel Corners, these mountains and their threatening rains are introduced: "Juan glanced up at the sky. The air was still but up high a wind was blowing, bringing legions of new clouds over the mountains, and these clouds were flat and they were joining together and moving in on one another as they hurried across the sky" (p. 137). From this point onward, the clouds will be a constant reminder of the destruction hanging over the passengers. At the novel's end, however, the clouds will part and the western mountains will reappear as symbols not of danger but of hope.

As the experience of Steinbeck's travelers intensifies, the face of nature becomes dark and frightening, and the lovely "Sweetheart" becomes a reflection of the evil condition of her cargo:

> The clouds piled in gray threat on threat and a blue darkness settled on the land. In the San Juan valley the darker greens seemed

black and the lighter green of grass, a chilling wet blue. "Sweetheart" came rolling heavily along the highway and the aluminum paint on her gleamed with the evil of a gun. (p. 181)

At this point it is too late to turn back; the curtain has fallen, cutting off the line of retreat, and the passengers must push on toward their confrontations. The façade has fallen away, and the trip has become deadly serious.

Shortly after "Sweetheart" has begun her precarious detour along the old road, Juan succeeds in miring the bus in the mud. He abandons the bus and passengers and walks off toward a dream of the good life in Mexico, vowing, "I will never go back. . . . I will take off my old life like a suit of underwear" (p. 222). In abandoning the bus, Juan is also abandoning his role as "responsible and proud individual"; at the same time, he is shrugging off his role as savior for the souls aboard "Sweetheart."

While the driver is absent, the passengers come into intimate contact with one another in the stranded bus and within three "deep, dark caves" beneath the weathered word "Repent." The caves, natural limestone formations near the mired bus, are very old, having sheltered coyotes and grizzlies and bands of Indians and, finally, wandering white men. They represent a primitive world where delusive values hold no sway. The moment of salvation is at hand for the spiritual refugees; it is in the womblike enclosures of the bus and caves, beneath the word "Repent" which some "wandering preacher" has painted in black, that the passengers are offered their opportunities for spiritual rebirth. In this moment of truth, some of the passengers show promise of "flowering and growth," while others remain, in the end, trapped within their spiritually corrupt lives.

Though it is Louie rather than Van Brunt who is the Satan of this novel, Van Brunt is doomed by his rejection of all that is not dying as he is. There is no place for Van Brunt in this time of "flowering." In direct contrast to Camille, who radiates a strong life-force paralleling that of the environment, Van Brunt is the living embodiment of death. He rejects everything, refusing to go on the journey and refusing to be left behind. It is appropriate that, in the end, Van Brunt suffers a living death as he lies unconscious and gasping for breath on the seat of the old bus.

The Pritchards, too, are doomed—she by her physical and spiritual frigidity, and he by his inability to face the truth about their lives. When Pritchard is rejected by Camille, he returns to one of the caves and rapes his wife. We are not, as Ditsky suggests, "intended to approve this last crow of an old cock who is under the influence of young sexuality";[48] rather, the rape (and each character's reaction to it) is the final indication of the pathetic and hopeless sterility of this couple. With that scene, Steinbeck has barred the Pritchards inexorably from the "season of flowering and growth." It is evident that the Pritchards' "successful" marriage will go on just as it has in the past.

Norma and Pimples suffer an awkward and brief encounter in the mired bus when, encouraged by Norma's sympathy, Pimples attempts to make forceful love to her and is vigorously repulsed. Norma and Pimples, however, though both deluded by questionable values in the form of Hollywood fantasies and Mother Mahoney's Home-Baked Pies, have a glimmer of hope at the end of the novel, primarily because they are young and capable of development. Norma has a wise mentor in Camille (who, nonetheless, thinks of Norma as an "incipient millstone"). Pimples has Juan, who at the last moment remembers to call Pimples by the new name, Kit. As Howard Levant has suggested, in these two relationships rests the possible flowering of the adolescents.[49]

Ernest Horton's only outstanding virtue (as his name implies) is his honesty, but because of it he is one of the elect of this assemblage. His advances toward Camille are straightforward, and she reacts with appreciation of his honesty. Camille, though scarred by life, both literally by the forceps marks on her jaws and figuratively by her cynical perspective, remains spiritually unblemished and physically unviolated throughout the novel, as her name would lead one to expect.

The relationship between Mildred and Juan is the literal climax of the novel. After walking a short distance from the bus, Juan takes refuge from the rain in an abandoned barn and is soon joined by Mildred, who has pursued him. After making love in the old barn, Juan and Mildred walk out together into the evening light. Each of these characters responds to the other honestly and directly here near the end of the book, and their lovemaking, rather than being a ploy to sell the novel, as critics have suggested, is the natural culmination of the theme of sexuality running through the novel. By the time Mildred enters the barn, Juan has already decided to return and free the bus. He has had his moment of decision and has accepted his responsibility—in the tradition of Steinbeck "heroes," Juan demonstrates the virtue of commitment. As the couple walks out of the barn, the western mountains are reintroduced and suggest now, rather than rain and threat, the positive note on which the novel will end. Mildred tells Juan, "Look, the rain has stopped. Look at the sun on the Mountains. It's going to be beautiful" (p. 289). The sun is setting on the coast range: "The sun touched the western hills and flattened itself, and its light was yellow and clear. The saturated valley glittered under the light. The clean, washed air was crisp. In the fields the flattened grain and the thick, torpid stems of the wild oats tightened themselves, and the sheathed petals of the golden poppies loosened a little" (pp. 295–96). The powerful sexuality of nature is reinforced again in this highly phallic description, and the imagery serves to underscore the positive nature of the relationship between Juan and Mildred.

The western mountains appear one last time just before the sighting of the exotic lights of San Juan de la Cruz and the end of the novel, and their symbol of hope cannot be missed: "There was a little rim of lighter sky around the edge of a great dark cloud over the western mountains, and then as the cloud lifted the evening star shone out of it, clear and washed and steady" (p. 312). The evening star is Venus, goddess of spring, bloom, beauty, and passion. Her appearance "clear and washed and steady" tells us that this springtime season of "flowering and growth" is once again as it should be. The taint is gone from the land, and "Sweetheart," with passion and nature in harmony, is free to roll happily toward the heavenly city.

This unmistakably "happy" ending poses some questions for critics and readers of *The Wayward Bus*. Nowhere else in Steinbeck's fiction, for example, do the western mountains—recurrent symbols of death—appear as symbols of life and hope. Nor is there any suggestion here that these characters will live happily ever after, for none of them is substantially changed by what has taken place. As Peter Lisca has suggested, the most any of them has gained is a "measure of self-knowledge." It is even difficult to find much consolation in Antonia Seixas's suggestion that "we are not deserted; the Juans walk back and dig us out, and the battered old bus lumbers on. But though we go forward, it is only to more of the same."[50] In spite of such reservations, however, there is a strong sense of triumph and resolution, which Steinbeck has taken great care to insure, in the climax of this novel.

The Wayward Bus ends with a celebration of nature, much as it began, because the message that Steinbeck is delivering is simply the most optimistic of all: life will go on; the hills will take in rain and flower and grow, as will certain individuals such as Juan and Mildred. Steinbeck is affirming the faith that life and the earth, as aspects of the whole, are comprehensive enough to contain both the periodic, seemingly destructive rampages of nature and the twisted, destructive urges of men and women. Just as in the midst of death there is life, from the western mountains—symbols of death—comes a promise of life. The hope upon which the novel ends echoes the conclusion of an earlier, greater novel, *The Grapes of Wrath:* the river will always abate, the flowers will unfurl their petals, and the evening star will shine again because this abiding, regenerative fertility is part of the undying whole. Like Camille, nature is forever unviolated in the midst of violence and apparent corruption. The several moments of truth for the passengers have altered nothing; they simply serve to illuminate more clearly the pathetic condition of much of mankind—they do not change that condition. The novel is not, as Ditsky suggests, about the "restoration of realistically revised dreams";[51] the dreams are not realistically revised, and this does not matter.

According to Steinbeck, this novel was first "projected in Mexico" and at that time was called *El Camion Vacilador*. Of this title he wrote: "The word *vacilador* or the verb *vacilar*, is not translatable unfortunately, and it's a word we really need in English because to be '*vacilando*' means that you're aiming at some place, but you don't care much whether you get there" (*Life in Letters*, p. 284). It does not matter whether the bus arrives at San Juan de la Cruz; what matters is the quality of the journey. This is the clue in the epigraph from *Everyman*: "How transytory we be all daye." When F. W. Watt says, "How utterly removed from the dignity of permanence are the daily lives of these modern pilgrims,"[52] he is touching upon Steinbeck's key: there is no permanence for man—dignity must be found in transit, as Juan finds it. The "one inseparable unit man plus his environment" is permanent; floods and individuals are not.

The novel ends on a note of triumph precisely because nothing has changed. Steinbeck's message is that this is the way things are, and in spite of this the world will endure and flower and grow.

Steinbeck's own doubts about the novel, including his confession that "it was a paste-up job and I should never have let it go out the way it did,"[53] were well founded. *The Wayward Bus* suffers from the intrusive allegorism so damaging to much of Steinbeck's later fiction, an allegorism which, unlike that of Hawthorne, strains awkwardly against the well-crafted realism of such a character as Juan Chicoy. The result is that Juan seems to have been lifted from one of Steinbeck's "objective" novels such as *In Dubious Battle* and set down in the driver's seat of a half-finished allegory that remains pathetically bound to a mundane microcosm, an everyday world unable to slip its moorings into the cosmic realm of a Hawthorne or Melville.

II.

THE VALLEYS

The Salinas Valley imprinted itself deeply upon the consciousness of John Steinbeck, so deeply that the valley setting came to dominate his fiction and to shape his vision of America. The long, amazingly fertile Salinas Valley, with its alternately rampaging and disappearing river and its shifting, wind-driven soils, epitomized the ambiguous Eden that Steinbeck felt at the heart of the American Dream. That the valley lay close up against a dark range of mountains marking the western edge of the continent could only make this westering, Edenic quality more unmistakable and intense. If Eden were not to be found here at the fertile farthest extent of the westward trek, surely it was not to be found at all. And thus Steinbeck's valleys, large and small, became studied Edens wracked by doubt and human weakness. In these valleys Steinbeck examines, probes, tests the Eden myth, putting it under the biologist's microscope and understanding it for the illusion it is. Steinbeck searches out and exposes within his valleys the fatal flaws of the American Eden.

It was the valley setting, with the emotionally charged Eden theme and complex of symbols which it evoked, that provided the soil for Steinbeck's greatest fiction. In the ironic Edens of Steinbeck's valleys flowered the psychologically penetrating stories of *The Pastures of Heaven,* the mature craftsmanship of *In Dubious Battle* and *Of Mice and Men,* the deft precision of some of the stories in *The Long Valley,* and the crowning achievement of *The Grapes of Wrath;* and out of the intricate complexity of Steinbeck's feelings for the valley of his birth and for California's place in American thought grew the ponderously ambitious, confused, and disappointing summing-up: *East of Eden*.

The Pastures of Heaven: Illusions of Eden

In *The Pasures of Heaven* (1932), Steinbeck's third work,[1] he set a novel for the first time exclusively in a California valley. The valley called Las Pasturas del Cielo is located in Steinbeck Country amidst the jumble of hills at the end of the Santa Lucia range near Carmel, "hugged jealously against the fog and the wind." The families of the valley "lived prosperously and at peace. Their land was rich and easy to work. The fruits of their gardens were the finest produced in central California" (p. 3). Like all of the valleys in Steinbeck's California fiction, this heavenly valley constitutes an ironic and fallen Eden where man forges his own fate out of his personal strengths and weaknesses. The valley is distorted by illusions, both the private illusions of its inhabitants and the greater illusion of the American Eden. And, as it was in *To a God Unknown*, Steinbeck's concept of "is" thinking is an important key to an understanding and penetration of these illusions.

In the first chapter of *Pastures*, Steinbeck describes the discovery of the valley by a Spanish corporal who has been dispatched to capture and return twenty runaway Indians to the clay pits of the Carmelo Mission. The Indians' futile flight toward freedom takes place "sometime around 1776," a date which, as Peter Lisca has pointed out, has great significance in American history and in this novel. Rather than being an ironic coincidence, this date carefully suggests the microcosmic qualities of the small valley and merges its history with that of the nation to the east of it. As Clifford Lawrence Lewis has suggested, "The opportune date . . . implies that the discovery and expectations were not limited to a California scene, that the failure of the American Dream was determined by our European mentality of which

74

slavery was one consequence." It should be further noted that the discovery of this microcosmic America, as Steinbeck describes it, illustrates what Richard Slotkin has called "the fatal opposition, the hostility between two worlds, two races, two realms of thought and feeling" which are "at the source of the American myth."[2]

When he discovers the valley while pursuing a deer, the corporal is overwhelmed by the beauty of the scene and cries out, "Holy Mother! . . . Here are the green pastures of Heaven to which our Lord leadeth us" (p. 2). A man "who had whipped brown backs to tatters" and "whose rapacious manhood was building a new race for California," this corporal dreams of returning to the valley, looking forward "with sentimental wistfulness to a little time of peace before he died, to an adobe house beside a stream, and cattle nuzzling the walls at night" (p. 3). Before he can realize this dream, however, the corporal dies a hideous death from pox he has received from an Indian woman. Within the corporal is a twisted shadow of the American hero of which Slotkin has written, "An American hero is the lover of the spirit of the wilderness, and his acts of love and sacred affirmation are acts of violence against that spirit and her avatars."[3] The corporal's dream is the first illusory dream in a book of illusory dreams, and the contradiction represented by this brutal, religious man drives back to the very foundations of America's idea of itself.

For the first time in his writing, Steinbeck set out in *Pastures* to study carefully a Garden of the West; what he discovered and held up to view was that, in the words of *Paradise Lost,* "The mind is its own place, and in itself / Can make a Heav'n of Hell, a Hell of Heav'n."

The Eden symbolism of *Pastures* seems to have escaped few readers or critics. Lewis perceptively concludes that "Steinbeck's stories show that an earthly Eden is an impossibility," and says, "Set in California, the pastures symbolize the American Dream itself." Peter Lisca calls the valley the world "after the fall of man." Joseph Fontenrose points out that "the Eden idea is symbolized in gardens and orchards" throughout the book. And Howard Levant calls the Pastures "the usual post-Edenic exile." John Ditsky moves beyond most critics who deal with this work when he places the novel in the larger context of Steinbeck's career, calling it "in its embodiment of the Eden motif, a major step towards the themes of Steinbeck's mature works." Interestingly, only Lewis clearly makes the important connection between the failure of the American myth and the individual failures within the valley of the Pastures, a connection essential to an understanding of this work.[4]

The question of whether *Pastures* is merely a collection of stories set within a framing device or a recognizable novel has caused much attention to be focused on the work's possible unity. While accepting the term "novel" for this work, Levant finds it lacking in any essential unity, claiming that "Steinbeck writes out of merely a simple, unqualified certainty that the Monroes *will* unify the novel. They do not." A more useful approach than Levant's is Lisca's guarded assertion that "although *The Pastures of Heaven* is probably the most loosely knit of any of Steinbeck's novels, it is more profitably approached as a whole rather than as a series of separate short stories."[5] Indeed, a careful examination of the work as a whole indicates that the novel is unified to an impressive degree by the ironical use Steinbeck makes of the Monroe family—the supposed agents of the valley's "curse." Not only do the Monroes supply a unifying principle through their involvement in each of the stories or chapters, but by causing us to view events in the valley through the illusion of the supposed curse, Steinbeck weaves a complex web of illusion that involves not only all of the unfortunate inhabitants of the Pastures, but us, as readers. Thus the illusion of the curse serves to unify the novel on a much broader level than has heretofore been supposed. If the characters in the novel are able to free themselves of the illusions they are struggling under, they may survive emotionally or physically and even prosper; if we fail to pierce the illusion of the curse, we will fail to grasp the human import of Steinbeck's stories and thus of the novel as a whole. Contrary to Levant's assertion, the Monroes do unify the novel, though not precisely in the way most critics have suspected.

Steinbeck's intentions in *The Pastures of Heaven* are well documented and worth repeating here:

> There is, about twelve miles from Monterey, a valley in the hills called Corral de Tierra. Because I am using its people I have named it Las Pasturas del Cielo. The valley was for years known as the happy valley because of the unique harmony which existed among its twenty families. About ten years ago a new family moved in on one of the ranches. They were ordinary people, ill-educated but honest and as kindly as any. In fact, in their whole history I cannot find that they have committed a really malicious act nor an act which was not dictated by honorable expediency or out-and-out altruism. But about the Morans there was a flavor of evil. Everyone they came in contact with was injured. Every place they went dissension sprang up. There have been two murders, a suicide, many quarrels and a great deal of unhappiness in the Pastures of Heaven, and all of these things can be traced directly to the influence of the Morans. So much is true. (*Life in Letters*, pp. 42–43)

As with Steinbeck's own claims for the origins of *The Red Pony*, it would be easy to merely accept the author's explanation as the basis for our understanding of the book, and this appears to be what critics have often done. Such reading provides Levant with the basis for his criticism of the novel's structure. However, as in *The Red Pony*, it should become obvious from the very first pages of the novel that Steinbeck's artistry and fascination with the American myth and the psychology of his characters have outstripped his announced intentions. Were we to accept the author's seemingly straightforward account here, we would have to accept his account of the naming of the work: "Because I am using its people I have named it Las Pasturas del Cielo." Such an explanation glibly sidesteps the obvious implications of the title he has chosen for the valley and, were we to accept it, would encourage us to overlook the heavy irony involved in the name change. *Corral de Tierra*, which Steinbeck translates in *East of Eden* as "fence of earth," is a long way removed from *The Pastures of Heaven*. One name suggests the impounding of earthly imperfections, while the other implies a heavenly perfection. The reality lies somewhere in between.

The "peculiar evil cloud" that seems to follow the Monroes is the result of carefully orchestrated coincidences and seeds of unhappiness or tragedy planted in the valley long before the Monroes move to the Battle farm. Steinbeck himself suggested this alternative view of the Monroes and the events in the valley in a letter to a friend, George S. Albee. In this letter Steinbeck described the feeling he wanted to evoke in a reader: "I'd like that feeling to be one of warmth and almost—tolerance. There are no villians only . . . circumstances and coincidences."[6] Here, Steinbeck is suggesting a non-teleological or "non-blaming" reading of the stories, a reading that eventually makes the work richer and more rewarding than would a literal acceptance of the concept of a "Monroe curse."

The idea of the "evil cloud" or curse is firmly planted in the reader's mind in the second chapter of the novel, when Steinbeck describes the mysterious and fatal history of the Battle farm. The history of the Battles, the family who built the farm, foreshadows the subsequent history of the valley and at the same time links the farm and valley securely to the American myth. In the archetypal American tradition, "George Battle came west in 1863" and settled in the Pastures. George marries a woman whom he considers "a good investment," and she bears him a son, John, before going mad and being confined in a mental asylum. The son inherits the farm from his father and "both the epilepsy and the mad knowledge of God" (p. 7) from his mother. In a parody of our Puritan ancestors' struggle with Satan in the wilderness, John does battle with a serpent in the wilderness of the Pastures. Ironically, this serpent is very real and John Battle's illusion kills him, striking him "three times in the throat where there were no crosses to protect him" (p. 8). Thus, in the first story of a family in the Pastures, Steinbeck has introduced the idea of the curse, the theme of destructive and even fatal delusion, and the theme of insanity which will reappear in the story of Helen Van Deventer. He has also reinforced the microcosmic quality of the valley, for if there is a curse on the farm it is the curse of an illusory belief in the valley (America) as a battleground with Satan. John's fatal illusion mirrors the illusion upon which the nation was founded. At the same time, the irony of John Battle's death, coupled with the ironic vignette of the Spanish corporal's discovery and naming of the valley, establishes the tone of irony that runs throughout the book, assuming even greater dimensions in the final chapter. As Lewis has suggested, the history of the Battles also establishes a perspective for the remaining stories by implying that "abnormal behavior is to be ascribed to psychological rather than supernatural causes."[7] George Battle made the mistake of looking for "a good investment in a woman," placing materialistic considerations first; the wife and son he received are the consequences of this failing. The son's delusion and death result from the insanity inherited from the mother. The so-called curse is the product of greed and insanity.

After he provides us with the ironic history of the Battle farm, Steinbeck introduces the Monroes, chronicling the series of failures that have led Bert Monroe to settle with his family on the Battle farm "half convinced that a curse had settled upon him" (p. 17). When Bert suggests to a gathering of the valley's farmers that "maybe my curse and the farm's curse got to fighting and killed each other off," T. B. Allen, the store's owner, replies ominously, "Maybe your curse and the farm's curse has mated and gone into a gopher hole like a pair of rattlesnakes. Maybe there'll be a lot of baby curses crawling around the Pastures the first thing we know" (p. 20). Once this semiserious prophecy has been made, it is extremely difficult not to view each failure or tragedy which occurs in the valley as the birth of another "baby curse," and this is the course most critics have taken. In accepting the reality of the Monroe curse, Peter Lisca states, "It soon appears that the curses have indeed 'mated,' and the Monroes become agents of the progeny." Levant asserts that "in reality, the curses merge, strengthen, and turn outward to the community." Even Joseph Fontenrose, who perceptively suggests that to blame the Monroes for each instance of tragedy "strains the evidence," concludes nonetheless that there actually is a Monroe curse which "affected every resident, whatever his virtues, faults, or condition"; and Fontenrose adds, "As the principal unifying device, the curse is the central mythical construct of *The Pastures*." Warren French sees the Monroes as bearers of a curse of a different nature, but a curse nonetheless: "Their curse . . . is that they never know the right thing to say or do; therefore, they have the calamitous effect of upsetting the precariously maintained equilibrium of insecure people."[8]

As Lewis points out, no curse led to the fatal termination of the Battle family's ownership of their farm, and a close study of what happens in each chapter of *The Pastures of Heaven* suggests that, to take Fontenrose's assertion further, to blame the Monroes for *any* of the misfortunes in the valley "strains the evidence." Fontenrose, in fact, underscores the key to the novel—illusion—when he states: "The valley had a kind of idyllic charm before the Monroes came, but it was a paradise built on illusions, neuroses, evasion—an unstable Eden."[9] The Monroes not only bring no curse to the valley, they may at times benefit the inhabitants of the valley by forcing certain individuals to discard crippling illusions and face reality, harsh though that reality may be.

If we approach the stories in *Pastures* keeping in mind Steinbeck's claim that "there are no villains," it becomes apparent that rather than the supposed Monroe curse, a variety of illusions are responsible for whatever tragedies take place. For example, as Lisca has suggested, Shark Wicks's fall from his position of imagined wealth is due to the fragile illusion he has so carefully nurtured. Levant is misinterpreting Wicks's attitude toward his daughter's virtue when he claims that Wicks "discovers financial value in his daughter's virginity" and therefore "ceases to be human."[10] However, Wicks is responsible for his own misfortune and is much better off after he has been exposed, for at the end of the story he has a strong, supportive wife and an opportunity to make real money by real application of his talents and to win real self-esteem. Steinbeck makes it clear that Wicks *is* financially astute, for he tells us that Wicks gave "startlingly good advice" to his neighbors on financial matters. If Monroe's coincidental involvement has had any effect on Shark Wicks, it has been a positive one in ridding him of his self-defeating illusions.

Molly Morgan also nurtures a carefully maintained illusion concerning her absentee father. Molly lives in a world filled with illusions, as is shown by her need to romanticize the outlaw Vasquez. Molly refuses to allow Bill Whiteside to accompany her on a visit to Vasquez's hideout, reasoning quite correctly that "if Bill comes along, it won't be an adventure at all. It'll just be a trip" (p. 147). Bill sees with the eye of everyday reality, complaining that Vasquez was actually a thief who "started in stealing sheep and horses and ended up robbing stages" and "had to kill a few people to do it" (p. 149). While Molly's desire to maintain an aura of romance in everyday life might ordinarily be applauded, it is a destructive force in her life, paralleling the illusion she desperately clings to about her father, who was, in Bill's words, "kind of an irresponsible cuss" (p. 146). The necessity to maintain the illusory vision of her father drives Molly from the Pastures and the happiness she had discovered there.

Molly's fondness for illusion also has a tragic effect on another inhabitant of the valley, Tularecito. Molly and the society of the Pastures are both responsible for Tularecito's imprisonment in the mental institution. Molly, whose own illusions are so fragile, acts irresponsibly when she suggests to Tularecito that fairies and gnomes really exist and awakens in him a sharp dream of escape from his loneliness and alienation. Of all of the valley's inhabitants, Molly most of all should have realized the dangerous power of such illusions. The community as a whole is ultimately even more responsible for Tularecito's tragedy because it has not the greatness of vision or heart to recognize and accept Tularecito's difference, instead forcing him to attend school in a parody of social normality. The seeds of Tularecito's unhappiness are planted in the blindness of middle-class values of the people of the Pastures. Like Pepé in "Flight," Lenny in *Of Mice and Men*, and Frankie in *Cannery Row*, Tularecito suffers because he is different, a natural rather than social creature forced to confront a social environment with which his instincts cannot enable him to cope. Just as later, in *The Grapes of Wrath*, Noah will confess "I know how I am" before disappearing alone down the river, the only happiness for Tularecito or any of Steinbeck's "naturals" lies in separation from society. Tularecito is not allowed to maintain that necessary separation.

Helen Van Deventer moves to the Pastures to isolate her insane daughter from the dangers of the city. Helen has an obsessive need to feel she is sacrificing herself for others—her dead husband or her mad daughter. This need leads her to refuse a possibility for her daughter's cure and to work hard at retaining the painful memory of her husband's death. In the Pastures, Helen attempts to construct a garden of innocence for her sexually awakened daughter, a mock Eden with a "beautiful log house." Of this house and the garden surrounding it, Steinbeck writes, "The carpenters had aged the logs with acids, and the gardeners had made it seem an old garden" (p. 71). Helen's house and garden are a parody of the American myth, and like those who first looked at America and dreamed of a new Eden, Helen is trying to ignore human reality. She realizes the impossibility of her dream only when the daughter tells of Bert Monroe's visit and of her crazy plan to run away. Shortly thereafter, Helen Van Deventer murders her insane daughter. Before this act, however, Helen has been changing, beginning to feel herself a part of the life of nature surrounding the house. Steinbeck states, "A change was stealing over Helen," and Helen thinks, "But now I'm looking forward to something, I'm just bursting with anticipation. And I don't know what the something can be" (pp. 78–79). What Helen is sensing is a kind of rebirth, a shedding of her illusions as she rids herself of the memory of her husband and her need for the dependence of her daughter. Levant argues that the violent conclusion to the story "is really a means of avoiding the deeper irony . . . that Mrs. Van Deventer is as insane as her daughter."[11] The greater irony, however, exists in the fact that Helen's rebirth, from the repression of the old life into the freedom of the new, takes place in "Christmas Canyon" in the Pastures of Heaven, and the sacrifice that frees Helen consists of the murder of her daughter, the only murder that takes place in the book. This is the central irony of the story, one that Steinbeck carefully underscores.

The story of Junius Maltby is one of the most complex in the book. Maltby and his son are obvious victims of the illusion maintained by the people of the Pastures that to be happy and respectable one must be materialistically productive and properly clothed. Thus, when Mrs. Monroe tries to give the clothes she has purchased to Robbie, Maltby's son, she forces the valley's illusory values upon the child and destroys his former innocence and happiness. It should be noted, however, that long before the Monroes moved to the valley, the women of the Pastures have plotted to "give the poor little fellow a few things he never had" (p. 96) as soon as Robbie was of school age. The fact that it is Mrs. Monroe who has paid for the clothes simply shows her generosity, but makes her no more responsible than the rest of the valley's residents. At the same time, Junius Maltby must bear a share of the responsibility for the unhappy ending to the idyll in the Pastures. He has originally come to the valley to escape from life, declaring the name of the valley to be "either an omen that I'm not going to live . . . or . . . a nice symbolic substitute for death" (p. 86). Junius wants to believe that the Pastures are not a part of the real world: though he comes closer than anyone else in the book to creating his own Eden, in the end the illusion is too fragile and crumbles easily in the face of plain reality. Junius's illusion is dangerous as well as delicate, for it has allowed him to dangle his feet in a stream while his wife's children lay dying, and it has left Robbie unprepared to deal with the real world which closes in on the farm from all sides. Junius prefers to avoid responsibility, and when reality intrudes he scurries back to the city, abandoning Eden. It is appropriate that the one adult in the valley who approves of the Maltbys' life is Molly Morgan, herself about to flee in panic rather than exchange her illusion for a truth.

Joseph Fontenrose has pointed out that "in the postscript to the separate publication of the story, 'Nothing So Monstrous,' he [Steinbeck] imagines that Junius and Robbie returned to the Pastures, occupied a cave in the outlying wilderness, and renewed their old way of life."[12] Steinbeck concluded this fantasy with the statement "I don't know if this is true. I only hope to God it is." As author, Steinbeck was too true to his materials to force such an ending onto the story and thus turn irony into sentimentality. While in wish-fulfillment he could imagine such a conclusion, in *The Pastures of Heaven* he made clear the tenuous and dangerous quality of Junius's attempt to recreate Eden in the fallen world of the valley.

The Lopez sisters, Rosa and Maria, like Tularecito and the Maltbys, suffer when the values of the society of the Pastures are forced upon them. Bert Monroe's unthinking joke merely provides the women of the valley with the opening they need to have the sisters' "restaurant" closed. While it seems that this intolerance is responsible for driving the innocent sisters to San Francisco and the lives of "bad women," in actuality the sisters are victims of their own illusions. It could only have been a matter of time before the women of the valley—women who, as we have seen in the case of the Maltbys, know what their neighbors are up to—put a stop to what was essentially a three-tortilla whorehouse. Like all of the illusions festering in the valley, the illusion nurtured by Maria and Rosa could not stand very much reality.

Of all of the stories in *The Pastures of Heaven*, that of Raymond Banks builds the best case against Bert Monroe. It is tempting, in fact, to agree with Warren French that "in the story of Raymond Banks, Bert Monroe wantonly and quite intentionally sets out to destroy another man's peculiar but socially harmless illusions in order to protect himself from an examination of his own depraved motives and behavior."[13]

Raymond Banks owns a chicken farm, the "most admired" farm in the valley, and Steinbeck tells us that "there was never any of the filth so often associated with poultry farms about Raymond's place" (p. 155). Raymond's approach to life is epitomized in the precise cleanliness of the farm; Raymond does not allow the reality of life's violence or shamefulness to intrude upon his life. He executes his chickens with clinical precision and sometimes invites his neighbors to a barbecue at his farm, where he broils "little chickens," as Steinbeck tells us, carefully turning "the little carcasses over the fire" (p. 164). In his descriptions of the fare at the barbecue, Steinbeck emphasizes the disturbingly delicate and "clean" attitude that Banks has toward death. Steinbeck describes Raymond "grilling little chickens" and returning to the pits "to cook some more for those fine men who might require a second or even a third little chicken" (p. 164). Mrs. Monroe is pictured "shrilling pleasantries around the gnawed carcass of a chicken" that Banks has given her (p. 167). The language of the story forces us to view Banks in an uneasy, disturbing light.

Banks discloses to Bert Monroe the fact that occasionally he goes to San Quentin to watch an execution, and at Monroe's request Raymond obtains an invitation for Monroe to attend the hanging. Raymond, we learn, goes to the hanging because he "had developed an appetite for profound emotion" and he enjoyed the excitement among the witnesses at the execution. He is neither cruel nor morbid but feels nothing at all for the condemned man. In contrast, Bert Monroe's fascination with the idea of witnessing a hanging *is* morbid and is a convincingly normal human reaction. Bert is fascinated and terrified because he knows he will identify and empathize with the dying man and will experience the inevitable feelings of terror, awe, and revulsion. "I'd be sick. I know I would," he confesses as he is backing out of the engagement; "I'd just go through everything that poor devil on the gallows did" (p. 174). Raymond's response at this point is "I tell you it isn't as terrible as that, when you see it. It's nothing" (p. 174). As in "Flight," *The Red Pony, To a God Unknown,* and *The Pearl,* death represents a mysterious and profound experience in Steinbeck's writing, whether it be one's own death or that of another. When Banks attempts to repudiate Monroe's fascination with the horror and mystery of death with the words "It's nothing," he is denying the most profound experience that man can have in Steinbeck's fiction. Bert Monroe's explanation of why he cannot witness the hanging does, as French claims, destroy Raymond Banks's illusion that death is a "clean" and pleasantly exciting event. Afterwards, Banks decides to invite the warden down to the farm to drink beer rather than attend another hanging. However, rather than wantonly destroying Banks's illusions, Monroe has, by his very human reaction, interjected into Banks's sterile world a greater awareness of the enormity of death. Banks may now find the "profound emotion" in everyday life that he previously sought in the executions. Banks's illusions, like the others in the valley, are no match for the reality Monroe forces upon the farmer, and by opening Banks up to this much deeper emotional perception Bert Monroe has made Banks a greater human being in the process.

Like the other inhabitants of the valley, Pat Humbert lives in a world governed by illusion. Pat develops and nurtures his illusion about Mae Monroe out of a scrap of conversation, and his illusions are born out of the crippling influence of his dead parents. Because his parents had forced him to live "in an atmosphere of age, of . . . aches and illness" (p. 177), the warp is permanently set in Pat's character long before he sees Mae Monroe. Whatever effect Mae has on Pat is, in fact, positive, for because of Mae he is able to rid himself of the debilitating influence of his dead parents. When Pat returns home after his illusion concerning Mae has been destroyed, he goes to the barn "to hide for a while, to burrow into some dark place" (p. 201). Pat avoids the house because "he was afraid he might lock up the door again" (p. 201) and let the spirits of his parents return. It is important here to recognize that, even with his illusion destroyed, Pat is fighting for the new life he has made, making a conscious effort not to bury himself in the old life once again by locking the parlor door. Though he wants to "hide for a while," there is no indication that Pat has buried himself again, that he will remain in the barn. Rather than being the victim of the Monroe curse, Pat Humbert has been freed from the curse of the dead parents because of Mae Monroe.

Illusions are also the foundation of the would-be Whiteside dynasty in the Pastures of Heaven, and they bring about the collapse of the dynasty just as they have other dreams in the valley. When he first sees the valley, Richard Whiteside imagines his future home there in an "uncertain and magical light" (p. 203), with "a whole covey of children." He attempts to impose this uncertain and magical vision upon the reality of the valley, and he fails. He plans to build "a structure so strong that neither I nor my descendants will be able to move away" (p. 205). His dream fails when his wife can bear only one living child and that son's wife, in turn, becomes barren after one child. When the grandson Bill, the realist of the Molly Morgan chapter, decides to marry Mae Monroe and move to town, the illusory Whiteside dynasty is finished. When the Whiteside house burns to the ground, the fire is testimony to the delusion upon which the would-be dynasty was founded, not, as Richard Astro has suggested, to "the defeat of the agrarian ideal."[14] The tragedy of the story is due to Richard Whiteside's mistaken belief that he could control the future by trapping his descendants in his personal "uncertain and magical" dream. Commitment to place is desirable in Steinbeck's fiction, but the desire to entrap others in one's personal and private illusion is not.

The final chapter in *The Pastures of Heaven* introduces the second part of the framing device as the passengers of a sightseeing bus discover the Pastures of Heaven. The theme of illusion that began with the dream of the Spanish corporal and permeated each of the chapters in the book is reinforced here at the end as each passenger sees the valley in a unique and illusory vision as a kind of garden where fulfillment and peace conform to one's private dreams. One man would subdivide the valley and live contentedly in the middle of the subdivision. Another sees sanctuary from the struggles for name and success that lie before him. The priest blindly sees "no poverty, no smells, no trouble," a place where "nothing dirty nor violent would ever happen . . . to make me sorry nor doubtful nor ashamed" (p. 241). Still another sees the valley as a kind of haven where "nothing would ever bother me . . . and I could think" (p. 242). The sightseers' discovery of this imagined Eden repeats the discovery that has been going on throughout the nation's history since the first settlers looked at the eastern shore and envisioned a New World paradise. Their failure to see the real valley that lies below them echoes the failures of the valley's inhabitants and the failure of the American myth on a national scale.

Steinbeck wrote *The Pastures of Heaven* while the troublesome *To a God Unknown* was having no success finding a publisher and shortly after his eventful meeting with Ed Ricketts in 1930. *The Pastures of Heaven* was born between the original writing of *To a God Unknown* and the final rewriting of that novel in accordance with the non-teleological thinking Steinbeck and Ricketts were exploring. While Astro argues that "there is perhaps less of Ed Ricketts in this . . . than in any of the novelist's prewar works after *Cup of Gold*,"¹⁵ it seems highly likely that *The Pastures of Heaven* would reflect the kind of philosophical thought Steinbeck was becoming increasingly absorbed in at this time. And if we look at *Pastures* as a non-teleological work, the meaning of the book and what Steinbeck was attempting become much more clear. In *To a God Unknown* we, along with Joseph Wayne, were required to divorce ourselves from a causal or teleological perspective in order to understand, as Joseph finally does, man's place in the "overall pattern." Those readers who failed to make this philosophical transition were trapped in shortsighted teleological thought that would cast Joseph as a literal priest of nature and his self-sacrifice as the cause of the rain that falls. Similarly, if we simply accept the idea of a Monroe curse as the supernatural cause of the problems in the valley, we are committing ourselves to the same kind of partial vision that Joseph had to transcend. Once we have accepted a "non-causal" or "non-blaming" viewpoint, we can see the crucial fact that "there are no villains" in this novel, and this, in turn, allows the novel a psychological complexity otherwise denied it.

If we fail to approach the novel in a non-teleological fashion, we allow ourselves to become mired in illusions just as are the people of the valley and the people on the bus. Steinbeck asks us in this novel, as he did in *To a God Unknown*, to work toward an understanding that transcends illusions and sees things as they really are. The central message here is that there are no Edens, for that is the most American and most dangerous illusion of all.

In Dubious Battle:
The "Recording Consciousness"

With *In Dubious Battle* (1936) Steinbeck created what has often been called his most objective work, a "non-blaming" study of a strike in a small orchard valley in California. While critics have often clashed in their evaluations of most of Steinbeck's works, this study of fallen man in a fallen Eden has won nearly universal praise and has, as Warren French states, "often been called the best novel about a strike ever written." Most critics would probably agree with Joseph Fontenrose that "in no other book has [Steinbeck] so completely avoided subjective statement" and with Peter Lisca's claim that "it is Steinbeck's most objective novel."[16] What to do with this objective novel has proved to be something of a problem for critics, however, a problem made more complex by the fact that Steinbeck's voice and philosophy are unmistakably present in the novel in the form of Doc Burton; yet Steinbeck claimed that "there is no author's moral point of view," and stated, "I wanted to be merely a recording consciousness, judging nothing, simply putting down the thing" (*Life in Letters*, pp. 105, 98).

Taking their cue from the novel's title and epigraph, both Lisca and Fontenrose have discovered extensive parallels between *In Dubious Battle* and *Paradise Lost*. Fontenrose says simply, "Satan's rebellion has everything to do with *In Dubious Battle*," and proceeds to find direct correspondences between characters in the two works: Satan is the Party and can be represented by either Mac or Jim; London, the "big guy" who is the strike's figurehead, is Beelzebub; Dakin, who is overly attached to his material possessions, is Mammon; Dick, the handsome bedroom radical, is Belial. Lisca largely agrees with these parallels and, like Fontenrose, points out Jim's simultaneous role as a Christ-figure. Fontenrose suggests that "the theme of war in heaven is interwoven with that of the sacrificed god-king. Jim as Party member is Satanic; as a person he is a Steinbeckian Christ." Lisca elaborates on this point: "Jim Nolan is but one of many Christ figures in Steinbeck's fiction—from Joseph Wayne in *To a God Unknown* to Ethan Allen in his last novel, *The Winter of Our Discontent*. No matter how different their conditions and actions, their lives take on significance by their engaging in the most essential attribute of Christ—sacrificing their lives for the benefit of mankind."[17]

There can be little doubt that Steinbeck, so acutely conscious of the structural possibilities in myth, intended for these parallels to be recognized. Mac and Jim are obviously Satanic in their ruthless manipulation of the ignorant strikers, and their battle against the seemingly omnipotent growers in the valley reflects the "dubious" nature of Satan's battle on the plains of Heaven. The fact that they are both highly aware that this is but one small skirmish in a very extended war with capitalism suggests Satan's "eternal hate" and eternal war. At the same time, the theme of sacrifice is heavily underscored in the novel, and Jim, like Joseph Wayne, is indisputably a sacrificial figure and strongly equated with Christ. This is made clear by the cocks that crow before Jim is killed (p. 263), by his ability to see Mary in the woman combing her hair with a "wise smile" (p. 273), and by the kneeling position in which he remains after he has been killed (p. 312). It is also suggested by Doc's recognition of "something religious" in Jim's eyes, something he says is "the vision of Heaven" (p. 182). Still another time, Doc abruptly sees Jim and Lisa and the infant together and declares, "This looks like the holy family" (pp. 218–19). The theme of blood and blood-sacrifice is woven through the novel and underscored by the sacrifices of Joy, old man Anderson, and finally Jim.

Steinbeck's central concern in *In Dubious Battle* is once again with the theme of commitment, the theme he discovered and carefully developed in *To a God Unknown*. Both the Satanic and Christian symbols and allusions are integral elements in Steinbeck's investigation of the phenomenon of commitment in this novel.

In a letter discussing *In Dubious Battle*, Steinbeck wrote: "I have used a small strike in an orchard valley as the symbol of man's eternal, bitter warfare with himself" (*Life in Letters*, p. 98). This valley, with its extensive apple orchards, is called the Torgas Valley in the novel and is another of Steinbeck's fallen Edens. The purpose of the title and epigraph is quite simply to underscore the dubious quality of the strike which is taking place, a strike which symbolizes the war originating in man's imperfect nature. Steinbeck is careful not to make the strikers admirable. They are at times cowardly, envious, lazy, and cruel. At the same time, the growers are depicted as ruthless, cruel, and greedy. Mac, a brilliant agitator, is at times convincingly humanitarian and at times a cold and callous exploiter of men for the "cause." That Steinbeck was interested in something other than the immediate phenomenon of the strike is indicated in a letter in which he declared: "I'm not interested in [the] strike as a means of raising men's wages, and I'm not interested in ranting about justice and oppression, mere outcroppings which indicate the condition" (*Life in Letters,* p. 98).[18]

The war between the strikers and growers, or communists and capitalists, illustrates the theme of "man's eternal, bitter warfare with himself," a theme that is underscored when Doc tells Jim, "The other side is made of men, Jim, like you. . . . We fight ourselves and we can only win by killing every man" (p. 230). Steinbeck's primary interest, however, is in exploring the nature and effects of commitment and noncommitment in the characters of Jim Nolan and Doc Burton. Ironically, it is through nonintellectual commitment to a dubious cause which eventually dehumanizes and destroys him that Jim finds fulfillment and happiness for the first time in his life. Just as ironically, it is through his intellectual desire to see "the whole picture" that Doc finds only an inability to commit himself to any group and the loneliness and unhappiness that accompanies such noncommitment.

As Howard Levant, among other critics, has pointed out, Jim Nolan's conversion to the Party represents a kind of rebirth, "a symbolic passage from death to life."[19] Before joining the Party, Jim tells Harry Nilson, the Party man, "I feel dead. Everything in the past is gone" (p. 7). Later, he explains his reason for joining: "I feel dead. I thought I might get alive again" (p. 7). Jim's conversion, however, what Doc describes as his "vision of Heaven," leads him farther and farther from humanity in the course of the novel. In the beginning Jim instinctively likes old Dan and has to be told by Mac, "Don't waste your time on old guys like that" (p. 65). Likewise, he is drawn to old man Anderson and, again, Mac must admonish him: "Don't you go liking people, Jim. We can't waste time liking people" (p. 103). By the end of the novel, however, it is Jim who castigates Mac for liking him (Jim) too much to use him properly, complaining, "You're getting just like an old woman, Mac" (p. 169). And it is Jim who supports Mac after Mac has pulverized the face of a high school boy associated with the vigilantes. "Don't worry about it," Jim says. "It wasn't a scared kid, it was a danger to the cause. It had to be done, and you did it right. No hate, no feeling, just a job" (p. 248). Mac's response illustrates the reversal which has taken place: "You're getting beyond me, Jim. I'm scared of you. . . . God Almighty, Jim, it's not human. I'm scared of you" (p. 249). In spite of Mac's callousness and Jim's growing inhumanity, neither loses completely his hold on humanity. Mac, whom Doc calls accurately "the craziest mess of cruelty and hausfrau sentimentality" (p. 187), demonstrates his humanity through his growing attachment to Jim and his genuine remorse for Anderson's ruin. The lasting traces of Jim's humanity are indicated by his desire, just before death, to "just sit down in an orchard" and "to sit all day and look at bugs" (p. 298).

In spite of the faint traces of human warmth left in Jim, it is appropriate that when he is killed his face is erased by the shotgun. Jim has lost his individual identity in his absolute commitment to the cause at the same time that he has increasingly lost his ties to humanity. Fontenrose suggests that Jim is "faceless" because "he has become Everyman."[20] In "Flight"—a story of Everyman's flight from and toward death—Pepé became faceless when an avalanche delicately covered his face at the moment of death. In that story, Pepé's facelessness signified his return to the "whole" symbolized by the mountains. In *In Dubious Battle*, Jim loses his identity in the process of total commitment; unlike Joseph Wayne or Pepé, Jim does not become a part of "the whole thing, known and unknowable"—he becomes a faceless part of the "cause." The emphasis is not on man's relationship with the "whole" in this story, but on the isolated and stark fact of commitment.

After Jim is killed, Mac carries the faceless body to the platform in the strikers' camp and "uses" Jim as the blood-sacrifice necessary to inspire the men to more violent and hopeless resistance. Mac's, and the novel's, last words echo what seems to be a Party cliché, the same words Mac used when Joy was killed by the vigilantes: "Comrades! He didn't want nothing for himself—" (p. 313). Ironically, the words in Mac's half-finished sentence are not only a Party cliché, they are also true and underscore Jim's totally selfless devotion to the cause. Warren French declares that "Jim has not only been used in life and death; he has been wasted." Calling *In Dubious Battle* Steinbeck's most pessimistic work, French adds, "Even had Jim survived the strike, his commitment to the 'cause,' Steinbeck intimates, would have dehumanized him."[21] The tremendous tension in this final scene, however, derives from the irony and ambiguity of Mac's final words. The Party cause has consistently been shown to be "dubious" at best, pursued by cruel and inhuman means; and to this dubious cause Jim has sacrificed himself. Mac's calculated and cold use of Jim's body, in the same way that he has used old Dan, Lisa in childbirth, Anderson, and the dead Joy, emphasizes again the "dubious" aspect of the strike. At the same time, however, Mac's words ring with moving sincerity, for there can be no doubt that Mac knows that what he is saying is deeply true for Jim and that Mac felt a strong bond, even love, for Jim. Thus, in one tightly knit scene, Steinbeck has brought the human and inhuman values of the novel into direct and unresolvable tension and made Mac the vehicle for this tension. No judgment is provided by the author; the character is left to bear the burden of ambiguity alone.

Doc Burton stands in direct contrast to Jim throughout the novel. Doc tells Mac, "I don't believe in the cause, but I believe in men" (p. 176). He will attempt to help the men involved in the strike all that he can, but Doc is totally unable to commit himself to the cause. Though Richard Astro has suggested that Doc is "modeled directly on Ed Ricketts," perhaps a more accurate definition of Doc's role in the novel is provided by Lisca, who says of Steinbeck, "As author, his stance toward the novel is close to that of Doc Burton . . . toward the strike situation: that of open-minded observer whose involvement transcends the particular and immediate terms of what is taken as a conflict of universal forces—'the whole thing.'" In fact, Doc's statement, "I want to see the whole picture. . . . I don't want to put on the blinders of 'good' and 'bad,' and limit my vision" (p. 130) may call to mind the philosophy of Ed Ricketts, but it also closely echoes Steinbeck's stated desire in writing this book to be "merely a recording consciousness, judging nothing, simply putting down the thing." Lisca asserts, "That Burton's ideas reflect those of the novelist is seen clearly through reading *Sea of Cortez.*" Astro has effectively shown that it is at best difficult to attribute much of the philosophy in *The Log from the Sea of Cortez* to Steinbeck alone, and if we depend upon that work it could easily be argued, as Astro does, that Doc Burton's ideas reflect the thinking not of Steinbeck but of Ed Ricketts.[22] However, we need go no further than Steinbeck's letters to find indisputable evidence that the theories advanced by Doc Burton were, by the time of the writing of *In Dubious Battle,* Steinbeck's own.

Of group-man Doc says, "A man in a group isn't himself at all, he's a cell in an organism that isn't like him any more than the cells in your body are like you. . . . People have said, 'mobs are crazy, you can't tell what they'll do.' Why don't people look at mobs not as men, but as mobs?" (p. 131). In a letter to a friend, George Albee, just before writing *In Dubious Battle,* Steinbeck wrote, "You must have heard about the trickiness of the MOB. Mob is simply a phalanx, but if you try to judge a mob nature by the nature of its men units, you will fail just as surely as if you tried to understand a man by studying one of his cells" (*Life in Letters,* p. 80).[23] Clearly, at the time of this letter Steinbeck felt

the group-man theory as he expressed it to be his own. Similarly, Mac tells Doc, "The trouble with you, Doc, is you're too God-
damn far left to be a communist" (p. 131). This is a definition
Steinbeck claimed for himself: "A Communist told me the other
day that I was so far left that I would be shot by the most rabid
nihilist as a danger to the nihilist order."[24]

Doc is the spokesman for Steinbeck's point of view in this
novel; his detached, intellectual position of noncommitment
mirrors the novelist's relationship to his materials. Doc resists
such an easy definition, however; he is a deeply ambiguous
character. Doc illustrates clearly Steinbeck's belief that "man is
lonely when he is cut off. He dies. From the phalanx he takes a
fluid necesary to his life" (*Life in Letters,* p. 81). Doc tells Mac,
"I'm lonely, I guess. I'm awful lonely. I'm working all alone
towards nothing" (p. 232). Critics have consistently noted Doc's
alienation. Levant says, "Doc suffers bitterly from his scientific
detachment. He is unable to join with men or to have any deeply human contacts." Astro concludes that "Doc drifts off into the
night, a lonely, defeated man, whose defeat is the direct result of
his inability to reconcile his non-teleological world-view with a
teleological program of meaningful social action." A third critic,
Linda Ray Pratt, exalts Mac as "the only character who balances
a capacity for morality and action with self-examination and
doubt" and declares with some accuracy that "Doc is the only
alternative to Mac . . . an alternative . . . with which Steinbeck
himself perhaps identifies sympathetically."[25]

Pratt convincingly argues that "Doc . . . offers no easy alternative, for though his gentle humanism is emotionally attrac-
tive, his inability to make a commitment to belief reduces him
to despair and thus undermines the validity of his point of
view." In his most pessimistic utterance, Doc declares that "man
has engaged in a blind and fearful struggle out of a past he can't
remember into a future he can't foresee nor understand. And
man has met and defeated every obstacle, every enemy except
one. He cannot win over himself. How mankind hates itself" (p.

230). Of these sentiments Pratt says, "Doc's thinking erases all distinctions which make human existence meaningful. . . . His belief that 'mankind hates itself' forces Doc into such a negative perspective that he sees humanity as ignoble and pathetic. For Doc, the distinctions necessary to a moral commitment are too difficult to make."[26]

In view of Doc's loneliness, isolation, and despair, and his pathetic disappearance into the night, it is easy to agree with Pratt's evaluation, an evaluation which the structure of the novel seems to support. However, a distinctive and very different light is cast upon Doc and the novel as a whole when we realize that the very sentiments Pratt condemns Doc for are Steinbeck's as well as his character's. In the same letter in which he declared his desire to be "merely a recording consciousness," Steinbeck stated that "man hates something in himself. He has been able to defeat every natural obstacle but himself he cannot win over unless he kills every individual. And this self-hate which goes so closely in hand with self-love is what I wrote about" (*Life in Letters*, p. 98). Following Pratt's argument, it would seem that, for Steinbeck as well as Doc, "the distinctions necessary to a moral commitment are too difficult to make." On the other hand, if we accept the claims of both the author and his character, it is obvious that both Steinbeck and Doc are carefully and rigidly avoiding moral commitments or judgments here in order that each may see "the whole picture" of the phenomenon that each is studying—the picture that Mac and Jim are unable or unwilling to see.

Steinbeck claimed that three layers of interest existed in *In Dubious Battle*: "surface story, group-psychological structure, and philosophical conclusions arrived at, not through statement but only through structure." Citing this statement, Clifford Lawrence Lewis argues that "Steinbeck failed in the latter effort to eliminate statement. Doc Burton's psychological and philosophical theories nearly destroy the novel and Steinbeck's tendency to add statements to his later works seriously mars his achievements."[27] If we heed Steinbeck's declaration that "this is a pretty carefully done [manuscript]" (*Life in Letters,* p. 105) and look very closely at the structure of this novel, it should become apparent that Lewis is misinterpreting the vital role which Doc, with his psychological and philosophical theories, plays in the novel. The surface story is that of the strike and its ramifications; the group-psychological structure is found in the novel's study of the "phalanx," a theme which provides the novel with much of its dynamic force and which is voiced at times by several characters, from old Dan to London, Mac, Jim, and Doc; the philosophical conclusions arrived at through structure are conclusions regarding man's need for commitment, conclusions that reverberate through all of Steinbeck's fiction both before and after *In Dubious Battle.*

Although Doc's philosophical viewpoint concerning the strike and mankind as a whole is unmistakably Steinbeck's viewpoint as well, the structure of the novel condemns Doc by bringing him into a tense psychological conflict with the "phalanx" which demands a commitment Doc cannot make. The structure of the novel implies that commitment—even the pure impulse toward commitment untouched by moral considerations—is necessary and that he who cannot make this commitment is cut off and dies, regardless of the correctness of his stance. This is simply the way it is.

Doc's theories, which express his need to see "the whole picture," provide the necessary counterbalance to the emotional momentum of the strike and its leaders. At the same time, the strike and particularly Jim cast doubts upon Doc's position of detachment, forcing us to acknowledge the fatal flaw in Doc's intellectual apartness. The "frightful kind of movement" and "terrible order" which Steinbeck claimed for this novel (*Life in Letters,* p. 99) arise from the ominous momentum of the group-psychological structure, but they are more than that; they stem from the careful balance of the irreconcilable tensions that work against one another to prevent the book from falling into any kind of moral framework. Neither author nor reader is allowed to make definitive moral judgments. The strike tactics and the actions of group-man are at best dubious, as is the entire conflict, and exemplify "man's eternal, bitter warfare with himself"; yet through his total commitment to this dubious cause Jim becomes a Christ-figure and his life and death take on meaning. Jim is coldly dehumanized and undergoes a religious transformation at the same time. Doc sees the "whole picture" and correctly recognizes the dubiousness of the Party's tactics and philosophy, yet because of his ability to see clearly Doc is lost in loneliness and despair. Finally, because Steinbeck sets himself the task of recording without judgment, of seeing his material the way Doc sees the strike, as author he is by implication as lonely and isolated from his material or subject—mankind—as Doc is from the life-giving warmth of the phalanx.

The only conclusion that stands out clear and certain in this complex and ambiguous novel is that commitment is a necessity for man, commitment even to the point of self-sacrifice and even for a cause of questionable merit. It is the only conclusion that can refute Astro's claim that this novel "ends in self-neutralizing ambivalence."[28]

In Dubious Battle is the most tightly knit of Steinbeck's works, illustrating a highly complex harmony between structure and materials. It is perhaps his most artistically successful novel and a key work in the whole of his fiction, for it marks an important turning point in the direction of two other great works: *Of Mice and Men* and *The Grapes of Wrath*. In *In Dubious Battle*, Steinbeck balances a pure non-teleological perspective against the necessity for commitment and finds commitment of first importance. It is therefore fitting that his next novel, *Of Mice and Men* (1937), while objective in method, should take as its central theme man's loneliness and isolation and the need for commitment between men as a way out of this despair. The work that follows *Of Mice and Men* is *The Grapes of Wrath*, Steinbeck's greatest achievement and one of his least objective works. In that novel the theme of group-man is welded to the theme of commitment to the whole—man plus his environment—and a moral vision is paramount. The late thirties, from the nonjudging *In Dubious Battle* to the jeremiad of *The Grapes of Wrath*, are the years of Steinbeck's mature and lasting fiction, and these years demonstrate a rapid movement away from the "recording consciousness" of the strike novel toward the unmistakably "moral point of view" in the story of the Joads. The unasked question that haunts *In Dubious Battle*—"Am I my brother's keeper?"—becomes the central question in *Of Mice and Men* and rises to epic dimensions in the final scene of *The Grapes of Wrath*, and in both of these novels the answer is an unwavering yes.

Of Mice and Men: The Dream of Commitment

The Eden myth looms large in *Of Mice and Men* (1937), the play-novella set along the Salinas River "a few miles south of Soledad" (*Of Mice and Men*, p. 1). And, as in all of Steinbeck's California fiction, setting plays a central role in determining the major themes of this work. The fact that the setting for *Of Mice and Men* is a California valley dictates, according to the symbolism of Steinbeck's landscapes, that this story will take place in a fallen world and that the quest for the illusive and illusory American Eden will be of central thematic significance. In no other work does Steinbeck demonstrate greater skill in merging the real setting of his native country with the thematic structure of his novel.

Critics have consistently recognized in Lennie's dream of living "off the fatta the lan'" on a little farm the American dream of a new Eden. Joseph Fontenrose states concisely, "The central image is the earthly paradise. . . . It is a vision of Eden." Peter Lisca takes this perception further, noting that "the world of *Of Mice and Men* is a fallen one, inhabited by sons of Cain, forever exiled from Eden, the little farm of which they dream." There are no Edens in Steinbeck's writing, only illusions of Eden, and in the fallen world of the Salinas Valley—which Steinbeck would later place "east of Eden"—the Promised Land is an illusory and painful dream. In this land populated by "sons of Cain," men condemned to wander in solitude, the predominant theme is that of loneliness, or what Donald Pizer has called "fear of apartness." Pizer has, in fact, discovered *the* major theme of this novel when he says, "One of the themes of *Of Mice and Men* is that men fear loneliness, that they need someone to be with and to talk to who will offer understanding and companionship."[29]

The setting Steinbeck chose for this story brilliantly underscores the theme of man's isolation and need for commitment. Soledad is a very real, dusty little town on the western edge of the Salinas River midway down the Salinas Valley. Like most of the settings in Steinbeck's fiction, this place exists, it *is*. However, with his acute sensitivity to place names and his knowledge of Spanish, Steinbeck was undoubtedly aware that "Soledad" translates into English as "solitude" or "loneliness." In this country of solitude and loneliness, George and Lennie stand out sharply because they have each other or, as George says, "We got somebody to talk to that gives a damn about us" (p. 15). Cain's question is the question again at the heart of this novel: "Am I my brother's keeper?" And the answer found in the relationship between George and Lennie is an unmistakable confirmation.

Of Mice and Men is most often read as one of Steinbeck's most pessimistic works, smacking of pessimistic determinism. Fontenrose suggests that the novel is about "the vanity of human wishes" and asserts that, more pessimistically than Burns, "Steinbeck reads, "*All* schemes o' mice and men gan *ever* agley'" [my italics]. Howard Levant, in a very critical reading of the novel, concurs, declaring that "the central theme is stated and restated—the good life is impossible because humanity is flawed."[30] In spite of the general critical reaction, and without

101

disputing the contention that Steinbeck allows no serious hope that George and Lennie will ever achieve their dream farm, it is nonetheless possible to read *Of Mice and Men* in a more optimistic light than has been customary. In previous works we have seen a pattern established in which the Steinbeck hero achieves greatness in the midst of, even because of, apparent defeat. In *Of Mice and Men,* Steinbeck accepts, very non-teleologically, the fact that man is flawed and the Eden myth mere illusion. However, critics have consistently under-valued Steinbeck's emphasis on the theme of commitment, which runs through the novel and which is the chief ingredient in the creation of the Steinbeck hero.

The dream of George and Lennie represents a desire to defy the curse of Cain and fallen man—to break the pattern of wandering and loneliness imposed on the outcasts and to return to the perfect garden. George and Lennie achieve all of this dream that is possible in the real world: they are their brother's keeper. Unlike the solitary Cain and the solitary men who inhabit the novel, they have someone who cares. The dream of the farm merely symbolizes their deep mutual commitment, a commitment that is immediately sensed by the other characters in the novel. The ranch owner is suspicious of the relationship, protesting, "I never seen one guy take so much trouble for another guy" (p. 25). Slim, the godlike jerkline skinner, admires the relationship and says, "Ain't many guys travel around together. . . . I don't know why. Maybe everybody in the whole damn world is scared of each other" (p. 43). Candy, the one-handed swamper, and Crooks, the deformed black stablehand, also sense the unique commitment between the two laborers, and in their moment of unity Candy and Crooks turn as one to defend Lennie from the threat posed by Curley's wife. The influence of George and Lennie's mutual commitment, and of their dream, has for an instant made these crippled sons of Cain their brother's keepers and broken the grip of loneliness and solitude in which they exist. Lennie's yearning for the rabbits and for all soft, living things symbolizes the yearning all men have for warm, living contact. It is this yearning, described by Steinbeck as "the inarticulate and powerful yearning of all men,"[31] which makes George need Lennie just as much as Lennie needs George and which sends Curley's wife wandering despairingly about the ranch in search of companionship. Whereas Fontenrose has suggested that "the individualistic desire for carefree enjoyment of pleasures is the serpent in the garden" in this book,[32] the real serpent is loneliness and the barriers between men and between men and women that create and reinforce this loneliness.

Lennie has been seen as representing "the frail nature of primeval innocence"[33] and as the id to George's ego or the body to George's brain.[34] In the novel, Lennie is repeatedly associated with animals or described as childlike. He appears in the opening scene dragging his feet "the way a bear drags his paws" (p. 2), and in the final scene he enters the clearing in the brush "as silently as a creeping bear" (p. 110). Slim says of Lennie, "He's jes' like a kid, ain't he," and George repeats, "Sure, he's jes' like a kid" (p. 48). The unavoidable truth is, however, that Lennie, be he innocent "natural," uncontrollable id, or simply a huge child, is above all dangerous. Unlike Benjy in *The Sound and the Fury* (whom Steinbeck may have had in mind when describing the incident in Weed in which Lennie clings bewildered to the girl's dress), Lennie is monstrously powerful and has a propensity for killing things. Even if Lennie had not killed Curley's wife, he would sooner or later have done something fatal to bring violence upon himself, as the lynch mob that hunted him in Weed suggests.

Steinbeck's original title for *Of Mice and Men* was "Something That Happened," a title suggesting that Steinbeck was taking a purely non-teleological or nonblaming point of view in this novel. If we look at the novel in this way, it becomes clear that Lennie dies because he has been created incapable of dealing with society and is, in fact, a menace to society. Like Pepé in "Flight," Tularecito in *The Pastures of Heaven*, and Frankie in

Cannery Row, Lennie is a "natural" who loses when he is forced to confront society. This is simply the way it is—something that happened—and when George kills Lennie he is not only saving him from the savagery of the pursuers, he is, as John Ditsky says, acknowledging that "Lennie's situation is quite hopeless." Ditsky further suggests that Lennie's death represents "a matter of cold hard necessity imposing itself upon the frail hopes of man." Along these same lines, Joan Steele declares that "Lennie has to be destroyed because he is a "loner" whose weakness precludes his cooperating with George and hence working constructively toward their mutual goal."[35] Lennie, however, is not a "loner"; it is, in fact, the opposite, overwhelming and uncontrollable urge for contact that brings about Lennie's destruction and the destruction of living creatures he comes into contact with. Nonetheless, Steele makes an important point when she suggests that because of Lennie the dream of the Edenic farm was never a possibility. Lennie's flaw represents the inherent imperfection in humanity that renders Eden forever an impossibility. Lennie would have brought his imperfection with him to the little farm, and he would have killed the rabbits.

When Lennie dies, the teleological dream of the Edenic farm dies with him, for while Lennie's weakness doomed the dream it was only his innocence that kept it alive. The death of the dream, however, does not force *Of Mice and Men* to end on the strong note of pessimism critics have consistently claimed. For while the dream of the farm perishes, the theme of commitment achieves its strongest statement in the book's conclusion. Unlike Candy, who abandons responsibility for his old dog and allows Carlson to shoot him, George remains his brother's keeper without faltering even to the point of killing Lennie while Lennie sees visions of Eden. In accepting complete responsibility for Lennie, George demonstrates the degree of commitment necessary to the Steinbeck hero, and in fact enters the ranks of those heroes. It is ironic that, in this fallen world, George must reenact the crime of Cain to demonstrate the depth of his commit-ment. It is a frank acceptance of the way things are.

Slim recognizes the meaning of George's act. When the pur-suers discover George just after he has shot Lennie, Steinbeck writes: "Slim came directly to George and sat down beside him, sat very close to him" (pp. 118–19). Steinbeck's forceful prose here, with the key word "directly," and the emphatic repetition in the last phrase place heavy emphasis on Slim's gesture. Stein-beck is stressing the significance of the new relationship be-tween George and Slim. As the novel ends, George is going off with Slim to have a drink, an action Fontenrose mistakenly in-terprets as evidence "that George had turned to his counter-dream of independence: freedom from Lennie." French suggests that "Slim's final attempt to console George ends the novel on the same compassionate note as that of *The Red Pony*, but Slim can only alleviate, not cure, the situation."[36] Steinbeck, howev-er, seems to be deliberately placing much greater emphasis on the developing friendship between the two men than such in-terpretations would allow for. Lisca has pointed out the circular structure of the novel—the neat balancing of the opening and closing scenes. Bearing this circularity in mind, it should be noted that this novel about man's loneliness and "apartness" began with two men—George and Lennie—climbing down to the pool from the highway and that the novel ends with two men—George and Slim—climbing back up from the pool to the highway. Had George been left alone and apart from the rest of humanity at the end of the novel, had he suffered the fate of Cain, this would indeed have been the most pessimistic of Steinbeck's works. That George is not alone has tremendous significance. In the fallen world of the valley, where human commitment is the only realizable dream, the fact that in the end as in the beginning two men walk together causes *Of Mice and Men* to end on a strong note of hope—the crucial dream, the dream of man's commitment to man, has not perished with

Lennie. The dream will appear again, in fact, in much greater dimension in Steinbeck's next novel, *The Grapes of Wrath*.

In *The Long Valley*

The whole range of Steinbeck's symbolic topography is to be found in *The Long Valley*, Steinbeck's only collection of short stories, written over a period of several years and published in 1938. Because of the diversity of settings in this volume, the title is somewhat misleading, and Richard Astro is correct when he argues that "it is pointless to seek a unifying thematic thread connecting the eleven stories in *The Long Valley*." Astro goes on, however, to assert incorrectly that "all but 'Saint Katy the Virgin' are vignettes set in California's Salinas Valley."[37] In actuality, only a few of the stories are set in the valley, and in this fact can be found the basis for the lack of thematic unity in the volume as a whole.

"Flight" and the stories that make up *The Red Pony* are set on the western and eastern slopes of the Santa Lucia Mountains, and these mountains are the dominant symbols and thematic force in each of these stories. "The Snake" is set not in the valley but in Dr. Phillips's laboratory on Cannery Row in Monterey, and the sea with its strong symbolic ties to the unconscious is the major topographical force here, as it is in other Steinbeck writings set near the sea. Because these stories are dominated by settings very different from that of the valley which gave this collection its name, I have discussed them in the sections entitled "The Mountains" and "The Sea." "Breakfast," a fragment that is of interest primarily because it later found its way into *The Grapes of Wrath*,[38] is of no thematic significance to this discussion and thus, along with the burlesque "Saint Katy the Virgin," has been omitted from discussion here. Of the remaining stories, it is possible to say that "The Chrysanthemums," "The White Quail," "The Harness," and "Johnny Bear" are all very

probably set in the "long valley" and take on thematic significance and unity because of this setting. "The Murder" is, like
"Flight" and *The Red Pony* and *To A God Unknown*, set in the
Santa Lucia Mountains, and this fact undoubtedly determined
the central role death plays in the story. However, as Peter Lisca
and Roy Simmonds have both shown, it is likely that this story
was conceived originally as part of *The Pastures of Heaven*, another work with a valley setting, and to this intended setting
can be attributed the strong thematic similarity between this
story and the other stories set in the Salinas Valley. Because of
this marked similarity, "The Murder" is discussed in this section. The settings for "The Raid" and "The Vigilante" are inde-
terminant and have little or no thematic significance in the stories. They may well be set in the valley, but thematically both
stories look back toward the themes of group-man and commitment in *In Dubious Battle* and forward to the same themes in *The
Grapes of Wrath*. These two stories contribute little to whatever
thematic unity may be discovered in this volume, but because
they do reflect the thematic concerns that engrossed Steinbeck
in his major valley fiction—especially the central theme of commitment through sacrifice—they are also discussed here.

Warren French has found a unifying element in the theme of
frustration running through several of the stories in *The Long
Valley*, and Fontenrose has suggested that "Steinbeck's title indicates a topographical unity," and that "in *The Long Valley* the
mythical theme of the garden is fused with the central theme of
all mythologies, cosmos against chaos." Reloy Garcia has elabo-
rated on the garden theme, suggesting that "there is a common
context, the garden, and a common theme as well, which derives
from the context and amplifies it. This theme is the brutal initiation into the world of disappointment, loneliness, manhood,
knowledge, evil, and death; in short the world of man. . . . Over
and against the painful awareness each initiation induces, character after character attempts to create a static, child's garden
which walls out the chaotic world of man." While such readings

are extremely helpful in understanding some of the stories in the volume, it is a mistake to attempt to harness the entire volume with a single thesis. It is with great difficulty, for example, that the theme of initiation can be made clear in such a story as "The Chrysanthemums," or that *The Red Pony* can be understood as "cosmos against chaos." On the whole it is more useful to admit, as Fontenrose does elsewhere, that the volume is primarily "a series of unconnected stories," or to agree with Brian Barbour that "for the most part, the book's order seems random; stories do not comment on or deepen each other. . . . The book lacks a center."[39]

The exception to this apparent lack of unity can be found only in the group of stories unmistakably set in the valley for which the collection is named. If there is a thematic dominance in the volume, it is generated by the thematic continuity found in these stories. To attempt to impose a strict unity on the volume as a whole is to ignore the realities of the work—that it serves most obviously as a way for Steinbeck to capitalize on the fame he had suddenly begun to achieve with the publication of *Tortilla Flat*, *Of Mice and Men*, and *In Dubious Battle*. It is a patchwork volume, as such inclusions as "Breakfast" and "Saint Katy" should clearly illustrate.

"The Chrysanthemums": Waiting for Rain

Of the first story in *The Long Valley*, "The Chrysanthemums," Steinbeck wrote: "It is entirely different and is designed to strike without the reader's knowledge. I mean he reads it casually and after it is finished feels that something profound has happened to him although he does not know what nor how" (*Life in Letters*, p. 91). In light of the eagerness with which critics have rushed to praise this story, calling it "Steinbeck's most artistically successful story," and "one of the world's great short stories,"[40] it seems that most critics would agree that "something profound" happens in "The Chrysanthemums." And the great difficulty critics have encountered when trying to explain the "what" and "how" of this story suggests that Steinbeck's design has been very effective, has led, in fact, to what Roy Simmonds refers to as "a small critical industry" grown up around this story.

Like each of the stories in *The Long Valley* actually set in the valley, "The Chrysanthemums" is about the repression of powerful human impulses, the repression that would be necessary in any would-be Eden set in the fallen world of the valley. And like the subterranean current of the Salinas River that Steinbeck describes in *East of Eden,* these human urges throb just below the surface of everyday life and occasionally burst through to the surface in sudden floods. This theme of repression (which French labels "frustration") is introduced in the opening imagery of "The Chrysanthemums" when we are told that "the high grey-flannel fog of winter closed off the Salinas Valley from the sky and from all the rest of the world. On every side it sat like a lid on the mountains and made of the great valley a closed pot" (p. 9). In this fog-lidded valley, it is "a time of quiet and of waiting" (p. 9). We enter here the lifeless winter of T. S. Eliot's *The Waste Land,* and the fertilizing rain is not likely to come soon, for, as we are told, "fog and rain do not go together" (p. 9). Like the plowed earth which waits "to receive the rain deeply when it should come," Elisa Allen cultivates her flower garden in a kind of suspended life, awaiting the fertilizing imagination of the tinker.

The difficulty posed by the "what" and "how" of this story is indicated in the fact that most Steinbeck criticism has tended to touch only briefly upon the story in passing. French is satisfied to call Elisa Allen "the victim of an unscrupulous confidence man," but he fails to shed any significant light on the story. More recent and comprehensive studies have been achieved in Mordecai Marcus's essay "The Lost Dream of Sex and Childbirth in 'The Chrysanthemums,' " Elizabeth McMahan's " 'The Chry-

109

santhemums': Study of a Woman's Sexuality," and William V. Miller's "Sexuality and Spiritual Ambiguity in 'The Chrysanthemums.'" As the titles suggest, each of these essays stresses the unmistakable significance in the story of Elisa's sexual frustration. The essays differ, however, about the importance of Elisa's frustrated maternal instinct. In a still more recent article, "The Original Manuscripts of Steinbeck's 'The Chrysanthemums,'" Roy Simmonds argues against the popular interpretation of Elisa's character, suggesting that "there is a case for suspecting that Elisa is the one who is unable or unwilling to satisfy her partner sexually."[41]

According to Marcus's reading of the story, Elisa's unfulfilled yearning for children gives birth to the tremendous current of frustration running through the story. Marcus argues that when the tinker coldly discards the flowers, "her feminine self, her capacity for fructification and childrearing, the very offspring and representative of her body, have been thoughtlessly tossed aside." McMahan, arguing correctly that no critic "has yet adequately explained the emotional reasons underlying [Elisa's] frustration," contends that "Elisa's need is definitely sexual, but it does not necessarily have anything to do with a longing for children"; instead, McMahan proposes that Elisa is discontented: "She is a woman bored by her husband, bored by her isolated life on the farm." Miller, in a more comprehensive and persuasive approach, locates Elisa's dream of fulfillment on three levels: "the conventional, the sexual, and the 'romantic.'"[42] Miller's reading would thus include the possibilities of sexual and maternal frustration (though Miller chooses to stress the former and to downplay the latter), while also accommodating McMahan's theory of "boredom." There is yet, however, a still more comprehensive basis for the tension and frustration which permeates this story, a basis involving once again the theme of commitment that runs in a steady current through Steinbeck's fiction.

It is obvious that these critics would all agree that "something profound has happened" in "The Chrysanthemums," and just as obviously they would not agree precisely about what has happened or how it happened. To argue as McMahan and Miller do that Elisa's frustrated yearning for "fructification" does not play a very central role in this story is to ignore the full meaning and impact of the imagery of the story, imagery that introduces and reinforces the theme of procreation in the form of the ploughed land waiting for rain. Elisa, in middle age, is implicitly compared to the plowed furrows in winter, and to say that Elisa is simply bored with her life is to miss the force with which the opening paragraphs establish this parallel and the note of nearly hopeless expectancy dominating the story's atmosphere. At the same time, the theme of repression is very pronounced in the opening imagery and in Steinbeck's description of Elisa's "hard-swept looking little house" and her "over-eager, over-powerful" trimming of last year's flowers. Elisa's response to the tinker is violently sexual once he has made a connection between himself and the chrysanthemums, but only *after* he has made this vital link between himself and Elisa's "flower-children." The sexuality of Elisa's response to the tinker becomes unmistakable when she intones, "When the night is dark—why, the stars are sharp-pointed, and there's quiet. Why you rise up and up! Every pointed star gets driven into your body. It's like that. Hot and sharp and—lovely" (p. 18). Finally, Steinbeck has forced the sexual tension of the scene to such a pitch that Elisa becomes a parody of a bitch in heat: "She crouched low like a fawning dog" (p. 18).

While critics have been unanimous in recognizing the theme of repressed sexuality in this story, it is a mistake to attempt, as McMahan does, to limit the story's thematic significance to this alone. In Elisa the sexual and maternal impulses are blended into a single, frustrated urge, a longing for deep fulfillment. It is difficult not to see the "strong new crop" of flowers Elisa nurtures as surrogate children in her barren world. At the same time, the tinker's exotic life does symbolize a kind of escape for

Elisa from the barrenness of the farm, an appeal to what Miller terms Elisa's "romantic" dream of fulfillment. All of these needs and urges come together, however, in the single powerful and unfulfilled yearning for the fertilizing potential inherent in deep human contact and commitment, the most significant symbols of which are sex, childbearing, and sacrifice. While the themes of sex and procreation are strong throughout the story, the theme of sacrifice is introduced in the story's conclusion.

After Elisa has seen the discarded flowers—evidence of the tinker's broken faith—she asks her husband, Henry, about the fights he has mentioned earlier. "I've read how they break noses," she says, "and blood runs down their chests. I've read how the fighting gloves get heavy and soggy with blood" (p. 23). Elisa's sudden interest in the fights which seemed to repulse her earlier has been seen as a rising desire for "vicarious vengeance" upon men, or simple "vindictiveness."[43] Such readings seriously undervalue the complexity of the story, however, and of Elisa's emotional response to what has taken place. Although Elisa does ask, "Do the men hurt each other much?" the emphasis here is not upon simple vengeance upon mankind or vicariously upon the tinker; nor does it necessarily indicate Elisa's need for a "sense of dominance over the male" as Roy Simmonds suggests.[44] Elisa's primary interest is in the blood. Coupled with her strong desire for wine at dinner, this imagery suggests another theme—that of commitment through sacrifice. Blood, as Mac knows well in *In Dubious Battle* and Joseph Wayne discovers in *To a God Unknown,* is the supreme symbol of commitment, and wine, of course, calls to mind the supreme Christian sacrifice. Elisa yearns here, in the wake of her abrupt awakening and disappointment, for a kind of futile sacrament—reacting to the arousal and frustration of her deepest needs, Elisa is seeking symbols of commitment in a world of physical, spiritual, and emotional isolation and sterility. Like so many of Steinbeck's characters, she is acting out of a profound loneliness.

"The Chrysanthemums" is Steinbeck's finest story precisely because he does not tell us the "what" or "how" and because the powerful imagery of the story is woven brilliantly into a single fabric with theme and character. Elisa, on her isolated ranch in winter, waiting for the fructifying rain which is not likely to come, matched with a capable but not deeply sensitive husband, is cut off from fulfillment. In this story, the theme of human isolation and commitment central to *Of Mice and Men* is imbued with a strong current of repressed sexuality and maternity, and the result is the most emotionally forceful and subtly crafted of Steinbeck's stories.

"The White Quail": Inside the Garden

Perhaps the most unmistakable Eden in all of Steinbeck's writing is Mary Teller's garden in "The White Quail," the second story in *The Long Valley*. Unlike Elisa Allen's chrysanthemum garden, no powerful sexual current flows through Mary's Edenic garden, for Mary has willed her garden into being as a barrier between herself and all contact with the world outside. Mary's garden is an attempt to construct an unfallen Eden in a fallen world, a neurotic projection of Mary's self.

Mary's garden is cut off from the imperfections of the ordinary world of mankind by the fuchsias that wall out "the dark thickets of the hill," thickets which to Mary represent "the world that wants to get in, all rough and tangled and unkempt" (p. 32). Like the garden, Mary is, as her husband Harry says, "kind of untouchable" (p. 20). Harry tells her, "You're kind of like your own garden—fixed and just so" (p. 20). Joseph Fontenrose says, "Mary's garden is a Platonic heaven, changeless and eternal, a cosmos inhabited only by a creator, eternally admiring his (her) handiwork." "The hillside," Fontenrose adds, "represents the world, including human society. That is, our cosmos is Mary's chaos."[45] Our world is, in fact, the actual fallen world, and Mary's garden is, like Elisa Allen's, very vulnerable to intrusions from that imperfect world regardless of the barriers she has willed into being.

Mary has been called "pathological," "narcissistic," and even a symbol of the Romantic artist "whose sublimination of all other values to her private vision is an act ultimately destructive of them."[46] While each of these readings does provide some insight into Mary's character, the key to this character and the story may once again be found in the theme that dominates Steinbeck's writing during the thirties: the necessity for human commitment as a wasteland of human isolation and loneliness. Mary attempts to exclude sexuality, a vital aspect of human commitment (as was seen in "The Chrysanthemums") and a symbol of imperfection in a perfect garden, from her make-believe Eden. We learn that, as a child, Mary was warned not to taste the "marvelous candy from Italy," because "it's prettier than it's good" (p. 39). Mary strives not to taste forbidden fruit, to keep experience out of the garden of her life; to achieve this end, she locks her door against Harry: "The lock was an answer to a question, a clean, quick, decisive answer. . . . It seemed to make him ashamed when he turned the knob and found the door locked" (p. 36).

As Fontenrose has suggested, Harry is one of the "devils" in Mary's paradise, a constant threat to the carefully crafted innocence of the garden.[47] Like the threatening gray cat, Harry represents the real world that Mary cannot keep forever from her garden. When Harry deliberately shoots the white quail, he is intuitively attacking the very center of Mary's Edenic illusion, what she describes as "an essence boiled down to utter purity" (p. 38). Mary reacts angrily to Harry's suggestion that the quail is an albino with "no pigment in the feathers, something like that" (p. 41). "Albino" indicates the opposite of the perfection Mary seeks; it suggests a missing element, an incompleteness. The quail thus very accurately represents Mary's essence, for she too, like the much more diabolical Cathy of *East of Eden*, lacks completeness.

Like "The Chrysanthemums," "The White Quail" is a story about human isolation. Harry's poignant cry, "I'm lonely. . . . Oh, Lord, I'm so lonely" (p. 42), echoes Elisa's predicament and Doc Burton's lament in *In Dubious Battle*. It reiterates two central themes in Steinbeck's fiction: the futility of holding to the Eden myth—even the danger of the illusion—and the necessity for commitment. To see Mary as a symbol of the isolated artist does not conflict with this reading of the story, nor does it strain the thematic structure as Brian Barbour has suggested.[48] That Steinbeck was very aware of and concerned with the role of the artist at this point in his career is obvious in his treatment of Doc in *In Dubious Battle;* that he felt that the artist must be actively committed to and a part of humanity is demonstrated by the increasingly subjective role of the author in *The Grapes of Wrath* and *East of Eden* and by the intense humanism of his Nobel speech.[49]

"The White Quail" is a weaker story than "The Chrysanthemums," and not as successful as other stories in *The Long Valley,* because Steinbeck too clearly left bare the "what" and "how" of his mechanism in this, his most mechanical Eden. Barbour is correct when he asserts that "the use of symbolism is heavy-handed, almost allegorical." He is less correct, however, when he claims that the shift in focus from Mary to the husband's frustration at the climax blurs the "force of the story."[50] While there is no resolution, no sense that either the husband or the wife grasps the complexity of their predicament the way Elisa does in "The Chrysanthemums," the story ends with a statement of the destructiveness of the Eden myth when it bars man from deep commitment to the world he inhabits, to "the one inseparable unit man plus his environment." Though Harry has brought the full force of imperfect reality to bear upon Mary's Eden the moment he has elected to kill the quail, the story ends with nothing truly changed. Though in his frustration Harry has struck at the heart of Mary's illusory garden, he finally permits her illusion to live on while taking upon himself the guilt for what he perceives to be a criminal act: "What a skunk I am . . . to kill a thing she loved so much" (p. 42). Harry is left lonely and ashamed, an exile from the unreal Eden which he has not the courage to destroy. Like "The Chrysanthemums," this story offers a portrait of an emotional wasteland without any certain hope for fructification, spiritual or physical.

"The Harness": The Good, Fallen Man

The parallel themes of loneliness and illusion, which are central to both "The Chrysanthemums" and "The White Quail," appear again in "The Harness," another of the stories in this volume set in the valley.[51] While Emma Randall has not tried to create an Edenic garden on the small farm she shares with her husband Peter, she has forced Peter to live within the strictures of an illusion she has willed into being. Peter is Emma's garden, and with the harness and girdle that she forces him to wear, Emma attempts to deny the reality of human imperfection or change.

Peter, who resembles both Elisa of "The Chrysanthemums" and Harry of "The White Quail," is lonely and has an unfulfilled need for deeply felt human contact. His wife is cold and sickly, "a little skin-and-bones woman" who "was sick most of the time" (p. 111). Steinbeck describes the Randall house as being "as neat and restrained as its owners" (p. 112), and adds, "Emma had no children. The house was unscarred, uncarved, unchalked" (p. 113). It is a cold and barren existence in which Peter is cut off from warm human contact with his wife by her very nature and from the rest of the world by the illusion his wife forces him to maintain. Peter's deep sexual and spiritual starvation sends him on his annual trips to the "fancy houses" of San Francisco.

When Emma finally dies, Peter is freed of her strictures; he rips the harness and girdle off and declares, "I'm a natural fool! For twenty years I've been pretending I was a wise, good man—except for that one week a year" (p. 120). Peter's profound need for sensation, for color and warmth, is reflected in his immediate decision to plant the whole farm in sweet peas after his wife's death. As we learn near the end of the story, however, he has been unable to enjoy the sweet peas because the gamble with a delicate and unpredictable crop has worried him terribly the whole time. As Joseph Fontenrose has shown, the irony of this story lies in the fact that there is, after all, only one Peter Randall: Peter the respectable farmer who existed beneath Emma's harness. In the final scene of the story, we learn not only that Peter has not been able to enjoy the flowers, but also that he is once again "busting loose" in San Francisco and preparing to return home and do penance on the farm by putting in electric lights. "Emma always wanted electric lights," he says (p. 129). Peter has not been able to change, and he attributes this fact to the belief that Emma is still controlling him. "She didn't die dead," he says, adding, "She won't let me do things" (p. 129). Peter's illusion prompts Fontenrose to suggest that Peter "needs Emma, alive or dead, to govern him, to save him from sinking into the chaos of instinct and sensual appetite." And Fontenrose adds, "Emma is a deity of a very Hebraic cosmos, and Peter is her faithful creature, subject, and servant."[52] In actuality, there is never any danger that Peter would "sink into the chaos of instinct and sensual appetite." The real irony of the story is that Peter is the "wise, good man" he pretended to be. In trying to deny Peter's "natural" slouch, and in apparently denying any emotional or physical commitment between Peter and herself, Emma was attempting to deny the possibility that Peter could be both good and flawed, or fallen. The truly good Peter was denied in favor of an illusion of unfallen perfection. Even after Emma's death, Peter is unable to free himself from the trap of Emma's illusion and see himself for what he really is: the good, wise, "ordinary" farmer. Perpetually harnessed by Emma's illusion, Peter maintains the illusion that man cannot be both good and fallen.

"Johnny Bear": Artist as Recorder

The destructive force of the Eden myth is again at the center of "Johnny Bear," still another of the stories in *The Long Valley* set in the Salinas Valley. In this story, the Hawkins sisters, Emalin and Amy, stand for spiritual and moral perfection in the midst of the "dirty little town" of Loma. The Hawkins sisters' aristocratic house, carefully walled in by a seemingly impenetrable cypress hedge, is the small town's unfallen garden, and the sisters bear the weight of this burden much as Peter Randall bore the harness of Emma's illusion. As it is in each of the other stories set in the valley, repression is again a key theme in "Johnny Bear," and, as it was in "The Chrysanthemums," this repression is symbolized by the fog that moves in upon the town from the "great black tule swamp" outside of town. The story is both about man's futile attempts to wall out reality in order to maintain an illusion of moral perfection and about the artist's role in laying bare the reality beneath the illusion.

Emalin and Amy Hawkins, we are told, are the town's "aristocrats, its family above reproach." They are "symbols" and "the community conscience." Of the sisters' role, the narrator says, "A place like Loma with its fogs, with its great swamp like a hideous sin, needed, really needed, the Hawkins women" (p. 158). Around the Hawkins house, the square "green barrier" of the cypress hedge appears "incredibly strong and thick" (p. 156). Appropriately, the narrator, slipping into the present tense, says, "There must be a small garden inside the square too" (p. 156). Like Mary Teller's little "symbolic trees"—the fuchsias—the hedge walls in the supposed Eden that serves to harness the town's symbols. Emalin and Amy are, above all, products of the town's need for the illusion—the town has willed them into being as much as Mary Teller willed into being her garden. The narrator suggests the painful repression of the sisters' lives when he sees them in their buggy and remarks, "It seemed to me that the check-rein was too short for such an old horse" (p. 157). The check-rein keeps the horse's neck arched, giving him the appearance of a young horse and maintaining an illusion of perfection that does not allow the old horse to fall into the posture dictated by age and nature. The check-rein is another version of Peter Randall's harness. Acting through the immediate presence of Emalin, the town serves as Amy's check-rein and eventually drives her to suicide. When Alex, the narrator's friend and the character who provides the necessary insight into the town's attitude toward the sisters, says, "There's something hanging over those people," he is inadvertently pointing to the force that the town's illusion brings to bear upon the women. Almost immediately, he adds, "They can't do anything bad. It wouldn't be good for any of us" (p. 163).

The fog, symbol of the pervasive repression, moves ominously in upon the town and the two women as the tragedy of Amy's suicide draws closer. When Alex stops the doctor's car and learns that something has happened to Amy, the narrator comments, "I was about to remark that the night was clear when, looking ahead, I saw the rags of fog creeping around the hill from the swamp side and climbing like slow snakes on the top of Loma" (p. 159). In this image, the fog represents both the repression forced upon the sisters and the serpent of experience, which coils about the town and finds its way into the Hawkins garden.

As Warren French has noted, "Johnny Bear" is one of Steinbeck's most haunting and least discussed stories. One of the first critics to deal with the story in any depth was Peter Lisca, who remarked perceptively that this story is "on one level an exploration of the artist's role in society," this role being to expose man's "hidden festers." Brian Barbour, in constrast, has argued that "no art literally holds the mirror up to nature. It doesn't reproduce the chaos of events. But Johnny Bear functions as little more than a super tape recorder, and attempts to show him as the artist revealing the community's secret soul to itself are not convincing."[53] If we examine Johnny Bear closely, however, it appears that Barbour's objections are not valid. Johnny Bear's role is not merely to hold the mirror up to nature; his recording consciousness is informed and guided by what he is aware that his audience will pay for in whiskey. Thus, he reflects the need and desires of his audience, an audience which needs to know the reality behind the illusion even as it desires desperately to maintain the illusion. The narrator indicates as much when he says of Johnny Bear, "It's not his fault. . . . He's just a kind of recording and reproducing device, only you use a glass of whiskey instead of a nickel" (p. 164). Later, the narrator points out the real relationship between Johnny and his audience when he says, after having plied Johnny with whiskey, "I was really responsible" (p. 161). And again, the narrator defines Johnny's role when he says of those listening: "Now those men really wanted to know. They were ashamed of wanting to know, but their whole mental system required the knowledge" (p. 165). Thus, Johnny Bear, another Steinbeck natural, provides a necessary function, that of the artist whom society pays to tell it what it does not want to know about itself but must, in fact, know.

Johnny Bear is John Steinbeck, a writer who, while writing his most pessimistic novel, *In Dubious Battle,* thought of himself as merely a "recording consciousness," and who spent a large portion of his career holding his audience's illusions up to the light to show their falseness and their danger. Like Samuel Hamilton in *East of Eden,* Steinbeck's finest works hold man's illusions up to him—particularly the illusion of Edenic perfection in the New World—in order to show their "dirt and danger" (*East of Eden,* p. 171). "Johnny Bear" is one of those works.

"The Murder": Illusions of Chivalry

"The Murder" is undoubtedly the most difficult and perplexing of the stories collected in *The Long Valley*. As its inclusion as an O. Henry Prize Story for 1934 suggests, the story contains unmistakable power, but the "what" and "how" of this story are as difficult to discover as they are in "The Chrysanthemums," the first story in *The Long Valley*, while the artistic fabric is much less successfully woven. Like Steinbeck's "Flight," "The Murder" is set in the coastal mountains of north central California, in Cañon del Castillo, "one of those valleys in the Santa Lucia range which lies between its main spurs and ridges" (p. 171). And like "Flight," this story is dominated by the theme of death. At the same time, "The Murder" clearly belongs with the other stories in *The Long Valley* in its incorporation of the themes of isolation and illusion, twin themes that form a continuous thread through "The Chrysanthemums," "The White Quail," "The Harness," and "Johnny Bear."

As Katherine M. Morseberger and Robert E. Morseberger have stated, "Seen only as a narrative, the story makes little sense except in terms of suspense and erotic violence, and Steinbeck critics have accordingly ignored it almost entirely." In an interesting reading that stresses what they term the "folktale quality" of the story, the Morsebergers outline the ritualistic aspects of "The Murder" and suggest that Jelka "embodies primitive passions that tie man to his biological primordial past." These critics go on to see the story as "a testament that mysteriously primitive passions and past are still with us." While such a reading provides a fascinating perspective on the story's emotional force and is much superior to Warren French's suggestion that the story is "an illustration of racial superiority," or Brian Barbour's claim that the story is "absurd," it still deals with only one aspect of the story while ignoring others equally crucial.[54]

Critics have consistently failed to examine very closely the

121

theme of illusion which is introduced in the opening description of the "strange accident of time and water and erosion" that has created the illusion of a "tremendous stone castle, buttressed and towered like those strongholds the Crusaders put up in the path of their conquest" (p. 171). To Barbour, this description "sounds an opening note of the eerie and that is all . . . it is just window dressing." To the Morsebergers, the illusory castle merely reinforces the "folktale quality" of the story.[55] America has produced no writer more acutely conscious of setting than Steinbeck. To assume that the carefully detailed introductory description in this story could be mere "window dressing" is to seriously misunderstand Steinbeck's method. To attribute the description somewhat vaguely to a desire for "folktale quality" is nearer to Steinbeck's method but seriously undervalues both technique and the importance of setting in Steinbeck's works.

As he does in other stories in this volume, Steinbeck introduces the theme of illusion in order to suggest man's failure to grasp a reality that conflicts with what he desires to believe. "The Murder" is heavily ironic because what Jim Moore wants to believe is that one should not beat one's wife, in spite of Jelka's father's advice that "he's not like a man that don't beat hell out of him" (p. 173). Jim's illusion consists of a kind of chivalry symbolized by the unreal castle—a chivalric code which dictates that it is barbarous and "foreign" to beat a wife even if the wife's culture has conditioned her to expect or even desire the beating. That the story embodies a conflict in cultural values has been pointed out by Roy Simmonds, who has shown that in the original draft of "The Murder" the protagonist was named Thomas Manuelo More, a name which was subsequently changed to Ernest More and finally to Jim Moore. As Simmonds states, the name More suggests "the intrinsic theme of the story: the clash between the comparative mores of two racial communities."[56] Because Jim refuses to recognize Jelka's foreignness, he cannot establish a deeply emotional or psychological commitment with her. The result is that there is "no companionship in her" (p. 173). His loneliness causes Jim to seek the noisy companionship of the girls in town and causes Jelka to seek that of one of her own people, her cousin. Jim Moore finds Jelka with the cousin; he ponders for a moment and then kills the cousin. Later, he beats Jelka severely with a bullwhip and establishes the emotional and psychological commitment that has been missing from the relationship.

In shooting the cousin, Jim acts accordingly to the accepted standards of chivalry for "Monterey County, in central California." The killing is condoned and even admired by Jim's neighbors and earns him respect in the nearby town. When Jim deliberately and dispassionately beats Jelka, he is bowing to what he now realizes are her expectations and needs, and when she asks expectantly, "Will you whip me any more—for this?" he replies carefully, "No, not anymore, for this" (p. 186). The implication is that the mores of Monterey County, which condone such a murder and even encourage it, are even more barbarous than those of Jelka's people, which require the beating of a wife. When he beats Jelka, Jim has fully accepted her difference. Katherine and Robert Morseberger make a very good point: "On a realistic level, the murder and the beating represent for Jelka the kind of absolute commitment she wants from Jim."[57] On a symbolic level, the butchered calf that brings Jim back to the ranch, the pig's blood that he remembers his mother catching in a bucket, and the murder all represent sacrifices which, as throughout Steinbeck's fiction, are symbolic of commitment.

In the end, it is obvious that Jim Moore's mores and his illusion of chivalry were as false as the sandstone "castle" at the canyon's head. Once he can approach Jelka on her terms, the barrier between them is dissolved and for the first time her voice has a "resonance in it" and her eyes "dwelt warmly on him" (p. 186).

In finding a troublesome "indefinite overall conclusiveness" in "The Murder," Roy Simmonds argues that the symbol of the illusory castle is "inadequately employed" and that "this carefully prepared ambiente is simply discarded."[58] It should be clear, however, once we have recognized the central theme of this story—the theme of illusion—that the ambiente is not only carefully prepared but that it introduces very effectively and subtly the idea of an illusory chivalry that is central to an understanding of Steinbeck's story. In preparing his ambiente, Steinbeck is careful to associate the murder of Jelka's cousin with the sandstone castle: "Below the castle, on the nearly level floor of the canyon, stand the old ranch house, a weathered and mossy barn and a warped feeding-shed for cattle" (p. 171). Almost immediately following this description, we learn that imagination has turned the site of the murder into a place of awe, where "boys tramp through the rooms, peering into the empty closets and loudly defying the ghosts they deny" (p. 171). The imaginary castle casts an ironical light over the entire story. The castle establishes the perspective through which we are to view events in the story; it informs the story and hovers over it as it does the abandoned farmhouse. Rather than being "simply discarded," the image of the castle is a highly effective device integral to the structural coherence of "The Murder."

However, in spite of Steinbeck's characteristically brilliant use of setting in this story, Simmonds is correct when he declares that " 'The Murder' is by no means one of Steinbeck's more successful stories." "The Murder" lacks the sense of precise control evident in such stories as "The Chrysanthemums" or "Flight," a difficulty particularly evident in the role of the animal imagery in Steinbeck's characterization of Jelka. Simmonds suggests that the animal symbolism in this story is "somewhat overstressed, so that eventually, so unremittingly is it hammered home, it begins to defeat its own purpose."[59] Throughout the story, Jelka is so closely and repeatedly associated with animal imagery as to become almost purely animal herself. At one point Steinbeck writes: "She was so much like an animal that sometimes Jim patted her head and neck under the same impulse that made him stroke a horse" (p. 173); and when Jim looks for her after the murder, he unerringly goes to the barn and finds her in the hayloft. Jelka's close association with animals is intended to suggest her strong need for unconscious, physical, and sensual communication with Jim. Whereas Jim misses conversation, Jelka misses the physical contact her cultural background has supposedly taught her to need even in the form of beatings.

So heavy-handed is Steinbeck's association of Jelka with the animal imagery of the story that she comes closer than any other Steinbeck character with the exception of such "naturals" as Tularecito and Johnny Bear to fulfilling Edmund Wilson's myopic claim that *The Long Valley* deals "mostly with animals," and that "Mr. Steinbeck almost always in his fiction is dealing either with the lower animals or with humans so rudimentary that they are almost on the animal level."[60] The flaw in Steinbeck's characterization of Jelka arises from the fact that Jelka is not a natural; her humanity is essential to the story's meaning. Like Lennie in *Of Mice and Men*, Jelka represents man's basic yearning for profound, unconscious commitment with his fellow man. While Lennie's animalism is carefully controlled, however, Jelka's becomes so overwhelming as to conflict awkwardly with her role as representative of a culture in conflict with the code of "Monterey County, in central California."

It is this uncertainty in Steinbeck's development of Jelka's character that pervades the story and causes it, in spite of its obvious power, to end on a disturbingly confused note. The unmistakable force of this story comes, however, not from characterization but from Steinbeck's painstaking integration of setting, symbol, and theme. From the first words of the story, and the description of the ominous "strange accident of time," Steinbeck introduces and underscores the theme of illusion, illusion that Jim Moore must transcend—even through murder—in order to realize a fundamental human commitment with Jelka. In spite of Steinbeck's apparent difficulties with Jelka's character, "The Murder" demonstrates an impressive structural coherence and power characteristic of the best of Steinbeck's stories in *The Long Valley.*

"The Raid": Commitment and Sacrifice

In contrast to the other stories discussed here, the valley setting plays no distinctive thematic role in "The Raid," Steinbeck's story about two communist organizers who bear the brunt of a vigilante raid. As Peter Lisca has shown, this story, while tightly organized and projecting a remarkable tension, is of note primarily because it echoes important themes in *In Dubious Battle* and looks forward to *The Grapes of Wrath.* Lisca's well-supported contention that "the story was originally conceived as an episode in [*In Dubious Battle*] or as part of Steinbeck's biographical sketch which evolved into that novel" is persuasive.[61] Thematically, the story parallels elements of both *In Dubious Battle* and *The Grapes of Wrath* in its emphasis on the theme of commitment expressed through self-sacrifice imbued with Christian overtones. Root's statement to the men who are beating him, "You don't know what you're doing" (p. 107), will be echoed almost verbatim by Jim Casy just before he is killed in *The Grapes of Wrath,* and his role as neophyte Party member who becomes quickly committed and is promptly "sacrificed" parallels that of Jim Nolan in *In Dubious Battle.* While the central theme of this story—commitment through sacrifice—is another expression of the primary theme of Steinbeck's fiction, "The Raid" is set apart from the other valley stories by the fact that there is no symbolic Eden and thus no illusion to be exposed and explored. "The Raid" appears, more than anything else, to be a valuable by-product of Steinbeck's strike novel.

"The Vigilante": Psychology of the Cell

In "The Vigilante" Steinbeck explores the psychology of the mob through the thoughts and emotions of one unit in that "phalanx." The story of Mike, who has just been part of a mob that has lynched a black man, reflects Steinbeck's acute interest during the thirties in the phenomenon of group-man. One of the "cells" of the mob, Mike knows that he has been part of something bigger than himself, but he cannot comprehend the thing: "Mike filled his eyes with the scene. He felt that he was dull. He wasn't seeing enough of it" (p. 134). As soon as Mike departs from the mob, he is not a part of the phalanx any longer and he feels cut off and lonely. When he meets the bartender, Welch, the two men instinctively group together in the loneliness that follows the breakup of the mob. They walk home together, seeking an ephemeral sense of commitment, but the sense of isolation deepens. In the end, after his wife accuses him of having been with a woman, Mike realizes that that is exactly how he feels. It isn't the lynching that has done this, however; it is the act of giving himself up to the larger whole—to the phalanx of the mob—that makes him feel this way.

"The Vigilante" explores the group-man theme of *In Dubious Battle* from the opposite perspective from that of Party leaders such as Mac and Jim. Acting again as merely a "recording consciousness," Steinbeck shows here the other side of the coin from "The Raid" and from the view of group-man we get in *The Grapes of Wrath*. It is Steinbeck's only attempt to delve into the mind of one of the common cells of the mob—recording without judging—and as such, it deals with a very different theme from the other stories in *The Long Valley*. Only the theme of isolation, of apartness resulting from the breakup of the group, echoes the primary theme of the valley stories. The message, like that of *In Dubious Battle*, is that man has an urgent and unconscious need to belong to something larger than himself, a

127

need to commit himself even if for only a moment to a cause as dubious as that of a lynch mob.

The Grapes of Wrath: Eden Exposed

The Grapes of Wrath (1939) is one of America's great novels and the zenith of John Steinbeck's career, a mature, extraordinarily ambitious and balanced statement of the major themes that dominated his life's work. Free of the heavy-handed symbolism of such an early work as *To a God Unknown,* and not yet en- snared by the excessive allegorism of the later works, *The Grapes of Wrath* combines the precise craftsmanship of the less am- bitious shorter works such as *In Dubious Battle* and *Of Mice and Men* with the scope and daring of the less successful *To a God Unknown* and *East of Eden.* The result is a tightly unified work of epic dimension moving its focus smoothly from American peo- ple—the Joads and other migrants—to America itself and back again. Malcolm Cowley accurately summed up Steinbeck's achievement in this novel when he declared, "A whole liter- ature is summarized in this book and much of it is carried to a new level of excellence."[62]

Critics have paid a great deal of attention to *The Grapes of Wrath* since its publication. Much of the critical discussion has centered on the group-man or "phalanx" theme in the novel, a theme which received its first statement in Steinbeck's fiction in *In Dubious Battle* (though it also figures briefly in *The Red Pony*) and which grows in *The Grapes of Wrath* to encompass the whole westering movement in America. Richard Astro has provided a careful and perceptive analysis of the marine biologist Ed Ricketts's influence on Steinbeck's thinking in *The Grapes of Wrath,* and other critics, most notably Martin Shockley, have debated exhaustively the Christian elements in the novel.[63] In spite of the disproportionate amount of critical attention paid to this novel, however, critics have generally paid too little attention to the uniquely American significance of *The Grapes of Wrath*. For in this book Steinbeck not only created one of the most powerful social tracts in our literature; he provided the most thorough evaluation and rejection of the American myth offered by any American writer. *The Grapes of Wrath* both condemns the illusion of Eden in the West and offers a way out of the wasteland created by that illusion.

Central to *The Grapes of Wrath* is Steinbeck's continued preoccupation with California as the ultimate symbol of the American Eden, and in this novel the Great Central Valley of California becomes the microcosm of the new Garden. Once again, a California valley is an ironic, fallen Eden, and the old dream of Eden is rejected in favor of a new dream of commitment. A dazzling cornucopia, the Central Valley lures the migrants westward from Oklahoma and the entire Dust Bowl region with the dream of the Promised Land, the same dream that drove their forebears across the Atlantic and across the continent. The journey of the Joads and the other migrants represents both a social phenomenon of the thirties and a recapitulation of the American westering movement with its echoes of the biblical journey toward Canaan—what Lester Marks has termed the "chosen people" motif of the book. Recognizing this obvious Exodus theme, Agnes McNeill Donohue has equated Steinbeck with Hawthorne here, claiming that both "as inheritors of the Puritan tradition use the journey as a complex symbol of fallen man's compulsive but doomed search for Paradise and ritual reenactment of the Fall."[64] While Donohue is correct in placing Steinbeck in the Puritan tradition in his obsession with the quest or journey theme, her interpretation, along with those of most other critics, fails to recognize the fact that for the first time in American literature an author has set out not only to demonstrate the fatal delusion implied in the Eden myth in America, but, more significantly, to replace that myth with a more constructive and attainable dream, the dream of commitment born in *To a God Unknown*—to place and to mankind, "the whole thing, known and unknowable." It is in this proffered solution to the problem of America that Steinbeck breaks rank with his predecessors in American fiction. Whereas many authors—including Hawthorne, Melville, James, even Fitzgerald—have offered visions of the danger inherent in the American Dream, only Steinbeck unhesitatingly offers to light the way out of this "doomed Paradise."

Finally, in *The Grapes of Wrath,* the myth that Steinbeck pursued and tested and systematically rejected for nearly a decade comes face to face with a crushing reality: Eden has been reached—one can go no farther westward on the American continent—and Eden has been found corrupt and indisputably fallen, the rotten fruit of the delusive myth upon which the nation was founded. All of Steinbeck's California fiction, all of his fiction to the time of this novel, points toward this final confrontation between myth and reality in the California Eden.

From the first pages of this novel we are faced with another American wasteland, another version of the master symbol given to the twenties by T. S. Eliot. Critics have generally failed to note, however, the stylistic dexterity with which Steinbeck simultaneously introduces this dustbowl wasteland and subtly foreshadows the structure of the entire novel in the opening paragraphs and first chapter of *The Grapes of Wrath.*

Paragraph one of the novel opens with an impressionistic swath of color reminiscent of Stephen Crane as Steinbeck intones, "To the red country and part of the gray country of Oklahoma, the last rains came gently, and they did not cut the scarred earth." He continues:

> The plows crossed and recrossed the rivulet marks. The last rains lifted the corn quickly and scattered weed colonies and grass along the sides of the roads so that the gray country and the dark red country began to disappear under a green cover. In the last part of May the sky grew pale and the clouds that had hung in high puffs for so long in the spring were dissipated. The sun flared down on the growing corn day after day until a line of brown

spread along the edge of each green bayonet. The clouds appeared, and went away, and in a while they did not try any more. The weeds grew darker green to protect themselves, and they did not spread any more. The surface of the earth crusted, a thin hard crust, and as the sky became pale, so the earth became pale, pink in the red country and white in the gray country.

A close look at this paragraph shows that following the panoramic, generalized opening, the paragraph begins to focus, to zoom in: "The plows crossed and recrossed the rivulet marks." And finally, from the impressionistic opening image our vision has closed the distance to focus very closely on not just "the growing corn" but the "line of brown" that spreads "along the edge of each green bayonet." At once the camera's eye begins to move back to register broader detail of clouds and generalized "weeds" until the paragraph ends where it began, with a panoramic image of the earth, which "became pale, pink in the red country and white in the gray country." In the second paragraph, the narrative eye again zooms in for a closeup: "In the water-cut gullies the earth dusted down in dry little streams. Gophers and ant lions started small avalanches." And again this paragraph expands to end with panorama: "The air was thin and the sky more pale; and every day the earth paled."

In these first paragraphs Steinbeck introduces the pattern upon which *The Grapes of Wrath* will be structured: a pattern of expansion and contraction—of a generalized, panoramic view of the plight of the migrants followed by a close-up of the plight of representative individuals, the Joads. Furthermore, here Steinbeck brings into the novel a naturalistic image central to the opening chapters, the ant lion. The minuscule trap of an ant lion is a funnel of finely blown dust or sand, a fact of nature from which the ant—struggle as he will—cannot escape. Similarly, the migrants cannot overcome the dust trap of the drought; the fact that they are dusted out is something they are powerless to alter and must simply accept. They must go on the road; there is no choice.

The influence of T. S. Eliot and the wasteland theme is first markedly apparent in Steinbeck's writing in the wasted land of *To a God Unknown,* and here, in the blowing, cropped-out earth and shriveled vegetation of the Dust Bowl, Steinbeck presents us with an even more powerful symbol of failed responsibility. Regardless of his professed admiration for the "Okies," not for a moment does Steinbeck exempt the sharecroppers from their portion of blame for the ruined and impotent earth. Like Americans for centuries before them, they have used up the land and now must move west following the archetypal American path. They have "cottoned out" the earth from which they derive their physical and psychological sustenance. Here, in what one critic has mistakenly termed "the land of innocence,"[65] the sharecroppers plead with the owners of the land for the chance to hang on—maybe there will be a war: "Get enough wars and cotton'll hit the ceiling" (p. 32). They are willing to barter death for a chance to further exploit the land. Chester E. Eisenger is undoubtedly right in claiming that the Jeffersonian agrarianism apparent in this novel "emanates from the Joads and other dispossessed farmers, from the people," and that Steinbeck "suggests a primitivistic conception of nature: that the farmer draws spiritual strength as well as sustenance from the soil."[66] However, it should be obvious that Steinbeck is also illustrating a belief that this kind of agrarianism is insufficient in itself; mere contact with the soil that supports them has not prevented the destruction of that soil by the sharecroppers. What Eisenger and other critics who find a strong Jeffersonian agrarianism in this novel have often missed is Steinbeck's condemnation of the sharecroppers and the American system of land exploitation, a condemnation implicit in the farmers' predicament and in their corrupt wish for a war to save them. It is not merely the drought or the creeping centralization of agribusiness that has ruined the farmers; their desire for a profitable war underscores this fact. The farmers have not learned the all-important lesson to be taught in this book: that spiritual and even physical survival

depend upon commitment to a larger whole, to "the one inseparable unit man plus his environment." The sharecroppers of
the Dust Bowl have failed in their responsibility to the land, and
they are sent on the road to learn a new commitment to one
another and to the place they will eventually claim in a new
land.

Steinbeck aligns the migrants firmly with the mainstream of
American history and the American myth when he causes the
characters to declare at various times that their fathers had to
"kill the Indians and drive them away"; and when the tenants
exclaim, "Grampa killed Indians, Pa killed snakes for the land"
(p. 34), we should hear a clear echo of the Puritans who
wrested the wilderness from the serpent Satan and had to kill
many Indians in the process. Though the tenants have tried to
persuade the owners to let them hang on, hoping for a war
boom in cotton, the tenant-voice also warns the owners: "But
you'll kill the land with cotton." And the owners reply, "We
know. We've got to take cotton quick before the land dies. Then
we'll sell the land. Lots of families in the East would like to own
a piece of land" (p. 33). It is the westering pattern of American
history laid bare: drive the Indians and serpent from the Promised Land only to discover that the Garden must lie yet farther
to the west. Reject the poor land, use up the good and move on,
destroying the Garden in the delusive belief that the Garden has
not yet been found. The barren remnants or the unproductive
soil are left for those who come behind. The Joads are firmly
fixed in this pattern of displacement, and they have no choice
but to follow the pattern until, along with the thousands of
other migrants, they reach the barrier of the Pacific. It is the
pattern which left Old Virginia farmed out by tobacco and
which still today lures thousands of Americans westward to the
deserts of Arizona, New Mexico, Nevada, and southern California.

The Eden symbolism in *The Grapes of Wrath* is prominent from
the novel's first chapter to its last. The owners tell the tenants in

Oklahoma, "Why don't you go on west to California? There's work there, and it never gets cold. Why, you can reach out anywhere and pick an orange" (p. 34). And the paean to California sounds again and again until the Joads reach the Golden State. Only Tom is aware from the first that California may not be the Edenic haven they are seeking. Very early, he tells Ma about a Californian who had told him the truth: "He says theys too many folks lookin' for work right there now. An' he says the folks that pick the fruit live in dirty ol' camps an' don't hardly get enough to eat. He says wages is low an' hard to get any" (pp. 93–94). Tom, however, is a pragmatist above all else, a man who says, "I climb fences when I got fences to climb." He realizes that the family has no choice but to move west, that they are trapped in the pattern, so he suppresses his foreknowledge and concentrates on getting the family to California. When they at least reach California, he again establishes a realistic perspective, looking at the mountainous desert waste near Needles and exclaiming, "Never seen such tough mountains. This here's the bones of a country." When Pa protests, "Wait till we get to California. You'll see nice country then," Tom punctures this illusion with "Jesus Christ, Pa! This here *is* California" (p. 211). While not a defeatist, Tom, like Melville's Ishmael, is "quick to perceive a horror." He is the "balanced" man of whom Melville wrote in *Moby Dick,* the man who will eventually grow to become a leader of the people and who does not succumb to illusion or myth. What hope and enduring strength is to be found in this novel comes precisely from this ability to pierce the surface and see the ugly reality beneath the façade of the Eden myth and still maintain and nourish a belief in the future.

The male Joads undergo a ritual cleansing in the Colorado River before making the desert crossing into the Garden of the Central Valley, but even during this casual baptism, reality intrudes in the form of a father and son returning from California. While the men are soaking in the river, these defeated Okies tell the Joads, "She's a nice country. But she was stole a long time ago" (p. 212). From the beginning, the reality of the Joads' situation and of the cultural pattern in which they are caught up has undercut any possibility of a new Eden to the west. Others have gone before them; there can be no unspoiled Garden. Only ignorance of the destructive pattern of which they are a part allows the Joads to naïvely expect a Promised Land in the West. Donohue goes so far as to declare that "although Steinbeck implies naivete rather than conscious evil in the Joads' hopes to assuage their hunger easily, their corrupted neighbors in California and hostile Nature oppress them as thoroughly as if their ignorance were culpable and Steinbeck hints that it is."[67] Donohue fails to realize, however, that the Joads' guilt of "naivete" is the collective guilt of a nation founded upon such a failure to see beyond myth. Their culpability has its roots in their Puritan forebears' vision of America.

Nowhere in American literature does California so magnificently fulfill its role of Promised Land as in the scene in which the Joads are introduced to the Central Valley. They stop the old truck atop Tehachapi Pass to look down the valley. It is dawn, the hour of rebirth: "They drove through Tehachapi in the morning glow, and the sun came up behind them, and then—suddenly they saw the great valley below them. Al jammed on the brakes and stopped in the middle of the road, and, 'Jesus Christ! Look!' he said. The vineyards, the orchards, the great flat valley, green and beautiful, the trees set in rows, and the farm houses." Pa's exclamation, "God Almighty!" is followed by a second catalogue: "The distant cities, the little towns in the orchard land, and the morning sun, golden on the valley." And the paean, reminiscent of Whitman, goes on: "The grain fields golden in the morning, and the willow lines, the eucalyptus trees in rows." And, "The peach trees and the walnut groves, and the dark green patches of oranges. And red roofs among the trees, and barns—rich barns." And finally, "The distance was thinned with haze, and the land grew softer and softer in the distance. A windmill flashed in the sun, and its turning blades

135

were like a little heliograph, far away. Ruthie and Winfield looked at it, and Ruthie whispered, 'It's California!' " Winfield brings the Promised Land into focus with the final comment: "There's fruit" (pp. 235–36).

In this heavily stylized hymn to the Promised Land, all of the possibilities inherent in the dream of a new Eden, from the distant vision of Captain John Smith to the Joads' precarious present, rush to fulfillment. We have indeed been allowed our Pisgah view of the New Canaan, a Garden rediscovered. And, appropriately, once again we encounter a serpent at the edge of Paradise. As the Joads begin to descend toward the valley in the rattletrap truck, "A rattlesnake crawled across the road and Tom hit it and broke it and left it squirming" (p. 238). The path into Paradise has been cleared, and Tom, echoing America's founders and perhaps thinking of the dead grandparents, exclaims, "Jesus, are we gonna start clean! We sure ain't bringin' nothin' with us" (pp. 238–39). It is the archetypal American Dream, and it would appear that the migrants have been reborn in the New Paradise.

It is with this descent into the rich garden of the valley, however, that the fortunes of the Joads, grim thus far, begin their downward flight toward the utter destitution with which the novel ends. Eden proves to be corrupted, its fruit of scientific knowledge rotting in fields and orchards, its lands lying fallow in the ownership of corporations and millionaires, its people divided and frightened and dangerous. And Steinbeck underscores the failure of the American Dream with heavy irony, describing the spring in California in rhapsodic tones recalling the time of "flowering and growth" in *The Wayward Bus*:

> The spring is beautiful in California. Valleys in which the fruit blossoms are fragrant pink and white waters in a shallow sea. Then the first tendrils of the grapes swelling from the old gnarled vines, cascade down to cover the trunks. Then the full green hills are round and soft as breasts. . . . All California quickens with produce, and the fruit grows heavy, and the limbs bend gradually under the fruit. (p. 360).

And when the fruit rots in the fields and orchards, Steinbeck takes on the voice of a modern Jeremiah to cry, "There is a crime here that goes beyond denunciation. There is a sorrow here that weeping cannot symbolize. There is a failure here that topples all our successes" (p. 363). The jeremiad ends with the warning, "In the souls of the people the grapes of wrath are filling and growing heavy" (p. 363). In the end, when Rose of Sharon offers her breast to the starving man, she is fulfilling the promise of nature which has been evoked in this description of spring, the season of rebirth.

Frederick Carpenter long ago pointed out Steinbeck's affinities in *The Grapes of Wrath* with "the mystical transcendentalism of Emerson . . . and the earthy democracy of Whitman, and the pragmatic instrumentalism of William James and John Dewey." And Carpenter concluded:

> For the first time in history, *The Grapes of Wrath* brings together and makes real three great skeins of American thought. It begins with the transcendental oversoul, Emerson's faith in the common man, and his Protestant self-reliance. To this it joins Whitman's religion of the love of all men and his mass democracy. And it combines these mystical and poetic ideas with the realistic philosophy of pragmatism and its emphasis on effective action. From this it develops a new kind of Christianity—not otherworldly and passive, but earthly and active.[68]

While there can be little doubt that faith in the common man—a faith tempered by realism—is central to Steinbeck's thought and to this book, and while Casy's love for the "whole thing" ("There was the hills an' there was me, an' we wasn't separate no more. . . . An' that one thing was holy") recalls the transcendentalism of the nineteenth century, Protestant self-reliance is not a sought-after quality in this novel. What the migrants must learn is to rely on the group above and beyond the individual, and to accept responsibility for all men rather than merely for the self or family. As Warren French has suggested, the migrants must learn to expand their consciousness and sense of responsibility beyond a "reductionist concept of 'family.'"[69] This process of expansion begins when the family takes in Casy, continues with the inclusion of the Wilsons, and culminates in Rose of Sharon's proffered breast. Again, the lesson is that which is central to Steinbeck's fiction: commitment to the whole. And it is insufficient to label this a new kind of Christianity, for while Christian allusions and symbols abound in the novel, to such an extent that critics have yet to agree about whether it is Tom or Casy who is the novel's Christ, the novel purposefully confuses these references in order, as in *To a God Unknown*, to isolate the vital element of commitment at the heart of Christianity and all other religions. We must go beyond even such persuasive "Christian" readings of the novel as Shockley's in order to recognize the new kind of faith Steinbeck is offering in place of the old myth.

A rebirth of consciousness is taking place throughout this novel as the Joads and other migrants shed their ties to the past and to the cultural pattern that put them on the road to California. The strongest ties to the old land for the Joads are severed when the grandparents die. Connie's desertion cuts away the only believer in the modern version of the American Dream— the illusory futures promised in magazine correspondence courses. The loss of Noah, who walks off down the bank of the Colorado River at the edge of Paradise, symbolizes an even more crucial severance, for Noah's name recalls the Old Testament myth of man's rebirth, or salvation from the doomed, corrupt world. With the disappearance of Noah, a symbolic link to the old mythical structure is cut; now survival for the migrants will depend not on divine intervention to save them from the flood that comes, but on mutual commitment. Emphasis has shifted from the Old Testament, with its Eden myth, to the New Testament and an emphasis upon the commitment symbolized by Christ. Finally, it is Rose of Sharon's stillborn child that symbolizes both the ultimate break with the old myth and the greatest hope for the future of the migrants and, in them, of mankind. Donohue suggests that "the child born to Rose of Sharon is no redeemer, but a stillborn messenger of death. In the fallen Eden of John Steinbeck, no redeemer comes."[70] However, the dead infant does serve as a kind of redeemer in this novel. It is, paradoxically, a symbol of rebirth and hope in the tradition of the vegetation cults that Steinbeck evoked in *To a God Unknown*. Like Adonis and other sacrificial deities, the infant undergoes a kind of "death by water" to prepare for new life. At the same time, in Uncle John's act of sending the dead child downstream in the apple box with the words, "Go down an' tell 'em" (p. 465), we cannot fail to see a stillborn Moses, or, as Donohue says, a "messenger of death." Like the loss of Noah (who, symbolically at least, would have certainly come in handy during the great flood), the dead Moses symbolizes the death of the old myth—there will be no further need for a Moses, for there is nowhere for the migrants to go. They are in the Promised Land already, and they must learn to survive both physically and spiritually in the place where they are. The dead child serves notice that the people will wander no longer.

Tom is reborn at this point in the novel to replace the rejected Moses as the leader of the people. As John Ditsky has pointed out, Tom is separated completely from his past in the "coal-black cave of vines" where he has hidden.[71] From this womb of nature, Tom is reborn as a new kind of leader who, like Casy, is committed to the people as a whole and to the place these people inhabit now, be it good or bad. Tom will help his people forge a garden from the inhospitable paradise in which they find themselves, but he will not lead them toward an illusory Promised Land that does not exist. In the words of Peter Lisca, Tom has completed the "movement from escape to commitment."[72]

On the literal level, the infant's death prepares for the powerful symbol of commitment—the proffered breast—upon which the novel will end. It prepares for Rose of Sharon's surprisingly sudden conversion from pathetic self-interest to a broadened consciousness and commitment to life as a whole, symbolized by the unknown old man. The archetypal "caritas" of the final scene symbolizes this commitment.[73] It is important to note here that Rose of Sharon's increasing identification with Ma Joad is designed to prepare her for this new role. When Donohue argues that the Joads' exodus "out of the wilderness to the land of promise is a journey of initiation into dark knowledge, from life to death,"[74] she is ignoring an important element of the journey. The Joads' exodus is from the fatal delusion of the American myth, with its inherent denial of commitment, into a knowledge that leads to commitment. It is a journey toward a mystical and non-teleological commitment leading to a pragmatic ability to survive in the American Eden that never was.

The novel does not carry the migrants, as another critic suggests, "from the innocence of the Oklahoma chapters, to the experience of the highway and California episodes to the higher innocence of the closing scenes,"[75] for while the migrants are for a long time naïve, they are never innocent, especially in the midst of their self-created wasteland. And in the end they are pragmatically committed to the survival of the whole of which they are integral parts. Nor can we say simply that the theme of the final scene and of the novel is that "the prime function of life is to nourish life."[76] For the primary message of the novel is much more complex; it is that the old values and the old myths are dangerously, even fatally, delusive and must be discarded to clear the way for a new commitment to mankind and place, here and now. It is a depiction of and a plea for a genuine rebirth of national consciousness, the mature statement of Steinbeck's major theme and the apex of his achievement.

East of Eden: The "New Eye"

To a God Unknown and *East of Eden* (1952) stand at either end of Steinbeck's career, both extraordinarily ambitious and both flawed, the former pointing the way into the difficult terrain of

Steinbeck's personal mythology, philosophy, and method, the latter looming as an immense terminus, a ponderous summing up. Though Steinbeck was to write several novels after *East of Eden,* he was correct in claiming that he put "everything" into this work. In the words of Warren French, *East of Eden* is Steinbeck's "plan for remaking the world,"[77] a plan toward which Steinbeck had been working throughout his career and which received its most cogent statement in *The Grapes of Wrath*. To Steinbeck, *East of Eden* was the "new eye" of which he had written more than twenty years before, "being opened here in the west."[78] Steinbeck called this novel "the whole nasty bloody lovely history of the world," and said, "Nearly everything I have is in it and it is not full. All pain and excitement is in it and feeling good or bad and evil thoughts and good thoughts—the pleasure of design and some despair and the indescribable joy of creation" (*Life in Letters,* p. 433). Steinbeck tried to put everything he had discovered during two decades of intense exploration into *East of Eden,* and it is this attempt which gives the novel what Lisca calls its "omnivorous, sprawling nature"[79] and which causes the book to fail, as it unmistakably does.

In *East of Eden* all of the major themes that wind their way in an unbroken stream through Steinbeck's California fiction are brought together in an attempt to provide the answer, to show the way with final certainty out of the snare of the Eden myth. Whereas the story of the Joads opened out to encapsulate the history of America, the story of the Trasks and Hamiltons spreads even wider to include the history of America and of all men. Steinbeck examines the foundations of the American consciousness in this novel, and he places an American Adam in the illusory Promised Land in order to demonstrate the failure of the myth of a new man in a new world. And as a replacement for the discarded dream of the Promised Land as well as a solution to the problem of man's isolation and loneliness Steinbeck once again proposes the ideal of man's commitment to man and place.

141

Setting is an active and determinant force in *East of Eden*. In tracing Adam Trask's path from Connecticut to the Salinas Valley, Steinbeck is tracing the symbolic westward trek of *the* American Adam toward the Eden which had eluded him throughout the country's history. The novel begins with a careful and precise establishment of place: "The Salinas Valley is in Northern California." As he does throughout his fiction, Steinbeck renders his setting in full and exact detail before he brings in his characters and begins his human drama. The opening paragraphs of the novel move quickly to establish a symbolic significance in the setting, a significance that not only permeates this novel but reverberates back through all of Steinbeck's fiction to the dark mythology of *To a God Unknown*. Steinbeck's description of the opposing ranges of mountains bears repeating here, for it defines the private topographical symbolism that does not vary throughout his writing, and it helps to define both the strength of the Hamilton dynasty in the eastern hills and the dark ambiguity of the valley where Adam Trask settles and makes his futile attempt to reconstruct Eden:

> I remember that the Gabilan Mountains to the east of the valley were light gay mountains full of sun and loveliness and a kind of invitation, so that you wanted to climb into their warm foothills almost as you want to climb into the lap of a beloved mother. They were beckoning mountains with a brown grass love. The Santa Lucias stood up against the sky to the west and kept the valley from the open sea, and they were dark and brooding— unfriendly and dangerous. I always found in myself a dread of west and a love of east. Where I ever got such an idea I cannot say, unless it could be that the morning came over the peaks of the Gabilans and the night drifted back from the ridges of the Santa Lucias. It may be that the birth and death of the day had some part in my feeling about the two ranges of mountains. (p. 1)

West, as in all of Steinbeck's writing, is the direction of the unknown, of death, and it is synonymous with Eden in the American psyche. If the illusion is to be overthrown, the American consciousness must turn about and commit itself to what it has traversed, to everything eastward of the Pacific shore. And in this eastward directionality, in the end of westering, is to be found commitment and the strength it brings, the strength found in Samuel Hamilton.

From the beginning of our acquaintance with Samuel, it is obvious that he embodies the life-force of the eastern hills. So close is Samuel's relationship with his environment that John Ditsky calls him "an agent of nature."[80] Because of his place in the Gabilans overlooking the Trask ranch, Samuel is beyond the reach of the illusory Eden that beckons from the rich valley floor. He has been forced to accept the harsh reality of his land, and he respects and loves the land. Samuel is the committed Steinbeck hero—committed to place and to man and free of illusion. French calls Samuel "a kind of fisher-king,"[81] and Samuel, waterdiviner and well driller, does assume a kind of fisher-king responsibility for the land—he even tries to blast through the hardpan of the valley in an attempt to "free the waters." Samuel is a Joseph Wayne who is never snared by the illusions that destroy Joseph; therefore, Samuel has no need of self-sacrifice as a means of "breaking through" to a vision of the whole. He is a successful Joseph who is able to see nature as it "is," accepting the dry years with the wet, the bare bones of the hills with the fertile valley. Samuel is able to be both dreamer and "is" thinker, seeing glorious visions of past and future at the same time that he brushes aside the illusions hanging over the Edenic valley to see the "black violence" that is upon it. He applies this same accuracy of vision to Adam Trask. Like Tom Joad, Samuel is the balanced man, able to perceive both good and evil.

Critics have often blamed the lack of unity in *East of Eden* upon Steinbeck's inclusion of Samuel Hamilton and the stories of the Hamilton clan. Peter Lisca states that "the two bodies of material [the Trask and Hamilton narratives] in no way influence or complement each other." French declares that "the decision to introduce the Hamiltons into a novel was unfortunate." Howard Levant contends that "the essential structural presumption is the necessity of a close, working parallel between the two families. Steinbeck does not provide any structure of this kind." In anticipation of such criticism, Steinbeck claimed that he had not "written two books and stuck them together," but that he had "written about one family and used stories about another family as well as counterpoint, as contrast in pace and color" (*Journal of a Novel,* p. 180). If we assume, along with Ditsky, that Steinbeck, a mature and very careful craftsman, "knew what he was doing," we should accept this claim by Steinbeck with a certain degree of authority.[82] And if we examine the role that Samuel and the Hamilton material play in the novel, it becomes apparent that both the author and his critics are correct: Samuel Hamilton is essential to the thematic structure of the novel because he stands in direct and necessary contrast to Adam Trask, in counterpoint, in the same way that the vitality of the eastern mountains stands in sharp contrast to the ambiguity of the valley and the darker unknown mountains to the west. Samuel takes a large measure of his significance from the setting with which he is identified, for in this novel setting goes a long way toward determining character—those who reside in the eastern hills (the Hamiltons) are above the illusions fostered by the rich promise of the valley, and those who settle on the valley floor must struggle through the illusions of Eden to an acceptance of the responsibility symbolized by Samuel. Thus, Samuel's dynasty in the barren hills thrives (with a few setbacks) while Adam's attempt to found a dynasty in the valley founders against the barrier of his illusion of "goodness." Samuel represents the man who has accepted the fact of the Fall and thus the responsibility for life as it really is, both good and evil. Adam, in contrast, clings to the Eden myth and seeks an unfallen garden in a fallen world. Samuel, like his biblical namesake, is the prophet and judge; Adam, like his namesake, is man on trial.

To say that Samuel Hamilton is essential to the novel is not to deny the problems created by the stories of the Hamilton family, stories which contribute little or nothing to the central theme of the novel and which negate the possibility of unity in the work. As Levant has suggested, there is no "close, working parallel" between most of the Hamilton material and the Trask plot. The most obvious example of Steinbeck's failure in judgment in this respect is the vignette concerning Olive Hamilton's airplane ride. Competely out of place in whatever thematic unity the novel possesses, this episode is reminiscent of the most damaging of Steinbeck's sentimental writing in the war dispatches later published as *Once There Was a War* (1958).[83] Perhaps, as French contends, Steinbeck was too close to his material to judge it accurately.[84] Other Hamilton episodes, such as the tragic story of Dessie and Tom, serve to reinforce the theme of man's struggle to cope with an imperfect world, but they offer no significant "counterpoint" or "contrast in pace and color" to the Trask plot, and they succeed in diverting much of the dramatic tension necessary to the furthering of the novel's central Trask narrative. The result is that the story of Adam's Fall and Cal's growth toward a responsible free will is desultory and curiously lacking in power. Cal, the "everyman" of the novel and the character of paramount thematic significance, emerges only near the end of the novel as a character with any meaningful depth, while Tom Hamilton steals much of the novel's thunder through Steinbeck's sensitive and intense portrait of a character of marginal importance.

Adam Trask is the most unmistakable Adam in American literature, an Adam who destroys or damages his own life and the lives of others through his blind refusal to see evil. Together, Adam and his brother Charles represent what Clifford Lawrence Lewis has termed the "split in American consciousness," that dialogue between good and evil which began with the first colonists. Adam symbolizes the American obsession with the idea of America as a new, unfallen world and embodies that train of thought and emotion that gave birth to the image R. W. B. Lewis has called "the American Adam."[85] Charles, on the other hand, represents the dark side of the American consciousness, the Puritan certainty of evil as a palpable absolute. His vision of evil is as unerring as Ahab's, and he is the Satan to his brother's Adam, a "bright being of another species" (p. 21) who can hurt or kill without ever being sorry. Both brothers stand for absolutes, and it is this element in the American consciousness—the illusion of absolute good and evil—that Steinbeck is isolating and condemning through these two characters.

To provide the psychological realism that underscores and attempts to make palatable the heavy, at times clumsy, allegory of the novel, Steinbeck introduces the biblical story of Cain and Able, the archetypal rejection myth. Of this story, Steinbeck wrote: "Without this story—or rather a sense of it—psychiatrists would have nothing to do. In other words this one story is the basis of all human neuroses—and if you take the fall along with it, you have the total of the psychic problems that can happen to a human."[86] As the scar on his forehead, the gift disdained by his Jehova-like father, his total apartness from mankind on the lonely farm, and his role of farmer all testify, Charles is the painfully obvious Cain of *East of Eden*. Adam, whose offering of a mongrel pup is cherished by the father, is Abel, beloved of the Almighty and destined to produce no lasting line of descendants—for mankind is descended not from Abel, who was killed by his brother before producing children, but from Cain, the guilty one. As the Adam/Abel figure, Adam Trask is without the guilt and insecurities resulting from rejection—without Cain's insecurities. He is incapable of recognizing evil as well as good and as such he is easy prey for one who is truly evil, such as Cathy. As he did with the Christ–Moses–John the Baptist parallels in *The Grapes of Wrath*, Steinbeck blurs the parallels between the Charles/Cain and Adam/Abel figures in *East of Eden*. It is Adam, for example, who becomes the outcast and wanderer, like the biblical Cain, while Charles remains at home on the farm. It is appropriate, however, that Charles becomes a marked man and an outcast from society on the farm and dies lonely and isolated. Steinbeck emphasizes this apartness when he writes: "He grew away from the village." And it is also appropriate that Adam, holding steadfastly to his certainty of innocence, takes his place in the historical pattern of westward expansion. Though he is careful not to kill, Adam nonetheless becomes a part of the paradoxical process by which Indians were killed or removed to clear the way for the trek toward the Promised Land and Garden of the West. Clearly establishing Adam's place in this dubious pattern, Steinbeck comments ironically: "It was not nice work, but given the pattern of the country's development, it had to be done" (p. 35).

The character of Charles suggests a major inconsistency that reappears in other central characters and damages the thematic structure of the novel. The problem with Charles is that we are asked to accept him as both evil by nature—as a Satanic "bright being of another species" who is essentially incapable of certain human emotions—and as the victim of rejection by his father. As a symbol of the dark side of the American consciousness, Charles embodies a kind of absolute evil, as his brutal and passionless beatings of Adam testify. He is a lesser monster than Cathy—he is even capable of missing his brother and loving his father—but Steinbeck suggests unmistakably that in Charles, too, "something is missing." As the rejected Cain figure, however, Charles must be supposed to be the victim of neurotic reaction and to be acting out of understandable jealousy and insecurity. Steinbeck makes this reading essential to the novel's central theme. There is thus a major conflict within the character of Charles between a kind of determinism and psychological realism, between the allegorical Charles and the "real" Charles, a conflict which cannot be resolved and which undercuts the *timshel* (free will) theme of the novel. The major example of this inconsistency, however, is Cathy, the representative of absolute and unwavering evil in *East of Eden*.

147

While the central theme of this novel—that man is free to choose good or evil and thus is responsible for his own nature— asks us to reject the illusion of absolutes or the deterministic concept of original sin, Cathy Ames can be read only as such an absolute, a kind of non-teleological fact of evil in the form of an unfinished, genetically misshapen "monster." Steinbeck prefaces his introduction of Cathy with the straightforward admission, "I believe there are monsters born in the world to human parents" (p. 72). As such a monster, Cahty represents a contradiction of Jim Casy's claim in *The Grapes of Wrath* that "there ain't no sin and there ain't no virtue. There's just stuff people do" (p. 23). Because of an apparent accident of creation, *timshel*—"thou mayest"—does not apply to Cathy. That Charles is a lesser version of Cathy is suggested by the similar scars they bear—the mark of Cain—and by her recognition of their kinship. When Charles, who sees through her façade easily, says, "I think you're a devil," she answers, "That makes two of us" (p. 117). Since, as Levant among other critics has suggested, the doctrine of free will is apparently "intended to unify *East of Eden*,"[87] the negation of free will inherent in the character of Cathy represents a serious contradiction in the novel. Steinbeck later hedges when he breaks in to confess, "When I said Cathy was a monster it seemed to me that it was so. Now . . . I wonder if it was true" (p. 184). And in Cathy's fascination with the Wonderland Alice and the illusion of being able to shrink to nothing, Steinbeck seems still later in the novel to be suggesting a paranoia and rejection complex complementing her role as another of the Cain-figures in the novel. However, the weight of the characterization throughout the novel argues against Steinbeck's attempt to humanize Cathy/Kate through a suggestion of a psychologically realistic basis for her thoroughgoing "badness." Cathy is evil; that's simply the way it is. She is consistently described in animalistic imagery, snarling and even ripping Samuel's hand with sharp-pointed "little teeth." Lee, the novel's spokesman/philosopher, suggests in a roundabout way

148

that Cathy may well be a demon (p. 189), and later tells Cal that
"there is something she lacks" (p. 448). Early in the novel Cathy's devilishness is strongly suggested in Steinbeck's description of her feet "almost like little hoofs." Steinbeck seems at a
loss to resolve the problem Cathy presents and to answer the
question he raises when he says, "It is easy to say she was bad,
but there is little meaning unless we know why" (p. 184). Attempting to free himself, his novel, and his readers of the Cal-
vinist certainty of evil, Steinbeck runs up against the age-old
difficulty of rationalizing unrepentant evil in any other way.
Wandering in the darkly complex realm of Hawthorne and
Melville, Steinbeck appears to lose his way; his attempt to answer the dilemma of evil fails. As Levant says, "Evidently Ca-
thy/Kate got out of the author's control."[88]

Joseph Fontenrose was among the first to recognize this major conflict in *East of Eden*. Pointing toward the problematical
question of why, if some characters suffer from a kind of moral
determinism, others may not also, Fontenrose focuses on the
fact that when Adam brutally rejects Cal's offering of money,
Lee tells Cal, "That's his nature. It was the only way he knew.
He didn't have any choice" (p. 544). Fontenrose asks perceptively, "Why doesn't 'thou mayest' apply to Adam as to other
men?"[89] The only answer to this question to be found in the
context of the novel is that in Adam Steinbeck is postulating an
absolute, deterministic "goodness" that stands in direct contrast
to Cathy's (and Charles's) absolute "badness." Thus, Adam and
Cathy represent the two halves of the illusory American myth
with its certainty of both evil and innocence, and neither is capable of functioning with any success in the real, good-and-evil
world of a fallen Eden. The difficulty with such a reading is that
it forces these characters into excessively narrowed roles as
what Steinbeck called "symbol people," and causes them to
contrast uncomfortably with the psychologically "real" characters in the novel, such as Cal and Samuel. Another possible
rationalization may be found in Steinbeck's attitude toward a

149

more vague kind of determinism. In a draft of *East of Eden*, Steinbeck wrote: "You see, what happened in Connecticut in the sixties and seventies is important because it seemed to make a channel in the blood line so that the generations right down to the present were affected. And since the line goes on, probably the tendencies are still there and will continue. I find the shadowy outlines of all my relatives in me, as you will in yourselves."[90] Steinbeck seems to be implying a kind of determinism that becomes diluted as it passes from one generation to the next. Because the emphasis in the early chapters is not on what happened in Connecticut as much as it is purely on character, what seems to actually "make a channel in the blood line" is Cathy-Charles's certainty of evil and Adam's equal certainty of goodness. Steinbeck as author seems unable to resolve the exact nature of this inherited determinism, a difficulty perhaps stemming from the nearly autobiographical nature of much of the novel.

When Adam Trask marries Cathy and takes her (unwillingly) west in pursuit of his Eden, he is not aware that she is a monster capable of burning her parents to death or driving a young teacher to suicide without a second thought. Nor is he aware that his brother's seed is within her, for on their wedding night Cathy, in an apparent ecstasy of "badness," had drugged Adam and slept with his brother. Adam settles with Cathy in the Salinas Valley, described as "that region which heaven unsuccessfully imitated" (p. 134). Intending to found a dynasty, Adam buys nine hundred acres that "straddled the river and tucked into the foothills on both sides" (p. 136). The setting for Adam's land reflects the valley's ambiguity, touching as it does both the western and eastern mountains—the symbolic landscapes of life and death. The ambiguity of the valley is further underscored by the river, which runs in a powerful underground current and can rise in the winter to rage destructively against the valley at the same time that it provides the water necessary to the valley's fecundity. Adam tells Samuel, "I mean to make a garden of my land. Remember my name is Adam. So far I've had no Eden, let alone been driven out" (p. 169). Samuel recognizes the danger inherent in Adam's illusion of an unfallen paradise and says, "It's my duty to take this thing of yours and kick it in the face. . . . I should hold it up to you muck-covered and show you its dirt and danger" (p. 171). Samuel realizes that Adam is refusing to see the realities of man and nature that he, Samuel, has been forced to come to grips with on his barren hill-ranch outside of the Edenic valley. Samuel recognizes that Adam's desire to believe in an unfallen garden is a dangerous and deadly state in a fallen world. As another in the long line of American Adams, Adam Trask reflects an image planted deeply in the American consciousness, of which R. W. B. Lewis has written, "It was an image crowded with illusion, and the moral posture it seemed to endorse was vulnerable in the extreme."[9] Like Tom Joad, Samuel is the balanced man capable, like Ishmael, the protagonist of another testament to America's dangerous pursuit of absolute good and evil, of seeing what is good while being "quick to perceive a horror." Samuel is the novel's guide to the way out of the moral wasteland implied in Adam's fallow mind, fallow children, and fallow land. In this role, Samuel plays the grail knight to Adam's fisher-king, attempting to cure the ailing king and restore the land. Like the grail knight, he must ask the right question, which in this story will destroy Adam's illusion of innocence and restore both his health and his vision of the real world of the valley.

Caleb and Aron, the twin sons born to Cathy, pick up the Cain and Abel theme introduced in the characters of Charles and Adam and carry it through to the end of the novel. The twins are each "born separate in his own sack" (p. 194), and it is impossible to determine their respective paternity. Like Charles and Adam, the twins represent still the split in the American consciousness. Aron, like Adam, maintains an unwavering and dangerously vulnerable certainty of "goodness" or innocence; he cannot cope with experience and remains unfallen until forced to face the reality of his whore-mother, Kate. This forced fall destroys Aron; he runs away to war and is killed. Cal, named after the biblical character who, we are told, "came to the Promised Land" (p. 271), grows up with an equal awareness of his own "badness." Like Charles, Cal feels rejected by his father, recognizing correctly that his father loves Aron better. In this artificial Eden, the test for the twins is whether each can pluck the fruit of knowledge of both good and evil; he who cannot will fail as surely as Adam fails. Again, determinism and psychological realism are confused in the characters of the boys. Is Cal bad because he may be descended from Charles, or is he bad because, like Charles, he feels rejected? Is it the "channel in the blood" that makes Cal different from the good Aron, or is it the father's response that determines each son's character? Steinbeck makes it impossible to determine who the boys' respective fathers may be. Cal is dark like Adam and has the small, delicate hands of Cathy. Aron looks most like his mother, but he resembles the ineffectual Adam in temperament. Unlike Adam, however, Aron is a tough fighter who does not know fear when he fights. Cal and Aron are the products of a marriage between good and evil, and the implication in these characters is that all men contain both good and evil and must accept this reality in order to survive in a fallen world—it is the lesson given in miniature in "The Harness." Because in the end Cal realizes that he can be "good," he survives; because Aron cannot accept full knowledge, he perishes. Steinbeck deliberately shifts focus away from the determinism that dominated the first Trask chapters of the novel in order to stress the theme of free will—*timshel*—that pervades the second half of the novel.

Of Cal, Steinbeck wrote, "Cal is my baby. He is the every man, the battle ground between good and evil, the most human of all, the sorry man."[92] In Cal, Steinbeck attempts to bring the divided consciousness of America together. Those characters in the novel who embody only one side of that division—Charles,

Cathy, Adam, Aron—perish by the wayside en route to Cal's final triumph. In the end, Cal, committed to full knowledge, plans to return to the valley land and to farm the land, freed of the illusion of Eden that destroyed his father and his father's dream-garden.

Integral to the Cain motif in *East of Eden* is the familiar theme of loneliness that haunts nearly every character in the novel. Cyrus, Charles and Adam's godlike father, dies "lonely and alone" in Washington, having rejected one son and been rejected by the other. Charles remains and dies alone on the farm, missing the brother he had tried to kill. Lee explains to Cal that Adam is lonely "because he has no lovely future to dream about" (p. 493), and even Lee, when he finally goes to San Francisco to open his bookstore, returns quickly and admits, "I've never been so goddam lonesome in my life," just as earlier he had admitted to Samuel that he was lonesome in the "hidey-hole" of his Chineseness. Cal prays, "I don't want to be lonely. For Jesus's sake, Amen" (p. 379), but part of Cal's full development is to accept loneliness: "Cal had to learn loneliness," Steinbeck writes (p. 442). While Cathy/Kate never admits to being lonely, there is no more isolated character in Steinbeck's fiction than the aging whore hidden away in the gray cave of her leanto, frightened and plotting revenge on the world for her own existence. Even minor characters in the novel are cursed with apartness and loneliness: Tom on the empty Hamilton ranch; Joe Valery in his cheap hotel room; Mr. Frenchel, the token German, in the isolation of racial ostracism.

Concomitant with the theme of loneliness and apartness, the theme so central to *In Dubious Battle, Of Mice and Men,* and *The Long Valley,* is the primary Steinbeck theme of commitment. Adam, wrapped in his failed dream of Eden, represents the un-committed man. Unable to commit himself to place in the East, he has followed the archetypal American path westward in pursuit of an illusion which bars him from commitment. He is a pathetic, unattractive figure completely lacking in the quality of first importance for the Steinbeck hero: the ability to commit himself. Samuel, one of the few characters in the novel who do not suffer from the pervasive loneliness, is the Steinbeck hero, fully committed to "the one inseparable unit man plus his environment."

To argue without strong reservation, as John Ditsky does,[93] that *East of Eden* is a successful novel is to see the good of the novel while ignoring what is bad. In *In Dubious Battle*, Steinbeck, through the character of Doc Burton, experienced and rejected the role of uncommitted "recording consciousness." In his next novels, *Of Mice and Men* and *The Grapes of Wrath*, Steinbeck moved from a non-teleological yet intensely sympathetic posture to a blatantly committed, moralistic position *within* his material, as the interchapters of *The Grapes of Wrath* and that novel's tone of moral outrage readily show. In *East of Eden* Steinbeck moves even further away from the kind of authorial stance that had once led him to tentatively entitle a novel "Something That Happened," until he became absorbed as an active element, a character, in his most ambitious and moralistic undertaking. The detachment that enabled him to produce his finest writing in the fiction of the thirties is gone; the careful balance of *The Grapes of Wrath* has vanished. No longer content to point out the way things "are" while subtly indicating a way out of the dilemma, in *East of Eden* Steinbeck simply presents us with his solution, the answer toward which he had been working all of his career: we should all be Samuels, wise, fallen men committed to seeing through the veil of illusion to the reality of our fallen world. And because Samuel loomed so large as Steinbeck's answer, he loomed gigantic in the novel and dragged his family along with him, effectively disrupting the novel's working out of the twin central themes of the Fall and Rejection. In place of the brilliantly integrated interchapters of *The Grapes of Wrath*, we find in *East of Eden* authorial intrusions that often break into what Lisca has accurately labeled "cliches, an essentially cracker-barrel philosophy."[94] Whereas in the earlier novels Steinbeck was a moralist by implication, in *East of Eden* he becomes an explicit moralist, telling rather than showing, and in so doing he loses touch with the power of his finest writing, the power of presenting detail that generates its own moral.

In *East of Eden*, Steinbeck ventured resolutely into the forests of Hawthorne and Melville's great ocean, and he lost his way.

III.

THE SEA

The ocean is a constant presence in Steinbeck's fiction, cutting at the edge of Steinbeck Country, marking the terminus of the westering impulse, lurking darkly beneath the valley floor and history in *East of Eden,* and threatening to devour the Torres farm in "Flight." The sea in Steinbeck's writing is an extension of the darkness, the unknown, death, and the unconscious symbolized by the western mountains that stand as a barrier between it and the continent. Those characters who live in this last realm of Steinbeck's fiction—in the area in and around Monterey on the California coast—are on the margins of the American experience, caught up not in the American myth of a new Eden or new Adam, but in the realm of instinct and the unconscious.

For Steinbeck, the ever-present sea beyond the western mountains retained always its archetypal association with the unconscious, an association explicit in this passage from *The Log from the Sea of Cortez:*

> For the ocean, deep and black in the depths, is like the low dark levels of our minds in which the dream symbols incubate and sometimes rise up to sight like the Old Man of the Sea. . . . We have thought often of this mass of sea-memory, or sea-thought, which lives deep in the mind. If one ask for a description of the unconscious, even the answer-symbol will usually be in terms of a dark water into which the light descends only a short distance. And we have thought how the human fetus has, at one stage of its development, vestigial gill-slits. If the gills are a component of the developing human, it is not unreasonable to suppose a parallel or

concurrent mind or psyche development. If there be a life-memory strong enough to leave its symbol in vestigial gills, the preponderantly aquatic symbols in the individual unconscious might well be indications of a group psyche-memory which is the foundation of the whole unconscious. (p. 32)

In the writing Steinbeck set at the sea's edge—"The Snake," *Tortilla Flat, Cannery Row, Sweet Thursday*—the focus is on marginal characters, those outside the boundaries of the American Dream; and the brooding, informing literal and symbolic presence of the sea is a constant factor. "The Snake" introduces into Steinbeck's writing both Steinbeck's first Ricketts character and the sea as a powerful symbol of the unconscious, as the story's protagonist, Dr. Phillips, is forced into a confrontation with his unconscious while the sea laps quietly at the pilings beneath his laboratory. The sea figures again, though only briefly, in *Tortilla Flat*, its significance in that novel growing as Danny becomes more deeply ravaged by the battle between his unconscious impulses toward a more simple past and his entrapment in a sophisticated present. As Danny prepares to sacrifice himself, he instinctively drifts down to the harbor and stares into the black water.

By the time Steinbeck came to write *Cannery Row*, major changes had taken place in his life. He had made the journey to the Sea of Cortez with Ed Ricketts and had become immersed for a time in both the life of the tide pool and the philosophy of Ricketts. Most important, he had been required to find words for his own and Ricketts's thoughts while writing the *Log*. While *In Dubious Battle* and "The Snake" both demonstrate Steinbeck's awareness of the tragic weakness in Ricketts's world-view and his concept of "is" thinking, it remained for *Cannery Row* to explore fully the strengths and weaknesses of the marine biologist's position.

Perhaps just as important, between *Tortilla Flat* and *Cannery Row* Steinbeck had gone to war across the Atlantic. As a correspondent for the *New York Herald Tribune*, he had spent months writing dispatches from England, North Africa, and the Mediterranean. He had returned from the war disillusioned and too disheartened to edit the dispatches into book form, and they were not published until 1958, under the title of *Once There Was a War*. [1] However, the collective dispatches in this volume demonstrate a remarkable unity, a unity that depends almost solely upon Steinbeck's fascination with the sea as symbol of the unconscious. [2] In the dispatches, Steinbeck's soldiers make a "night-sea crossing" in a ship unmistakably symbolizing the "belly of the whale," and they slip into a deeply unconscious dream-state from which they do not emerge during the dark violence of war. The sea shifts and sighs beneath the writing of the dispatches as it does under the floor of Dr. Phillips's laboratory in "The Snake." In the war dispatches Steinbeck makes his deepest journey into the sea of the unconscious, and it is significant that upon returning from the war he completed *Cannery Row* in a brief six weeks. [3]

"The Snake": The First Lonely Doc

"The Snake" (1935), collected in *The Long Valley* in 1938, introduced two crucial elements to Steinbeck's California fiction: the Monterey setting with its omnipresent sea-consciousness and the first fictional treatment of Ed Ricketts. The setting would shift slightly for *Tortilla Flat,* but it would reappear unchanged in *Cannery Row* and *Sweet Thursday.* The Ricketts prototype would make its second appearance in the form of Doc Burton of *In Dubious Battle* one year later and would hold center stage as Doc in *Cannery Row* and *Sweet Thursday.* "The Snake" establishes and defines the "Doc" character in Steinbeck's fiction, with strengths and weaknesses that would remain little changed for three novels and two decades.

While most critics have been content—and probably relieved—to pass over "The Snake" with minimal comment, two essays in the last decade have explored the story in some depth and have added valuable critical insights. In his explication of the story, Reloy Garcia suggests that the story's "unifying principle" is the "initiation theme," and that the story "is the introduction of the principle of evil, in the form of woman, into the life of a young man." In an echo of Joseph Fontenrose, Garcia claims that the laboratory is another version of the Edenic garden common to the other stories in *The Long Valley*. In another fascinating and thoroughly Jungian reading of the story, Charles E. May argues that "the inadequacy of scientific knowledge is the essential subject of 'The Snake,'" and that "the mysterious incident recounted in 'The Snake' is a reaction of the mythic world against the efforts of science to obliterate it."[4] While these two readings have little in common, they both share the key assumption that Dr. Phillips—the story's protagonist—is incomplete, that he lacks something essential to a full experience of life, be it knowledge of evil as well as good or an awareness of the power of the unconscious. Both of these readings are helpful in directing attention to the "lonely" and "set-apart" Doc who will appear in *In Dubious Battle* and *Cannery Row* and who will be caricatured in *Sweet Thursday*.

Dr. Phillips's lab is built "partly on piers over the bay water and partly on the land." It touches both worlds—the objective and subjective, rational and irrational, conscious and unconscious. The presence of the sea permeates the story, intruding quietly and subtly at frequent intervals to make its symbolic presence felt as it laps at the pilings beneath the floor. The story, which Steinbeck claimed was based on a real and poorly understood event,[5] tells of the visit to the marine biologist's laboratory of a woman interested in purchasing a male rattlesnake. Steinbeck carefully identifies the woman in appearance and action with the snake which she purchases and requires Dr. Phillips to feed. Phillips, meanwhile, is identified with the rat that the snake devours. A complex symbol, the snake at the center of the story may represent "the principle of evil," or it may symbolize rebirth.[6] In it are merged symbols of death and resurrection, just as the rattlesnake venom collected by the scientist may kill or, if used correctly, cure. Charles May points out that the mysterious woman is identified with both the snake and the sea—at one point the scientist does not know "whether the water sighed among the piles or whether the woman sighed."[7] Though May does not explore this dual significance at any length, the complex symbolism occurs because the serpent is also sometimes identified with the sea and thus with the mysteries of the unconscious.[8] Thus the woman, the snake, and the sea merge to surround Dr. Phillips with a threatening awareness of the unconscious, an overwhelming intrusion into the objective world of his laboratory—in May's words, "a reaction of mythic world against the efforts of science."

May asserts that "the anima force embodied in the woman rises out of the primeval sea, disrupts the doctor's methodical scientific process, upsets his calm and ordered existence, and then goes back to her sea home never to be seen by him again."[9] Without consigning the dark lady of this story exclusively to the realm of myth, as May does, it is nonetheless important to recognize her similarity to the old Chinaman of *Cannery Row*, for like that character she forces upon another a potent and deeply troubling awareness of the unconscious. When she jars the scientist out of the haven of his objectivity, she awakens him to the abyss of the unconscious that literally surrounds him. It is a momentary awakening felt in the heart the way the rat feels for an instant the fangs of the rattlesnake.

The key symbol of the deficiency of the scientist's life is the cat "crucified in the cradle and grinning comically." This parody of the crucifixion—the primary symbol of commitment in Western culture and in Steinbeck's fiction—underscores the scientist's lack of commitment to and comprehension of the "whole." The pun on "cradle" suggests a kind of still-born faith, a martyrdom without meaning. Whereas Joseph Wayne of *To a God Unknown* sacrificed himself in order to break through to or "live into" the whole, Dr. Phillips lives in a world disengaged from any kind of commitment to "the whole thing, known and unknowable."

His partial vision allows for only the known and knowable, and when, after his disturbing experience with the woman, Phillips realizes that he cannot pray, he recognizes his inability to voice his own "mystical outcrying." He is cut off and alienated from the whole of which his unconscious is an integral part. His admission, "Maybe I'm too much alone" (p. 86), underscores the central problem of his detachment, a problem that will torment Doc Burton in *In Dubious Battle* and "Doc" in *Cannery Row* and *Sweet Thursday.*

"The Snake" is important in itself as one of Steinbeck's finest stories, a well-crafted window between the known and unknown, conscious and unconscious realities, between the objective world of the laboratory and the subjective world below and surrounding it. It is also important because of the insight it provides into the Ricketts character so central to the novels. The aloneness of Dr. Phillips reappears as the tragic alienation of Doc Burton in Steinbeck's strike novel and develops into the detachment and loneliness of Doc in *Cannery Row.* It reappears in a diluted and sentimentalized form in *Sweet Thursday.*

The inability of the young scientist to acknowledge the significance of the "unknowable" or to pray becomes in the future "Docs" an inability to achieve a profound commitment to "the whole thing"—even while the vision of the whole picture is before them. It drives Doc Burton into the night and oblivion and tortures Doc with an awareness of his own incompleteness in *Cannery Row.* And when Steinbeck would later turn his vision toward the popular audience for the first time in his career, he would in *Sweet Thursday* attempt to solve the problem of Doc's detachment with a parody of romantic love.

Tortilla Flat: Camelot East of Eden

Since John Steinbeck's well-known letter to his agents pointing out the Arthurian parallels in *Tortilla Flat* (1935), the problem of such parallels in this novel has pained and perplexed critics. The pioneer Steinbeck critic Peter Lisca responded to the problem in *The Wide World of John Steinbeck* (1958) by suggesting that "Steinbeck may have exaggerated the book's parallel to Malory in order to impress some publishers." But in his most recent major Steinbeck criticism, *John Steinbeck: Nature and Myth* (1978), Lisca takes a different position, stating that "from the novel's preface to its last words . . . Steinbeck's use of Arthurian materials is clear, though perhaps not as obvious as he himself thought." Another major Steinbeck critic, Warren French, has also appeared to change his opinion of the significance of the parallels, stating in the second (1975) edition of his *John Steinbeck* (1961) that "too much ingenuity has been expended—in the previous edition of this book, among other places—in pointing out Arthurian parallels." Even Arthur F. Kinney, whose essay "The Arthurian Cycle in *Tortilla Flat*" (1965) provides the most thorough tracing of the Malory materials in the novel, seems to recant somewhat in *"Tortilla Flat* Re-Visited" (1975) when he claims that "there is no necessity to trace exact correspondences for Steinbeck's characters and episodes in Malory nor even to determine the degree of influence." Howard Levant dismisses Joseph Fontenrose's careful investigation of the parallels as "strained" and concludes that "the parallel operates only in minor and external details, and, hence, does not perform its intended function of unifying *Tortilla Flat*." The critical trend in recent years seems, in fact, to be toward a dismissal of the Malory parallels in *Tortilla Flat*, a trend justified by French's claim that "what actually occurs in *Tortilla Flat* has largely been obscured by a red herring dragged across the path by the author himself."[10]

This confusion of critical attitudes leaves us still with the problem of how to cope with the question of why Steinbeck insisted so strongly on the parallels, an insistence repeated as late as 1957. Fontenrose is persuasive when he suggests that "an author's own statement of his structural plan should be of prime importance for the study and interpretation of a book."[11]

If Steinbeck does indeed fail in providing a structure for *Tortilla Flat* through his use of the Arthurian cycle, and if the cycle is then of little significance to our understanding and appreciation of the thematic intent of the novel, we can dismiss his insistence as mistaken and at best a sort of wish fulfillment. No one has yet established a convincing case for such a failure, however.

In order to understand Steinbeck's use of the Arthurian myth in *Tortilla Flat*, it is helpful to reconsider his use of mythological structures elsewhere, particularly in *To a God Unknown*, published only two years earlier. In that novel, Steinbeck used the fisher-king myth in conjunction with older religious myths in order to isolate the central theme of commitment. The mythological structure in that novel was designed to provide an index of Joseph's growing commitment and confusion. In the end, Joseph rises above the confused trappings of myth to a transcendent awareness of his place in the larger "whole." Joseph, as we have seen, is never meant by Steinbeck to be accepted as a literal nature god or fisher-king or Christ—he is a man struggling to break through to an awareness of the larger picture. In other Steinbeck works it is the Eden myth that is treated ironically and must be transcended much like Joseph's nature worship. The central point here is that there are no nature gods just as there are no Edens in the real world of Steinbeck's fiction and there is no ideal Round Table or Arthur in *Tortilla Flat;* there are only illusions of such perfection, illusions which, in each novel or story, must be transcended by real men in a real, fallen world. The significance of the Arthurian materials in *Tortilla Flat* will not become clear until it is realized that Steinbeck is not simply recreating a modern version of the Round Table among the paisanos of Monterey. Such a recreation is impossible because there is no Arthur, as Steinbeck tells us clearly in the first chapter when Danny intones, "Where is Arthur Morales? . . . Dead in France. . . . Dead for his country. Dead in a foreign land" (pp. 23–24). The very name Arthur Morales should alert us to the fact that this is Arthur, the moral center of Camelot and the

Round Table. Arthur F. Kinney has suggested that "there is no moral norm" in this novel,[12] an observation which (though Kinney does not make this claim) may well stem from the fact that Arthur is dead and Steinbeck is not writing about a paisano version of King Arthur's world but about the *post-Arthurian* world of everyday man, the fallen world of fallen man situated to the east of Eden.

Steinbeck's very careful use of the litotes in his preface should also alert us to his method in *Tortilla Flat*. The preface begins quite simply with the statement, "This is the story of Danny and of Danny's friends and of Danny's house. It is a story of how these three became one thing." And Steinbeck continues: "For Danny's house was *not unlike* the Round Table, and Danny's friends were not unlike the knights of it" (p. 9, my italics). Rather than simply striving for an archaic effect, or somewhat heavy-handedly stressing the parallel, Steinbeck is carefully defining the relationship between the Arthurian and paisano cycles: we are not to interpret the parallel too closely. The ordering of statements in the preface is important as well, for this tells us that the book is first about the unity which formed about Danny and his house, about the all-important Steinbeck theme of commitment. The Arthurian materials are significant only insofar as they reinforce this central theme.

Because there is no Arthur in *Tortilla Flat*, Danny's Round Table is doomed from its inception. It is constructed not around a symbol of moral perfection, such as Arthur, but out of the flawed elements of the real, flawed world, and it is astride a split between two consciousnesses—the old paisano pastoralism and the world of capitalism into which the paisanos are emerging. It is the ownership of the houses which brings Danny's friends close to him and which at the same time destroys the old life for which Danny yearns. Danny, while no Arthur, is a knight errant, the only horseman amongst the paisanos, with his legs "bent to the exact curve of a horse's sides" by the time he was twenty-five (p. 12). He is a morally flawed Launcelot at best, unable to bear the weight of responsibility his property and the resulting fellowship have thrust upon him. The book is ultimately about Danny's failure; the tragedy is that of a man caught between cultures, unable to move back into the freer, more natural past and unable to go forward into the economic structure of the present and future. While the other paisanos, led by Pilon, adapt to their changing environment, Danny cannot and is destroyed. When, in the foreword for the 1937 Modern Library edition of *Tortilla Flat*, Steinbeck spoke of the paisanos as "people who merge successfully with their habitat," and wrote, "In men this is called philosophy, and it is a fine thing," he was of necessity excluding Danny. Pilon, not Danny, is the one who merges, the philosopher of *Tortilla Flat*; Pilon represents the transitional phase the paisanos find themselves in, as his name, which means "something thrown in when a trade is concluded," indicates. The trade is the old life in exchange for an uncertain new one, and Pilon will merge successfully while Danny perishes.

Kinney reveals a key insight into *Tortilla Flat* when he states, "It is not true, finally, that the paisanos combat capitalism or absorb its ways unknowingly; what we come to learn is that they actively embrace it."[13] The paisanos, Kinney suggests, are "capitalists at heart." Throughout the book, until the full flowering of the fellowship, paisano friendship almost invariably involves exploitation and self-interest. Thus, when Danny first encounters Pilon, his oldest and closest friend, his reaction is to avoid sharing his food with Pilon. Danny thinks, "I will pass Pilon by" (p. 21). It is not until Danny realizes that Pilon has something to drink that Danny becomes friendly and invites Pilon to share his pilfered ham and stale bread. It is then Pilon's turn to try to avoid Danny, scurrying away to escape his friend's clutches and declaring only when there is no escape, "Danny, I do not mind sharing my brandy with you, half and half. It is my duty to see you do not drink it all" (p. 23). This encounter establishes the pattern that holds true throughout most of the book.

The paisanos even attribute mercenary or selfish motives to one another as a form of respect. When Danny becomes involved with the dead Arthur's widow, Pilon defends Danny to Jesus Maria by saying, "Oh, don't think Danny is a fool. Mrs. Morales has two hundred dollars in the bank" (pp. 61–62). Danny rises above the pattern of mutual exploitation only when he impulsively cries, "Pilon, I swear, what I have is thine. While I have a house, thou hast a house. Give me a drink" (p. 26). At that moment the paisano's ill-fated Round Table is born, though Pilon is properly skeptical in his reply: "I must see this to believe it. . . . It would be a world wonder if it were so. . . . And besides the bottle is empty."

As the commitment between the paisanos grows, the friendships come to be founded less on mutual exploitation and more on a pure principle of friendship. The paisanos become, in one sense, better than they were; in the words of one chapter heading, they become "a force for good." The turning point is dramatically symbolized by the friends' invitation to the Pirate and his dogs to share their house. Though motivated solely by their desire to do the Pirate good by spending his money for him, the invitation brings about the first completely altruistic commitment between the friends. Up to this point Danny has "rented" one of his houses to Pilon in order to be free of one-half of the weight of property; Pilon has attracted the other paisanos to his house in order to foist off on them the responsibility for the never-to-be-paid rent. When the Pirate out-maneuvers the paisanos by placing his hoard of quarters under their mutual protection, however, he breaks the chain of irresponsibility. For the first time, the friends must take responsibility for someone else, and the Pirate's gesture welds the unit more tightly together: "The bag of money had become the symbolic center of the friendship, the point of trust about which the fraternity revolved" (p. 199). Never before had the paisanos been forced to commit themselves to such a trust. Steinbeck adds: "About this guardianship of the Pirate's money there had grown a structure of self-respect and not a little complacency" (p. 198). The paisanos take to the new responsibility with a vengeance, beating Big Joe with a cruelty seemingly out of character when he steals the bag of quarters. And later, though Pilon had not been at all loath to borrow Big Joe's pants to barter for wine at an earlier point, he becomes sincerely disturbed when Danny, in his madness, steals Pilon's shoes. Pilon cries out, "This is crime. They were not very good shoes, but it is a crime against friendship to take them. And that is the worst kind of crime" (p. 269).

Coupled with the paisanos' growing sense of commitment is a subtly increasing acceptance of the capitalist way of life; the fact that the symbolic center of the friendship is a bag of money is an ironic suggestion of this change. When they at last aid the Pirate in accomplishing his goal of buying the candlestick for St. Francis, the paisanos, led by Danny, celebrate by buying a feast of hamburger and onions and getting decorously drunk. Steinbeck comments: "The evening was a great good marker in their lives" (p. 211). It is a marker that cuts two ways, however, for while the evening marks the apex of the friends' comradeship and commitment to one another, it also marks the moment when the paisanos turn most fully away from the old "free" ways toward the new. Never before have the friends considered purchasing food that they could beg or steal; all money has previously gone without second thought for wine or love. From this day forward, the Pirate works not for celestial reward but for the paisanos' daily bread, using his quarters to purchase each day's food. Steinbeck writes ironically, "This was one of the best of times for the friends of Danny. The struggle for existence was remote." The friends simply wait each day for the Christ-like capitalist, Pirate, to provide "the daily miracle of food."

The paisanos are becoming civilized, a process of which Steinbeck wrote in 1930: "Probably the whole civilization process might be defined as a deadening of enthusiasms."[14] The episode concerning the corporal's baby illustrates this shift from the old chivalric code to the new economic values. When the corporal's baby dies, Pilon praises the young soldier for his failed but noble "plan of revenge." The paisanos assume that, according to the chivalric rules of revenge, the corporal intended that the "baby would grow up, and he would be a general; and in time he would find the capitan, and he would kill him slowly" (p. 184). The friends, in fact, express rage and a desire for vengeance against the capitan, emotions which the corporal does not feel. The corporal disclaims the imagined plan of revenge and tells the paisanos that he was thinking only in materialistic terms: "If that capitan, with the little epaulets and the little sash could take my wife, imagine what a general with a big sash and a gold sword could take!" (p. 185). A "long silence" and a revolution in the paisanos' thinking must take place before Danny can respond: "It is to be pitied . . . that so few parents have the well-being of their children at heart." The statement is an indication that Danny, too, is succumbing to the new "civilized" values. It is an important demarcation point in the civilization of the paisanos.

Appropriately, it is at the moment of greatest complacency among the paisanos that Steinbeck introduces the stories of Tall Bob Smoke, who accidentally shoots the tip of his nose off while pretending to commit suicide, and Old Man Ravanno, who accidentally hangs himself while also pretending suicide. Both stories are funny, but as Jesus Maria says, "when you open your mouth to laugh, something like a hand squeezes your heart" (p. 248). At the conclusion of the Ravanno story, "Broad smiles broke out on the faces of the friends. Sometimes, they thought, life was very, very humorous" (p. 256). In both stories, the victims were hurt or killed while trying to force some kind of commitment from others. Tall Bob thinks as he prepares to fake his suicide, "I will kill myself, and then people will be sad" (p. 246); and Old Man Ravanno tries to win the love of a fifteen-year-old girl because, as Jesus Maria points out, he "was lonely" and "didn't know how to take up his time"

171

after his son has married the girl's sister (p. 253). Both men are seeking what the paisanos have found: commitment. With these two stories, Steinbeck very adroitly alters the tone of *Tortilla Flat*. While retaining the "very, very humorous" quality, he introduces the hand that squeezes the heart. And he anticipates critical reaction to the chapters to come in the paisanos' reactions to these stories. Pilon complains about the story of Old Man Ravanno: "It is not a good story. There are too many meanings and too many lessons in it. Some of these lessons are opposite. There is not a story to take into your head. It proves nothing" (p. 257). Ironically, perhaps the earliest criticism of *Tortilla Flat* echoes Pilon's complaint. After reading the manuscript, Robert O. Ballou, Steinbeck's early publisher, wrote: "My feeling of disappointment at the end of it lay in the fact that all the way through I had been looking for and waiting for some important story or argument and found it nowhere."[15] Ballou might as well have said, "There is not a story to take into your head. It proves nothing." Steinbeck also anticipated another reaction, reminiscent of the feeling he claimed to have desired in readers of "The Chrysanthemums" when he wrote of that story: "It is entirely different and is designed to strike without the reader's knowledge. I mean he reads it casually and after it is finished feels that something profound has happened to him although he does not know what nor how" (*Life in Letters*, p. 91). This reaction is Pablo's, who says, "I like it because it hasn't any meaning you can see, and still it does seem to mean something. I can't tell what" (p. 257).

Chapter 14 is thus the pivotal chapter in *Tortilla Flat*. It carefully shifts the novel's tone back to the tone of the first chapter, in which Danny feels his loneliness and, in a faint *ubi sunt* theme, recalls his "lost friends." Simultaneously, it anticipates the readers' reactions to the major shift about to take place in the final three chapters. Concerning this shift, Howard Levant has claimed that the novel "is flawed in its conclusion by the imposition of an arbitrary, predetermined order on the events," and he adds, "Steinbeck cultivates this tendency in the future." Levant further concludes that "the weakness of Steinbeck's self-alleged debt to *Morte d'Arthur* is indicated clearly by the appendix which these final chapters constitute. They are detached from the harmonious relationship between structure and materials that characterizes the rest of the novel." The key to Levant's criticism of the novel's structure is his assertion that "Danny's madness does not derive from earlier events. It is a sudden turn of 'plot,' pasted onto rather than integrated into the economic theme and moral content of the novel."[16] What Levant and others have overlooked is the crucial fact that rather than being "pasted onto" the central theme of the novel, Danny's madness has in actuality been carefully prepared for from the first pages of the novel and is an inseparable part of the "economic theme and moral content" of *Tortilla Flat*. The novel is, as Steinbeck stated, a cycle, and it comes full circle with Danny's madness. When Danny "goes mad," he runs away from the house and the demand for commitment and responsibility which it entails, and he rages about the town breaking windows, fighting, and generally outraging everyone. This rage not only parallels Launcelot's madness (which precedes the collapse of the Round Table), it also reflects what Kinney calls Danny's "own wild attempt to find a freer, truer existence."[17] It is Danny's final struggle to break free of the encroaching complacency that has settled over the paisanos and to renounce the subtle capitalism that they are sliding into. Danny, the only knight among the paisano infantry, yearns for the old knightly freedom. When we first meet Danny, he is waging a glorious rebellion against the ownership of two houses that have been forced upon him by the death of his grandfather. Happiness comes to Danny only when he is arrested and placed in the familiar jail and allowed to forget his responsibility. Thus, both Danny's madness and his indefinable yearning are foreshadowed in the first chapter in his rebellion against property and his loneliness for a lost time and lost friends. And the loneliness and apartness that Danny feels lurk just below the surface of the entire novel, as Steinbeck suggests in his description of the night when Pilon and Big Joe walk along the beach after Pilon has stolen and returned Big Joe's pants: "The night was cold and aloof, and its warm life was withdrawn, so that it was full of bitter warnings to man that he is alone in the world, and alone among his fellows; that he has no comfort owing him from anywhere" (p. 151). This theme of loneliness and apartness will surface again in *In Dubious Battle,* and it will rise to dominate *Of Mice and Men,* Steinbeck's next two novels. In the friendship that flowers briefly among the paisanos, the men escape this loneliness for a moment.

Danny's ties to the old life are stronger than the ties of the other paisanos, perhaps because Pilon and the others—the paisano infantry—represent the paisano middle class while Danny stands for an older freedom. Danny is more in tune with his unconscious impulses—those impulses that lead him away from civilization toward his Indian past—than the other paisanos.[18] Danny feels the presence of the forest and sea strongly. Of the sea, a force in the background of this novel, Steinbeck writes: "The waves beat out the passage of time on the rocks." And he adds: "Danny began to feel the beating of time. . . . to dream of the days of his freedom. . . . He remembered that the name of Danny was a name of storm" (pp. 260–61). The sea—the unconscious—draws Danny away from his commitment to the friends and from those elements of property and civilization that the other paisanos are learning to adapt to and even embrace. In the novel's preface Steinbeck describes the paisanos as a marginal people, living "where the forest and the town intermingle . . . as embattled as the Ancient Britons are embattled in Wales" (pp. 10–11). The paisanos react differently to this marginality. While Pilon leads the others toward a successful merger with the world of property and responsibility, Danny moves in the opposite direction, toward the forest and sea.

Steinbeck wrote of the "group" in a letter dated June 21, 1933, two months before he began work on *Tortilla Flat:* "One could easily say that man, during his hunting period, had to give up the group since all game hunters must; and now that his food is not to be taken by stealth and precision, is going back to the group which takes its food by concerted action. That if one lives by the food of the lion he must hunt singly, if by the food of the ruminants he may live in herds and protect himself by his numbers" (*Life in Letters,* p. 76). Danny is pulled in the direction of the group by his Round Table, and he is torn from the group by his yearning for the old life when his food was "taken by stealth and precision"; he yearns for the "food of the lion."

Ironically, as Danny tries to tear himself from the unit that has been forged around him, his friends' commitment to him grows more intense and selfless. "Some harm will fall upon our friend in his craziness," they tell one another. "We must search through the whole world until we find him" (p. 264). When Danny finally returns to the house after his madness has passed, he is defeated; he has recognized that the old life is gone. Pilon says, "He is changed. . . . He is old" (p. 284). And Steinbeck at this moment intrudes to make the nature of Danny's failure clear as he intones: "But see, Danny! Thou art not alone. Thy friends are caught in this state of thine. . . . Thy life is not thine own to govern, Danny, for it controls other lives. See how thy friends suffer! Spring to life, Danny, that thy friends may live again!" (pp. 286–87). But Danny is not a fisher-king or Christ or Arthur. He fails in his commitment to the group because he cannot reconcile the twin necessities of his character: for the old life and for the group. Just as Danny's commitment to the friends has reached its lowest ebb, their commitment to Danny scales a transcendent peak when they decide to have a party for him. Steinbeck writes: "These friends were urged on by altruism more pure than most men can conceive. They loved Danny" (p. 288). Gone is the theme of mutual exploitation and gone are the mercenary impulses; and the theme of commitment reaches a height comparable to Joseph Wayne's self-sacrifice in *To a God Unknown* when the paisanos decide that they will work cutting squids for a day to finance the party. To save Danny, the friends enter the American work force with the rationalization, "One day would not be so bad—only one day" (p. 288). And Steinbeck comments, "It was a portent, like the overthrow of government, or even of the solar system" (p. 289). The irony is heavy, for in their self-sacrificing endeavor to save Danny, the paisanos move further away from Danny in the direction of the "system of American commercialism" (p. 11), though the taint is as yet slight. Just as the house is a symbol that cuts in two directions, bringing the friends together and wrenching Danny disastrously away from the old freedom, it is the job at Chin Kee's that formally announces the end of the old paisano world and the birth of the new economic order. Appropriately, when Pilon and Pablo go to find Danny on the night of the party they discover him "on the end of the dark pier," looking "into the deep, deep water" (p. 293). He is becoming more withdrawn into his unconscious; and the sea, as symbol of the unconscious, the unknown, and death, suggests what is to come for Danny as he turns inward to fight his ultimate battle.

The loneliness Danny felt in the first chapter, his lament for the "lost friends," surfaces again in his painful cry, "Am I alone in the world? Will no one fight with me?" (p. 300). When he rushes from the house to find "the Enemy who is worthy of Danny," he is rushing to confront the ghost of the old life which exists only within himself. The Opponent, which French has insightfully labeled "some kind of personal Moby Dick" and Maxell Geismar has, more accurately, called "the spectre of civilization within one's self,"[19] is the irreconcilable split within Danny, and by challenging it at last he, like Ahab, can defeat only himself. The lion and the group-man destroy one another within Danny, and thus the organism of the paisano Round Table dies.

Tortilla Flat is the study of the birth and death of an organism, or "phalanx," which, Steinbeck wrote, "break up in a fine imitation of death of the man unit" (*Life in Letters,* p. 81). And it is a study of a marginal people drawn both toward and away from the main current of American society. It documents an attempt, unconscious and for a brief time successful, to found a Round Table made up of fallen materials in a fallen world—as if after Camelot had gone to pieces Launcelot in all his weakness had inherited the castle and tried to reform the Round Table from the flawed remnants surrounding him. It is above all another statement of the theme that dominates Steinbeck's fiction: the need for commitment between men and between man and his environment. Even Pilon's discovery of the geodetic marker— the book's "Grail"—reinforces the theme of commitment to place: the treasure that Pilon and Big Joe unearth in the forest underscores their exact awareness of their place in Tortilla Flat and Monterey. Without the same surety, Danny perishes, caught between two worlds. Steinbeck's next two novels, *In Dubious Battle* and *Of Mice and Men,* both dramatize man's need for commitment to something larger than himself, be it a group of paisanos, a group of strikers, or a single human soul such as Lennie Small, and this theme rises to epic dimensions in the novel that follows these two: *The Grapes of Wrath. Tortilla Flat* ends with the failure of the dream as Pilon, Pablo, Jesus Maria, Big Joe, and the Pirate walk away from the burning house—the "talisman"—with the author's final words: "and no two walked together." It is remarkably unified and artistically successful novel, and, in spite of the laughter, it is perhaps the most pessimistic of Steinbeck's works, rivaled in its darkness only by *In Dubious Battle.* By the time Steinbeck had come to write *Of Mice and Men,* he was able to illustrate both the death of a dream and the birth of a new commitment out of that dream, for at the end of that novel George walks away not alone, but with Slim, the man of understanding.

177

Cannery Row: "An Essay in Loneliness"

Cannery Row has been called many things by critics, from a "sentimental" novel to a "poisoned creampuff," from a "glorification of weakness of mind and degeneration of character" to a "pastoral poem."[20] It has been labeled a "defense of poetry."[21] Steinbeck himself at times seemed little more certain about the novel than were his critics, calling it in various statements "a mixed-up book" with "a pretty general ribbing in it," a "kind of nostalgic thing" written for soldiers in the war, and "a relaxation from the war." Steinbeck's most intriguing comment on the novel, however, came in his response to Malcolm Cowley's famous "poisoned creampuff" remark. Had Cowley taken the time to read the book again, Steinbeck responded, "he would have found out how very poisoned it was." Steinbeck also seemed to contradict his own claim that the book was "mixed-up" when he wrote to Pascal Covici to say, "No critic has as yet stumbled on the design of the book."[22]

Steinbeck's agreement with Cowley should serve as adequate warning that this is not a "sentimental" novel or simply "a kind of nostalgic thing"; nor can it be considered a "glorification" of human weakness. It should also suggest that if *Cannery Row* is indeed indebted to the pastoral tradition, as Stanley Alexander has claimed,[23] it is to the very dark and, perhaps, poisoned pastoral hinted at in such a Shakespearean work as *As You Like It*— a pastoral perhaps, but from the perspective of an ambiguous Jaques.

It is scarcely necessary to read *Cannery Row* a second time to realize how deeply the poison runs in this novel. The most insightful description of the book remains, in fact, Ed Ricketts's assertion that the book was "an essay in loneliness."[24] Loneliness is the poison in the *Cannery Row* creampuff, and the novel continues Steinbeck's obsession with this theme.

The introductory portrait of Cannery Row insures that from the beginning we view the Row as a "whole," an organism with multiple interrelated parts like the tide pool Steinbeck later describes. It begins with a catalogue of particulars: "a poem, a stink, a grating noise, a quality of light, a tone, a habit. . . . tin and iron and rust and splintered wood, chipped pavement . . . sardine canneries of corrugated iron, honky tonks, restaurants and whore houses, and little crowded groceries, and laboratories and flophouses" (p. 1). By the end of this list, Dora's whorehouse, Doc's laboratory, Lee Chong's grocery, and the Palace Flophouse have been introduced generically into the setting in the last four elements in the list. The description then proceeds to show how the organism functions as a whole in a brief synopsis of a day in the life of the Row. And by the end of this second paragraph of activity, the central characters of the novel have been casually introduced: "The bums who retired in disgust under the black cypress tree come out to sit on the rusty pipes in the vacant lot. The girls from Dora's emerge for a bit of sun. . . . Doc strolls from the Western Biological Laboratory and crosses the street to Lee Chong's grocery for two quarts of beer. Henri the painter noses like an Airedale through the junk in the grass-grown lot" (p. 2). Already the novel's method has been ingeniously established. We are peering down into the inner life of Cannery Row the way Doc peers into the clarity of a tide pool, and Steinbeck uses the metaphor of biological collection to define his authorial method: "to open the page and to let the stories crawl in by themselves" (p. 2). It should already be obvious that the stories have begun to crawl in very subtly in the first two paragraphs and that the metaphor of the tide pool—what several critics have recognized as the "controlling metaphor" of the book—has been quickly and deftly established at the same time that Steinbeck has gone through his invariable routine of carefully establishing a detailed and fully realized setting.

The first story to crawl into the book is that which tells of Lee Chong's acquisition of the fish-meal warehouse and its subsequent appropriation by Mack and the boys. Lee Chong's grocery is the last "specimen" mentioned in the introductory sketch, and appropriately, the first sentence of the first chapter begins with the words "Lee Chong's grocery." The development most important to the narrative action of the novel in the first chapter is Mack's not-very-subtle blackmail of Lee in order to gain the warehouse as a home for himself and the other Cannery Row dropouts. The portion of the chapter that makes the deepest impression and determines the dominant tone of the chapter, however, is the story of Horace Abbeville's suicide, by which means Lee obtains the warehouse. The story of the suicide is one of complete despair, related in a disturbingly matter-of-fact and understated tone. And the disturbing manner in which the dropouts acquire their version of the *Tortilla Flat* "talisman"— the Palace Flophouse and Grill—subtly introduces the theme of what Steinbeck and Ricketts, in *The Log from the Sea of Cortez*, called the "great organism, Life," which "takes it all and uses it all" (p. 263). This theme will later be articulated in Steinbeck's description of the tide pool: "the whole sea bottom a fantastic cemetery on which the living scamper and scramble" (p. 99). The living who scamper and scramble on Horace's cemetery are the Flophouse gang, and while Lee and Mack and the boys may indeed have established a "commensal" relationship through the "renting" of the warehouse, this relationship is strongly colored by the way in which the warehouse was obtained. It is a rather inauspicious beginning for a sentimental novel or a pastoral "solidly in the comic vein."[25]

While chapter 1 introduces the "poison" of despair and suicide into the novel (a poison that will be reinjected at strategic intervals throughout the novel) and underscores the theme of the interrelatedness of life and death, chapter 2 offers further insight into Steinbeck's method as the author sings a paean of praise to Lee and Mack and the boys and demonstrates his power to lift them out of the real Monterey into the "cosmic Monterey." It is both a foreshadowing of the way in which the metaphor of the tide pool can expand to take in the whole picture of all of life—the cosmic tide pool—and a suggestion that we must be aware throughout the novel of both levels. Thus, when the author sings the praises of Mack and the boys, we are not to forget that below the cosmic level on which they are praised there is another, very real, level on which they are flawed and struggling human beings. Steinbeck is demonstrating the power of the author's words to control the "peephole" through which we view the tide pool of Cannery Row.

Lest we stray too far from the real Cannery Row into the cosmic realm, Steinbeck brings us back to the bitter reality of life amidst the marginal characters of the Row in chapter 3. In this chapter we hear about William, the pimp at Dora's house who kills himself out of loneliness and isolation. William tries to make friends with Mack and the boys, and when he is rejected he returns to the whorehouse and plunges an ice pick into his heart. The story is a stark lesson in the deadly effects of loneliness and apartness, and according to Steinbeck in "About Ed Ricketts," it was based on an actual event witnessed by Ricketts and related to Steinbeck. Ricketts labeled the real rejection by the bums "a piece of social cruelty which has never been bettered in Scarsdale" (*Log*, p. xxxii).

By the end of chapter 3, Steinbeck has burdened the air of Cannery Row with two suicides and a tense awareness of the fatal effects of loneliness. Thus he is ready, in chapter 4, to bring on the old Chinaman—a disturbing vision of man's essential loneliness and isolation. The Chinaman appears only at dusk and dawn—the marginal, timeless times of day—and he is mysteriously associated with the night sea, the archetypal symbol of the unconscious and death. When "one brave and beautiful boy" dares to challenge this apparition, the boy is plunged into a vision of man's ultimate and final isolation, an expressionistic vision of a realm of death reminiscent of the landscape through which Pepé moves toward his death in "Flight." The "desolate cold aloneness" in the Chinaman's eyes is a projection of the boy's own unconscious awareness of death and of the inexorable aloneness represented by the idea of death. Like the "dark watchers" of "Flight," the old Chinaman is a "dream symbol" rising from the dark night sea which "deep and black in the depths, is like the low dark levels of our minds" (*Log*, p. 32).

With the apparition of the Chinaman, the dominant tone of loneliness and isolation has been fully established in *Cannery Row*, the tone on which the novel will end. In the course of the novel, there will be three certain suicides mentioned and the possibility of a fourth: the drowned girl at La Jolla. And there will be a great deal of cruelty and pain illustrated in the interchapters (the cruelty of one young boy to another whose father has killed himself is a prime example). Peter Lisca has suggested correctly that the novel's interchapters "with their suicides, physical mutations, psychological maladjustments, and mental cruelties, serve as a built-in restraint on the tendency toward sentimentality."[26] The chapters go even deeper, however; they control the tone of the entire novel, allowing the plot to rise above the level of deep despair only at brief intervals.

The interchapters also provide commentary on the central narrative, as we see in the story of Mary Talbot. Though very poor, Mary loves parties and gives as many as possible while pressuring her friends to do the same. When no human parties are available, Mary slips into a carefully contrived world of make-believe and creates parties for the neighborhood cats: a "kind of satiric game," which "covered and concealed from Mary the fact that she didn't have very nice clothes and the Talbots didn't have any money" (p. 139). More important, Mary uses the parties and her gift for artificially induced gaiety "as a weapon against the despondency that lurked always around outside the house waiting to get in at Tom" (p. 139). Like Mary's, all of the parties in *Cannery Row* are weapons against the despondency that lurks just beneath the surface of life on the Row and which very frequently breaks through. This is illustrated by the despondent aftermath that surfaces after each party. The first party Mack and the boys attempt to throw for Doc is the foremost example of this fact, ending as it does with Mack's confession, "I been sorry all my life" (p. 119). We see this also in the party Mack and the boys have with the "captain" during the frog hunt, a party which ends with the host passed out and Mack saying from bitter experience, "We got to get out of here. He's gonna wake up feelin' lousy and it's goin' to be all our fault" (p. 86).

Even the strange interlude concerning the humorist, Josh Billings, provides wry commentary on the novel as a whole. After describing the town's outrage over the desecration of Josh Billings's "tripas," Steinbeck comments, "For Monterey was not a town to let dishonor come to a literary man" (p. 65). This may well be Steinbeck's only reaction within his fiction to the hostile treatment he had received at the hands of his neighbors during his career, especially at the time of the publication of *The Grapes of Wrath*. Steinbeck well knew that it was the "humorous" novel, *Tortilla Flat*, which had not only brought him recognition and financial reward but also awakened the esteem of his Monterey neighbors, an esteem slow to come even then and undoubtedly based on the fact that the novel brought tourists and dollars to the community. In *Cannery Row* Steinbeck was creating another novel that could and would be considered humorous only if readers did not penetrate the thin surface to see the poison. The Josh Billings episode is a commentary by Steinbeck on his ironic and temporary position as a "humorist" in Monterey after *Tortilla Flat*, a bitter comment and a wry jibe at those who could consider that novel and *Cannery Row* mere humor.

The dual vision, or twin "peepholes," of *Cannery Row* is illustrated in Steinbeck's treatment of Mack and the boys. On one level Steinbeck obviously admires these characters and through them criticizes the middle-class values they reject. This admiration is clear in Doc's description of them:

There are your true philosophers. I think . . . that Mack and the
boys know everything that has ever happened in the world and

possibly everything that will happen. I think they survive in this particular world better than other people. In a time when people tear themselves to pieces with ambition and nervousness and covetousness, they are relaxed. All of our so-called successful men are sick men, with bad stomachs, and bad souls, but Mack and the boys are healthy and curiously clean. (p. 129)

And it is obvious in Steinbeck's description of the bums as "the Virtues, the Graces, the Beauties of the hurried mangled craziness of Monterey and the cosmic Monterey" (p. 11). In Mack and the boys, Steinbeck is, as Fontenrose has stated, "attacking and satirizing the drive for success, as commonly conceived, as wealth, ownership, status." And, as Lisca suggests, the novel can be read on one level as "a philosophically based and impassioned celebration of values directly opposed to the capitalist ethic dominant in Western society." However, there is another side to the Flophouse castaways, a sad and less pleasing dimension of failure, rejection, and withdrawal. Fontenrose directs us toward this aspect when he says, "Behind the idyllic picture of pleasant loafers we glimpse the maladjustment which brings a man to Skid Row."[27] This maladjustment is made distressingly obvious in Mack's confession to Doc after the failed party. After Doc has hit Mack in anger—and, one suspects, out of despair resulting from his vision of the girl in the tide pool—Mack says,

> "It don't do no good to say I'm sorry. I been sorry all my life. This ain't no new thing. It's always like this. . . . I had a wife. . . . Same thing. Ever'thing I done turned sour. She couldn't stand it any more. If I done a good thing it got poisoned up some way. . . . She only got hurt from me. She couldn't stand it no more. Same thing ever'place 'till I just got to clowning. I don't do nothin' but clown no more." (p. 119)

Mack is in retreat from the world outside of the Row; he has failed in love and in any kind of deep commitment and has come to hide out from further commitment on Cannery Row.

Mack and the boys are the flotsam and jetsam of the American Dream, pushed to the edge of the continent and, as Mack makes clear, aware of their failure. Though they are "good," they have, as the authors of the *Log* put it, a "weak survival quotient" (p. 96). They are, in fact, not a large step removed from Frankie, whose insufficiency results in his final removal from society into an asylum. Mack's catastrophic attempt to do something nice in the form of the first party for Doc is paralleled by Frankie's attempts to help Doc by serving beer to Doc's guests—an attempt which results in spilled beer and a broken-hearted Frankie—and by stealing the clock statue of St. George as a gift for Doc—which results in Frankie's removal from even the marginal society of the Row. Frankie's purpose in the novel is to remind us again of the laws of reality, that those who are too weak do not long survive even on the Row. Doc's full realization that "there wasn't a thing in the world he could do" to help Frankie underscores this truth.

Another character who is afraid or incapable of commitment is Henri, the artist and boat builder. Henri is terrified of the ocean; therefore, he builds his boat again and again so that he can never complete it and be forced to confront his fear. That Henri is terrified of his own unconscious—again symbolized by the sea—is indicated in the horrifying vision he experiences of a man cutting a child's throat while the child laughs. Henri asks Doc, "Is it some Freudian horror out of me or am I completely nuts?" (p. 125). That Henri is afraid of commitment is also suggested by his love life: "And one after another his loves left him" (p. 123). Like Mack and the boys, Henri is an outcast from the heart of America; he too has a low survival quotient and, in *Sweet Thursday*, Henri will be driven in panic from the Row by Mack and the boys' pranks.

The "desolate cold aloneness" of Cannery Row enters in the figure of Doc, the most deeply ambivalent character in Steinbeck's fiction. Richard Astro provides valuable insight into the character of Doc, obviously modeled on Ed Ricketts, when he states that "*Cannery Row* contains Steinbeck's greatest statement of affection for Ed Ricketts as well as the novelist's objective portrayal of the inherent shortcomings of the marine biologist's complex philosophy of life."[28] These shortcomings take the form in *Cannery Row* of an intense, overriding loneliness. While there can be little doubt that, as Ricketts himself recognized, the book "is written in kindness" and constitutes a tribute to a friend Steinbeck greatly admired, Steinbeck casts a dark shadow over the character of Doc in this novel. While Doc is no "local deity" as has been suggested,[29] he is a wise, gentle, and much-beloved figure in the novel. He is also, however, a "lonely and a set-apart man" (p. 91).

In "About Ed Ricketts" Steinbeck wrote: "But for all of Ed's pleasures and honesties there was a transcendent sadness in his life—something he missed or wanted, a searching that sometimes approached panic. . . . It was like a deep and endless nostalgia—a thirst and a passion for 'going home.' " And he continues: "He was walled off a little, so that he worked at his philosophy of 'breaking through,' of coming out through the back of the mirror into some kind of reality which would make the day world dreamlike" (*Log,* p. liii). Mack senses this same transcendent sadness in Doc:

> In spite of his friendliness and his friends Doc was a lonely and a set-apart man. Mack probably noticed it more than anybody. In a group, Doc seemed always alone. When the lights were on and the curtains down, and the Gregorian music played on the great phonograph, Mack used to look down on the laboratory from the Palace Flophouse. He knew Doc had a girl in there, but Mack used to get a dreadful feeling of loneliness out of it. Even in the dear close contact with a girl Mack felt that Doc would be lonely. (p. 91)

Doc, like the Ed Ricketts Steinbeck describes in "About Ed Ricketts," is not lonely for a particular lost love or necessarily a woman; he longs rather for a wholeness of vision, to "break through" to a vision of "the whole thing" as Doc Burton called it in *In Dubious Battle*. And Doc achieves this vision for a brief moment when he kneels to look into the eyes of the drowned girl in the tide at La Jolla.

All of the characters in *Cannery Row* are closely in tune with their unconscious. Mack and the boys rely heavily on instinct in their daily lives, and Henri, though terrified, exists on the edge of his unconscious just as he does the edge of the sea. Doc, however, is more deeply in touch with his unconscious than the others, a fact symbolized by Doc's close relationship with the sea and, more important, with the tides. Doc's laboratory is, as Astro has pointed out, "a veritable extension of the tide pool,"[30] with at least part of it set on piles over the incoming tide. And Doc's life is ruled by the tides, as is indicated in the fact that, when he could find no one to accompany him to collect octopuses, "Doc had to go alone because the tide would not wait" (p. 93). Later, Steinbeck says, "He had been working in a tidal pattern so long that he could feel a tide change in his sleep" (p. 98). It is the tide that pulls Doc to the edge of the sea and his sudden vision of wholeness and terrible beauty in the face of the drowned girl at La Jolla.

Just before he brings Doc face to face with the drowned girl, Steinbeck provides a hauntingly beautiful description of the tidal zone, ending with a suggestion of the "whole picture": "The tide goes out imperceptibly. The boulders show and seem to rise up and the ocean recedes leaving little pools, leaving wet weed and moss and sponge, iridescence and brown and blue and China red. On the bottoms lie the incredible refuse of the sea, shells broken and chipped and bits of skeleton, claws, the whole sea bottom a fantastic cemetery on which the living scamper and scramble" (p. 99). With the appearance of the drowned girl, more "refuse of the sea," the tide-pool metaphor suddenly opens outward to engulf all reality, and Doc experiences his vision of the "whole"—he "breaks through."

The drowned girl is a complex element in this novel, a window between the microcosm and the macrocosm, between the small picture and the "whole." She is also another Ophelia—a drowned sacrifice to failed love—and she is related to the drowned god of *The Waste Land* and *The Golden Bough* and *To a God Unknown*. Steinbeck and Ricketts wrote of sacrifice and "wholeness" in the *Log:* "Perhaps among primitive peoples the human sacrifice has the . . . effect of creating a wholeness of sense and emotion—the good and bad, beautiful, ugly, and cruel all welded into one thing. Perhaps a whole man needs this balance (p. 121). When, for an instant, Doc achieves this wholeness of vision in the face of the "pretty, pale girl with dark hair," he "shivered and his eyes were wet the way they get in the focus of great beauty" (p. 100). Doc's breaking through to this terrible beauty is not without cost, for it forces him to confront the fact that he has missed something very valuable in his life. As a symbol of sacrifice and of love, the drowned girl is another of the many symbols of commitment throughout Steinbeck's fiction, a commitment Doc, like the others on the Row, has been unable or unwilling to achieve. The story of the gopher, coming as it does just before the final chapter and the novel's climax, is designed to underscore this point.

The penultimate chapter tells the story of a gopher that creates the perfect and perfectly secure home on Cannery Row—a "gopher's equivalent of Cannery Row," as Lisca says[31]—but is forced to give up his perfect home in order to find love amidst the traps and poisons of the world outside of the Row. Rather than simply teaching us that "the creature that lives by physical sensation must sacrifice security to the satisfaction of such desires—ones that probably doom him,"[32] the story of the gopher is a comment on the human inhabitants of the Row, including Doc, none of whom is able to find any kind of deep commitment on Cannery Row. Mack has fled to the Row from a failed love, Gay hides out in the Palace Flophouse from his tormenting wife, Henri's loves leave him in rapid succession, and Doc finds only increased loneliness and solitude in his loves. Cannery Row is a place of disengagement where the kind of commitment so highly prized in Steinbeck's fiction is not found. The unbreakable barrier of Doc's detachment prevents him from finding any kind of meaningful commitment even among his friends. As Levant points out, Doc's relationship with Mack and the boys is not one of deep commitment: "They are interesting to him, as everyone is, but his interest in them is much like that he pays to the specimens he finds in the tide pools. He helps them as much as he can, but he does not love them."[33] Doc is not, finally, a Steinbeck hero, for he does not embody the deep commitment to all of life found in a Joseph Wayne, Jim Casy, Tom Joad, or even Juan Chicoy. Astro points out Doc's strong resemblance to the tragic Doc of *In Dubious Battle:* "Both Docs are lonely, set-apart men, who, while able to break through to momentary insights of great understanding, are in the end sustained only by their melancholy."[34] While Doc is described as "half Christ and half satyr," it is not convincing to argue that he "embodies all the qualities which Steinbeck finds admirable," and that "in him all opposites are reconciled."[35] Doc has sacrificed a fullness of experience to seek a wholeness of vision.

The novel ends with Doc reading and reciting "Black Marigolds":

> Even now
> I know that I have savored the hot taste of life
> Lifting green cups and gold at the great feast.
> Just for a small and a forgotten time
> I have had full in my eyes from off my girl
> The whitest pouring of eternal light—

Doc's "girl" has been the girl in the tide at La Jolla, and the "eternal light" has been the momentary vision of the whole. As Doc experiences again the sense of wholeness inspired by his vision in the tide pool, he slips more deeply into his unconscious, and the world becomes more dreamlike, a state suggested by the tide: "Under the piers it was very high tide and the waves splashed on rocks they had not reached in a long time"

189

and "he could hear the waves beat under the piles" (p. 180). Doc, however, has not truly "savored the hot taste of life"; he is too set apart in his quest for the whole picture, and he is too lonely. The parties and the lonely trysts with women only reinforce this apartness. The novel ends therefore on a deeply ambivalent note, with Doc achieving a wholeness of vision at the same time that his essential apartness is sharply brought home to him. With the tide moving beneath the floor and the rattlesnakes staring into space "with their dusty frowning eyes," the novel ends on what, in the *Log*, Steinbeck termed a "harvest of symbols": "Symbol, the serpent, the sea" (p. 34). Doc is deeply in touch with his unconscious and deeply alone.

Sweet Thursday: Farewell to Steinbeck Country

John Steinbeck's *Sweet Thursday* (1954), the final, sad installment in the canon of Steinbeck's California fiction, is a funny novel, a romantic comedy written with one eye on the musical-comedy stage, where it would quickly appear in an adaptation by Rogers and Hammerstein.[36] However, the lighthearted comedy of *Sweet Thursday* loses a good deal of its sweetness when we realize that this late novel is a self-parody, a mockery by Steinbeck of the characters, symbols, and themes that run through his fiction from the first novel, *Cup of Gold*, in 1929 to *Cannery Row* in 1945. *Sweet Thursday* is Steinbeck's ritual cleansing, like the potlatch Mack and the boys attempt when they raffle off the Palace Flophouse (though *that* potlatch is conveniently rigged). Rather than a "continuation" of *Cannery Row*, as Steinbeck once called it (*Life in Letters*, p. 474), *Sweet Thursday* is a bittersweet farewell to Cannery Row and Monterey, to California and Steinbeck Country.

The motivation behind Steinbeck's rejection of the region that had produced all of his lasting fiction is not difficult to find. In October 1944, immediately after he had completed *Cannery*

Row, Steinbeck ended nearly two years of residence in New York by moving back to Monterey. Just before the move he wrote to his lifelong friend Carlton Sheffield: "We are getting out—going back to Monterey. I've had a wonderful sense of going home, but just lately I'm a little scared. . . . There must have been a change in me and in everyone else" (*Life in Letters,* p. 272). Steinbeck's foreboding would prove prophetic. Within a few months of returning to Steinbeck Country, he was writing to Pascal Covici to say, "There is no home coming nor any welcome. . . . This isn't my country any more. And it won't be until I am dead. It makes me very sad" (*Life in Letters,* pp. 280–81). Steinbeck had left Monterey and California for good, reversing the archetypal American journey westward so central to his fiction and heading east to finish out his life on the Atlantic coast. Steinbeck Country had rejected Steinbeck, and almost a decade later that rejection would bear bitter fruit in the novel ironically entitled *Sweet Thursday.*

In *Sweet Thursday* we find the bitter world of *Cannery Row,* the earlier novel so aptly described by Malcolm Cowley as a "poisoned creampuff," transformed into an idyllic world in which survival is not difficult and worries not very complex. Whereas the sea makes its presence felt in *Cannery Row,* as it did in Steinbeck's earlier story "The Snake," as a brooding symbol of the unconscious, in *Sweet Thursday* the tide laps pleasantly around the pilings of Doc's laboratory as he turns his attention away from the tensions of the tidal zone and toward Fauna's whorehouse and Suzy, the whore with a heart of gold. No longer in *Sweet Thursday* are Mack and the boys the tragicomic outcasts we find in *Cannery Row;* now the Palace Flophouse bums are respectable, their primary concern being not survival but how to throw a proper party for Doc and how to bring Doc together with Suzy, the object of his timid passion. Now Mack, the Flophouse leader, worries about the correct attire for Doc's party and proclaims, "Nobody gets in without he's got a necktie on" (p. 173). Even the representative paisano, Joseph and Mary

Rivas, who has replaced Lee Chong as the grocer of Cannery Row, is simply a successful and devoted capitalist who exploits his fellow paisanos with cheerful approval from the denizens of the Row and its author.

Steinbeck writes early in *Sweet Thursday,* "Change was everywhere. People were gone, or changed, and that was almost like being gone" (p. 4). The inhabitants of the previous Cannery Row are all changed, all gone. The tough and capable Dora of the earlier novel has been replaced by her marrying-missionary sister, Flora/Fauna, who runs a finishing school for prospective brides in the form of a virtuous whorehouse. Lee Chong, the grocer of *Cannery Row,* in an absurdly comic echo of the pirate Henry Morgan in Steinbeck's first novel, *Cup of Gold,* has gone buccaneering toward adventure and romance in the South Seas. The old man by the sea in Steinbeck's second novel, *To a God Unknown,* a lonely figure who sacrificed small animals at the death of each day in a noncausal "mystical outcrying," reappears in *Sweet Thursday* in the guise of a beachcombing, addle-brained "seer" who steals candy bars and preaches a doctrine of romantic love. The mystical outcrying of the earlier novel has become in this character merely a muted, vague yearning, and he bears an uncomfortable resemblance to Pimples Carson of Steinbeck's *The Wayward Bus,* another character tainted by an addiction to sweets.

The transformation which has taken place between *Cannery Row* and *Sweet Thursday* is most obvious in the characters of Mack and Doc. In the prologue to *Sweet Thursday,* Steinbeck establishes Mack in the role of critic, writing: "One night Mack lay back on his bed in the Palace Flophouse and he said, 'I ain't never been satisfied with that book *Cannery Row.* I would of went about it different. . . . I guess I'm just a critic'" (p. vii). That Mack has indeed become a critic is amply illustrated by the alteration in his speech between *Cannery Row* and *Sweet Thursday.* While in the former novel Mack was a deep thinker upon matters of pleasure and survival, his speech was that of a social dropout and Flophouse habitué. In *Sweet Thursday*, however, Mack has become painfully literary, dispensing fragments of Latin and verse with abandon, from *"Hoc sunt"* (p. 60) and *"Quod erat demonstrandum"* (p. 64) to "Doc lets concealment like a worm in the bud feed on his damask cheek" (p. 77). The novel even ends weakly with the newly sententious Mack spouting, "Vice is a monster so frightful of mien, I'm sure we should all be as happy as kings." This is not the sorry Mack of *Cannery Row,* the complex outcast who sought refuge from the American Dream near the sea's edge. This is a musical-comedy, literary Mack for whose critical approval the novel is offered. Through this characterization of Mack, Steinbeck makes it very clear that this novel is a departure, the first Steinbeck novel written explicitly with the intention of pleasing the popular audience and critic. Mack's portrayal suggests, in fact, that Steinbeck was quite conscious of the fact that this last of his California novels was, as French has called it, a "sellout."[37]

The distance between the tense, complex world of *Cannery Row* and the comic reality of *Sweet Thursday* is even more apparent in the character of Doc. In *Cannery Row,* Doc is described as a "lonely and a set-apart man" (p. 91), a man isolated from his community because of his non-teleological detachment—a figure suffering profoundly from the same incapacity for commitment to his fellow man found in Doc Burton in *In Dubious Battle.* In *Sweet Thursday* Doc's loneliness returns, but it is altered and rechanneled. Now the quest for a vision of the "whole picture" which haunted Doc in *Cannery Row* and *In Dubious Battle* has disappeared and Doc's yearning has become merely the causal factor in another lightweight love story. In this later novel, Steinbeck intentionally misremembers the Doc of *Cannery Row,* claiming that "before the war Doc had lived a benign and pleasant life" and "all in all, he had always been a fulfilled and contented man" (p. 21). The unhappy sage of the earlier novel, who

yearned to break through to some kind of transcendent understanding, has become a simple man in a simple, sentimental
world.

That Steinbeck had a very different kind of Doc in mind for
Sweet Thursday, and that he was in fact writing with the stage in
mind is further suggested in a letter he wrote to Henry Fonda,
star of the film version of *The Grapes of Wrath:* "You will remember also that when I was writing *Sweet Thursday* I had you
always in mind as the prototype of Doc" (*Life in Letters,* p. 603).
The vision has shifted from the tide pool to the stars of Hollywood for this final California fiction.

Not even Steinbeck himself escapes the mockery of *Sweet
Thursday,* for Steinbeck's self-parody becomes most acute in Joe
Elegant, the posturing, effeminate cook in Fauna's whorehouse,
this novel's novelist. As he sits in the whorehouse writing his
novel, obsessed with myth and symbol, Joe Elegant may indeed
suggest a young Truman Capote, as one critic has claimed,[38] but
he calls to mind even more sharply a young John Steinbeck,
author of such ponderously mythical novels as *Cup of Gold* and
To a God Unknown with their naïve and heavy-handed wielding
of symbols. When Joe Elegant paints a bullseye on Hazel's bare
bottom and sends him innocently off to Doc's party, Joe Elegant
is doing precisely what Steinbeck has done in this novel to all of
his characters. In this funny book, Steinbeck has carefully and
consciously targeted himself and all of his previous creations.

While in *Cannery Row* the metaphor controlling our vision
was that of the twin "peepholes," in *Sweet Thursday* our vision
of the Row is defined by the metaphor of the pinhole in Flora's
window shade which projects the life of the Row on Flora's wall
upside down. *Sweet Thursday* inverts the pathos of *Cannery Row*
and turns it into light comedy. To insure that we do not miss his
conscious distortion of this world, Steinbeck emphasizes a second symbol of perspective in this novel. While in *Cannery Row*
our perspective was that of the microscope with which Doc
studies and dissects the life of the tide pool—including Mack and

the boys—in *Sweet Thursday* the microscope gives way to the telescope that Mack and the boys mistakenly give to Doc. Like Gulliver, we experience a pronounced shift in our perspective, one which, like the telescope, enlarges and thus distances us from the minutiae of our subjects. With this new, musical-comedy perspective, we do not see the flaws, the pathetic failures, and the pain of Cannery Row; it is all glossed over. Steinbeck very carefully brings this major shift in perspective to our attention through the metaphors of the pinhole and telescope and provides us with keys to how to approach this novel.

The most sweeping mockery found in the humor of *Sweet Thursday* comes in the form of Mr. Deems, the godlike giver of roque courts who is sacrificed angrily each year by the residents of Pacific Grove in a parody of ancient sacrifice. "They make a celebration of it," Steinbeck writes, "dress up a life-like figure, and hang it from a pine tree. Later, they burn it" (p. 57). That Mr. Deems is meant to call to mind the hanged god of Frazer's *The Golden Bough* is unmistakable, for that ancient sacrificial figure, symbol of man's commitment to his environment, is also hung from a pine tree and often burned. Most important here, however, is the fact that the hanged god, together with the related sacrificial deities associated with that figure, is the most important symbol running through all of Steinbeck's fiction, from the nature worship and fisher-king of *To a God Unknown* to the Christ figures of *In Dubious Battle, The Wayward Bus, The Grapes of Wrath,* and even Steinbeck's last novel, *The Winter of Our Discontent.* In Mr. Deems, Steinbeck's self-parody is heavy, for this absurd sacrifice mocks the central thrust of Steinbeck's life's work; the metaphor for man's commitment to what Steinbeck termed "the whole thing, known and unknowable" has lost its force and its meaning.

If we look closely at the comic world of *Sweet Thursday,* it becomes clear that all of the themes and symbols central to Steinbeck's fiction have been parodied and cast off. No longer in this novel does California symbolize the American Eden and

195

terminus for the westering impulse; it is simply a middle-class setting with bums and whores the upholders of middle-class values. No longer does the sea suggest the unconscious, the unknown, and death. No grail knight like Joseph Wayne of *To a God Unknown,* or Kino of *The Pearl,* or Old Gitano of *The Red Pony* confronts the mysteries of the unconscious and death.

In *Sweet Thursday,* Steinbeck has shifted the foundation of his fiction to one day *before* Good Friday in order to create a less-than-serious world in which the necessity for sacrifice and commitment simply does not exist. As the title of this novel cleverly hints, this is a purely comic world devoid of the most meaningful symbol in Steinbeck's fiction and Western culture: the Christian sacrifice.

CONCLUSION: THE WINTER OF OUR DISCONTENT AND THE AMERICAN CONSCIENCE

Steinbeck would return to the themes and symbols, if not the setting, of his great work one last time in *The Winter of Our Discontent*, his final novel (1961). In this study of the American conscience, the dominant Steinbeck theme of commitment through sacrifice finds its symbolic statement in Ethan Allen Hawley's obsession with and intense feelings for Good Friday and his betrayal of the vaguely Christ-like Danny. "Why do they call it Good Friday?" Ethan asks, and his wife, Mary, answers for all of Steinbeck's fiction: "Spring." Commitment through sacrifice leading to rebirth—Steinbeck's answer to the way out of the spiritual and moral wasteland of the twentieth century. However, in this last novel there will be no resurrection, no spiritual rebirth for Ethan Allen Hawley. For the first time in Steinbeck's fiction, spring alone is insufficient.

The Winter of Our Discontent is a startlingly different novel for Steinbeck, one in which the author enters new and more difficult terrain.[1] For the first time in his long career, here Steinbeck attempts to come to terms with the moral dimensions of the isolated individual. Ethan Allen Hawley represents the modern American Everyman, and Baytown is microcosmic America, but Ethan, far more than any previous Steinbeck character, transcends the role of what Steinbeck earlier termed "symbol-people" and becomes fully human with all of the personal agony that entails. The result is that *Winter*, flawed as it is by a disturbing coyness,[2] breezy cynicism, and at times less-than-sparkling style, is nonetheless one of Steinbeck's most moving works.

Critics have in general not been kind to this novel. Contrasting the novel with the short story from which it grew, "How Mr. Hogan Robbed a Bank," Warren French in 1965 declared that "a delightful comic fantasy has been turned into a contrived melodrama." Joseph Fontenrose dismisses the novel as superficial and "improbable." Peter Lisca, in a 1965 attempt to explain what most critics saw as Steinbeck's serious decline as a writer, attacks the novel for its "reworked cliches and stereotyped situations."[3] Only in recent years has *Winter* begun to attract the serious and often positive criticism that it deserves, including perceptive readings in light of both Jungian elements and the influence of Eliot's *The Waste Land*.[4]

Weaknesses in *Winter* are not difficult to find. That Steinbeck is not writing at the height of his powers is evident in such awkwardnesses as the passage in which Mr. Baker and Ethan fill the reader in on Ethan's history:

> "I had my opportunity, Mr. Baker, more opportunity than good sense. Don't forget I owned this store right after the war. Had to sell half a block of real estate to stock it—the last of our business property."
>
> "I know, Ethan. I'm your banker. Know your business the way your doctor knows your pulse."
>
> "Sure you know. Took me less than two years to damn near go bankrupt. Had to sell everything but my house to pay my debts."
>
> "You can't take all the blame for that. Fresh out of the Army— no business experience. And don't forget you ran smack into a depression, only we called it recession. Some pretty seasoned businessmen went under."
>
> "I went under all right. It's the first time in history a Hawley was ever a clerk in a guinea grocery." (p. 12)

Never before has Steinbeck had to resort to such clumsy exposition to get his pertinent information across; such an episode smacks of haste or carelessness on the part of a writer who was seldom if ever hasty or careless. Similarly, Steinbeck's attempt to create a kind of offhand cynicism in such lines as "Once in a while, not too often, he took her out to dinner and laid her" (pp. 176–77) falls disturbingly flat. And when Steinbeck intrudes in chapter 9 of part 1 to have Ethan tell us, "He didn't say it meanly the way it looks in print" (p. 130), he slips in a way that Steinbeck has not slipped before, raising the confusing question of just who the author of the first book, with its mixture of first and third-person narrative, really is.

In spite of such failings, *The Winter of Our Discontent* is worthy of careful and serious study, for this novel is Steinbeck's final fictional statement and it brings together crucial threads of Steinbeck's philosophy—an argument spanning a career of more than three decades. Once again, in *Winter* Steinbeck examines America's idea of itself—the American Myth replete with images of Eden and innocence, rebirth and renewal. And again Steinbeck suggests that the myth is both deceptive and dangerous.

The Winter of Our Discontent was written while Steinbeck was stalled in his last great effort, the Malory "translation" that would appear posthumously as *The Acts of King Arthur and His Noble Knights,* a rough and unfinished creation. It is therefore not surprising to find that the Grail Quest central to Malory and to so much of Steinbeck's earlier work is again prominent in this last novel. Like *The Waste Land* and *Canterbury Tales* and Chretien de Troyes's *Conte du Grail*—the Grail version Malory based so much of his own work upon—*Winter* begins in April, "the cruellest month," the time of the year's rebirth and of the death and resurrection of Christ. That Steinbeck was thinking of Eliot and the Arthurian materials simultaneously once again, as he had been years before when he rewrote *To a God Unknown,* is suggested in a letter he wrote to the Malory scholar Eugene Vinaver in which he declared, "The Matter of Arthur is surely the Matter of Me. . . . The Wasteland was surely in the brilliantly dry and despairing mind of Eliot. Malory would have found it incomprehensible."[5]

Like Eliot, Steinbeck presents us with a picture of spiritual corruption and sterility in a modern wasteland, in *Winter* a world in which Easter eggs have replaced an understanding of the profound significance of Easter and in which the church service figures merely as a prelude to corrupt business deals. The world of *Winter* reflects Steinbeck's concern that "immorality is what is destroying us, public immorality. The failure of man toward men, the selfishness that puts making a buck more important than the common weal."[6] In this world, Ethan's store is his church, with its "diffused cathedral light" (p. 9), and money has replaced God, as Joey Morphy makes clear when he says, "Comes nine o'clock on the nose we stand uncovered in front of the holy of holies" (p. 132). The world of Baytown is one in which man's commitment to man—the commitment at the heart of Christ's sacrifice—has failed; it is a world in which individuals are sacrificed in the name of profit, from Danny and Marullo to the entire town administration. As Peter Lisca states, "The image of man, or, more accurately, the image of the American, which emerges is one of dishonesty, laziness, opportunism, and cynicism on all levels."[7] The seer of this moral wasteland is Joey Morphy, who knows everything and inspires Ethan with his dream of bank robbery. "The Morph" is Morpheus, god of dreams—in this case the American dream of easy gold. And Ethan awakens fully to the pervasiveness of this corruption only when he discovers near the novel's end that his son Allen has cheated in an "I Love America" contest.

Again, as in *To a God Unknown*, Steinbeck calls upon Frazer and Weston, Eliot and Malory, for his symbols and for the structural element of the Grail Quest. Margie Young-Hunt is, in Ethan's words, "a predator, a huntress, Artemis for pants" (p. 15), and she is Diana, goddess of the sacred wood wherein the old king—priest and murderer—must regularly be slain and replaced by the new.[8] Danny and Marullo are the old kings, both of whom have intimate relationships with this huntress, and Ethan is the new king whom Margie sets up to ascend to his position of power by destroying his predecessors. Simultaneously, Ethan is a fisher-king whose decline and spiritual impotence are reflected in the despair of both his family and his town. Finally, Ethan is Lancelot, flawed knight and father of Galahad, the perfect knight and Quester. That Ethan is the fallen, tainted knight is strongly suggested by the Knights Templar hat with its symbolically yellowed plume (which Ethan would like to bleach white again). Like that ancient knightly order, Ethan begins nobly but succumbs to the lure of wealth. We see this parallel most clearly when, as Margie is about to read the fortune that will send Ethan on his way toward irreversible corruption, Ethan descends the stairs (into a modern hell) with the tarnished Templars hat on his head.

Margie is not only Artemis/Diana, she is also, as Donna Gerstenberger has suggested, the Madame Sosostris of this novel, "a wicked woman with a Tarot pack."⁹ Madame Sosostris, in Eliot's *The Waste Land*, predicts the necessary death by water, thus foreseeing, in spite of her own debased condition, the necessary sacrifice leading to rebirth. In *Winter*, however, Ethan's ambiguous awakening is to the ubiquitous moral decay of the world on the day that, his Aunt Deborah says, "Jesus is dead" (p. 51).

Margie is also a witch, descended from a Russian witch sentenced to Alaska because "she raised storms." Steinbeck even suggests that Margie may haunt Ethan in the form of a cat that appears repeatedly at the back of the store, implying at one point that the cat may have mysteriously opened the storeroom door. "You hear me—aroint!" Ethan says to frighten the cat away, adding, "That must be a magic word" (p. 9). Later Ethan will use the same magic word against Margie (p. 153). Steinbeck is reminding us here that he is writing in and of New England, that place of witchcraft and guilt and the birthplace of the American myth. And furthermore, he appears to be stressing a positive element in Margie Young-Hunt's role. Rain represents a fertilizing potential in *The Waste Land* and throughout Steinbeck's own work—as we see, for example, in the rain that does not come to Elisa in "The Chry-santhemums." As an heir to someone who "raised storms," or "freed the waters," Margie possesses the ability to bring Ethan to life as, paradoxically, she initiates him into the world of corruption surrounding him.

Ethan, when we first encounter him in this novel, is, like the fisher-king in the Diu Crone version of the myth,[10] neither living nor dead. He uses his bantering wit as a defense against life, a barrier behind which he hides from meaningful commitment. Ethan's daughter, Ellen, accuses him of just this evasion when she cries, "You never listen, really listen," adding, "You'll be sorry" (p. 150). Ethan has cut himself off from life and the moral responsibility and risk life demands, as is evident in the corruption of Allen, his only son and namesake, which has occurred without Ethan's awareness. According to Jessie Weston, the Grail Quest should be viewed as an initiation story.[11] By assisting in Ethan's initiation into full knowledge, Margie causes Ethan to "spring to life" as fully human, with all the tragic potential this entails.

The past in this novel is symbolized by the *Belle-Adair*, "one of the last built and finest" of the whaling ships, a vessel owned in partnership by Ethan's grandfather and Mr. Baker's father, and burned for insurance money by his grandfather's partner. "Our people were daring men," Baker tells Ethan (p. 13), and a few pages later Margie exclaims, "I dare you to live up to it [Ethan's fortune] and I dare you not to. So long, Savior!" (p. 17). "Dare" suggests Christ's "awful daring of a moment's surrender / which an age of prudence can never retract" in *The Waste Land*, but ironically here the sacrifice Ethan makes is that of his self-respect and morality, and the result will be that the *Belle-Adair* is lost forever to him. Ethan has been attempting through his detachment to ignore evil, and once he is initiated into full knowledge he falls, unable to accept the dare central to *East of Eden*: that of remaining "good" while knowing evil (compare Melville's Ishmael: "Not ignoring what is good, I am quick to perceive a horror").

When Ethan says, "Town like this has got myths," Steinbeck is reminding us of America's myths, especially that most American myth of all: of beginning anew, recovering innocence. Ethan thinks as he plans his descent into corruption, "Temporarily I traded a habit of conduct and attitude for comfort and dignity and a cushion of security. . . . But my objective was limited and, once achieved, I could take back my habit of conduct. I knew I could" (p. 200). However, what Ethan is to learn is that there is no turning back, no way back into the Garden. Ethan would like to be reborn, resurrected with Christ, a desire that represents a profound need and a wish fulfillment, but not a real possibility. As he is thinking of Margie and the inescapable fortune, Ethan says, "The roosters up on Clam Hill had been crowing for a long time and I had heard and not heard. I wished I could stay to see the sun rise straight out from the Place" (p. 46). Like so many other roosters, from *The Waste Land* to *To a God Unknown* and *In Dubious Battle,* the roosters suggest Christ's betrayal and crucifixion, and here Ethan's betrayal of Danny. The conventional pun on "sun" is Steinbeck's hint that Ethan won't experience the resurrection. Instead, Ethan hurries home to make his plans for his un-Christian behavior, leading to the sacrifice of Danny, during the day when "Jesus is in hell" (p. 51). The Place is Ethan's womblike retreat at the ocean's edge, but in this passage it also suggests Christ's tomb, from which He rose. When the time comes for Ethan, who identifies with Christ, to rise, he will rise neither reborn nor saved.

The Grail of this novel is Ethan's talisman, the little stone "continuity thing" (p. 127) which can glow a deep red "as though a little blood had got on it" (p. 231), calling to mind the Grail as the chalice of Christ's blood. Like Ethan's talismanic stone, the Grail "radiates a blazing light"[12] and is a symbol of profound commitment and continuity. And like the Grail, the talisman has a bearer in Ellen, who, when she approaches the talisman, "seemed to have a glow, perhaps in her white nightgown" (p. 126). When Ellen holds the talisman, Ethan says, "The dim room seemed swimming with particles of brilliant light. . . . And it did seem true that a glow came from my daughter Ellen" (p. 128).

Like the Grail Maiden, Ellen is pure and chaste, declaring childishly, "I do hate boys." Ellen's name even suggests that of Elaine, daughter of Pelles the fisher-king and Grail Bearer in Welsh tradition.[13]

In addition to being the Grail Bearer in the novel, Ellen is Steinbeck's feminine Galahad, the promise of the future. According to Richard Cavendish, "Lancelot stands for Adam, the imperfect man, and Galahad for Christ as the Second Adam, or man perfected."[14] Ethan, whose house even has "Adam decorations" (p. 3), is the imperfect American Adam, and he is the Lancelot Steinbeck described in a letter to his agent, Elizabeth Otis:

> And now we come to the Grail, the Quest. I think it is true that any man . . . when he comes to maturity has a very deep sense that he will not win the quest. He knows his failings, his shortcomings and particularly his memories of sins, sins of cruelty, of thoughtlessness, of disloyalty, of adultery, and these will not permit him to win the Grail . . . Lancelot could not see the Grail because of the faults and sins of Malory himself. He knows he has fallen short and all his excellences, his courage, his courtesy, in his own mind cannot balance his vices and errors, his stupidities.[15]

Ellen is the Galahad described in Malory as the "Clean Maiden,"[16] the light bearer and Ethan's hope.

At the novel's end, Ethan has dared to engage life fully, but has failed and has realized the enormity of his loss and the corrosive horror of moral decay as exemplified in his son Allen, and he sees that, as he tells Mary, the crime is "everybody's" (p. 212). He has promised his grandfather, "I'll get that keel up—soon as I'm rich" (p. 265), but because the keel represents lost honor, Ethan will never resurrect it. When he goes once more to the Place to die, Ethan discovers that he "could see the third rock, but from the Place it did not line up with the point over the sunken keel of the *Belle-Adair*" (p. 280). He has lost his bearings, the sense of place that his grandfather had so carefully instilled.

And in this final scene a star appears: "Then I could see a star—late rising, too late rising over the edge" (p. 280). It is "too late rising" for Ethan, who knows now that he cannot go back. In contrast to the evening star at the end of *The Wayward Bus,* this star no longer assures renewal—a new responsibility has fallen upon the individual in Steinbeck's fiction. A boat appears as Ethan is preparing to die in this place of baptism and rebirth, and Ethan says, "I saw her mast light over the toothy tumble of the break water, but her red and green were below my range of sight" (p. 280). The light is that of Ellen, Marullo, the Grail, of hope. But the red and the green suggest the blood of sacrifice and the green of renewal, and these are out of Ethan's vision, no longer possible for him.

Ethan goes on to define a profound shift in Steinbeck's thinking: "It isn't true that there's a community of light, a bonfire of the world. Every one carries his own, his lonely own. . . . My light is out" (p. 280). Throughout his fiction, Steinbeck had insisted upon the necessity for commitment to and a merger with the larger whole, the "one inseparable unit, man plus his environment." In *The Winter of Our Discontent,* for the first time, Steinbeck shifts his focus squarely onto the individual and illuminates the enormous and lonely responsibility each individual bears for his own moral existence. It is here that Ethan as character achieves much greater impact than any previous Steinbeck character, surpassing in the power of his tragic implications such successful archetypes and symbols as Joseph Wayne, Jim Nolan, Lennie and George, Ma and Tom Joad. For, as Ethan says, in a statement that flirts with sentimentality, "It's so much darker when a light goes out than it would have been if it had never shone" (p. 281).

The Winter of Our Discontent ends on a positive note as the grail/talisman which Ellen has secreted in her father's pocket draws Ethan away from the sea and death and back toward his responsibility to the living. As he discovers the talisman, he sees that "in my hand it gathered every bit of light there was and seemed red—dark red" (p. 281). The blood-red stone pulls Ethan back to responsibility and commitment. His light is out—his own quest has failed—but, as he says in the novel's final words, "I had to get back—to return the talisman to its new owner. Else another light might go out."

On the heels of this final exploration of America's idea of itself, Steinbeck would return one last time to Steinbeck Country in *Travels with Charley in Search of America* (1962), and the experience would send him fleeing in despair back toward the new home in the East. As his hasty journey and quick retreat in that book make clear, the ties to California had long been irreparably severed and Steinbeck knew this. "What we knew is dead, and maybe the greatest part of what we were is dead," he tells an old Monterey friend. "What's out there is new and perhaps good, but it's nothing we know." What the troubled jeremiad of *Winter* and the sense of loss here suggest is that Steinbeck felt cut off not merely from California but from America, as if the nation he had spent his life studying, probing, had quietly passed him by.

Steinbeck would continue his movement eastward and away from California, reversing the archetypal American journey westward, crossing the Atlantic to research the work he died writing, his "translation" of Malory. Ironically, this final project would take Steinbeck full circle, back to the Arthurian materials so central to his first novel, *Cup of Gold,* and he would end up where he began, in the abstract realm of myth and legend far removed from the contemporary crisis acted out in his final novel.

Steinbeck's fiction constitutes the most ambitious and thorough examination of the idea of America yet produced by any writer. It is a life's work focused on the singular attempt to understand for America the great myth upon which the nation was founded, to illustrate the complexities of that myth in its major symbol—California—and to illuminate the way out of the modern wasteland brought so sharply to the American consciousness by T. S. Eliot and company in the twenties. That his writing fails when it seeks to tell rather than show does not detract from the daring of his attempt, and that it succeeded brilliantly in such works as *The Pastures of Heaven, Tortilla Flat, Of Mice and Men, The Red Pony, In Dubious Battle, The Long Valley, The Grapes of Wrath,* and *Cannery Row* should convince us that Steinbeck's fiction is worthy of close and careful study and that it will remain with us for a very long time. Like his heroes, Steinbeck was committed to a quest for understanding, an attempt to open the "new eye" in the West and throughout America. As his last poignant adventure with Charley suggests, Steinbeck's life was spent "In Search of America."

NOTES

Introduction

1. Steinbeck, quoted in Nelson Valjean, *John Steinbeck the Errant Knight: An Intimate Biography of His California Years* (San Francisco: Chronicle Books, 1975), p. 123.

2. Ibid.

3. Richard Astro, "From the Tidepool to the Stars: Steinbeck's Sense of Place," *Steinbeck Quarterly* 10 (Winter 1978): 5–11.

4. William Appleman Williams, "Steinbeck and the Spirit of the Thirties," in *Steinbeck and the Sea,* ed. Richard Astro and Joel W. Hedgpeth (Corvallis: Oregon State University Press, 1975), p. 43.

5. Frederic Carpenter, "The Philosophical Joads," in *A Casebook on "The Grapes of Wrath,"* ed. Agnes McNeill Donohue (New York: Thomas Y. Crowell, 1968), pp. 80ff.

6. Richard Astro, *John Steinbeck and Edward F. Ricketts: The Shaping of a Novelist* (Minneapolis: University of Minnesota Press, 1973), pp. 43–60.

7. Annette Kolodny, *The Lay of the Land: Metaphor as Experience and History in American Life and Letters* (Chapel Hill: University of North Carolina Press, 1975), p. 66.

8. Richard Slotkin, *Regeneration Through Violence: The Mythology of the American Frontier, 1600–1860* (Middletown, Conn.: Wesleyan University Press, 1973), p. 27.

9. Kolodny, *The Lay of the Land,* p. 7.

Chapter One: The Mountains

1. Astro, *Steinbeck and Ricketts,* p. 81.

2. For an account of the genesis of *To a God Unknown,* see Peter Lisca, *The Wide World of John Steinbeck* (New Brunswick, N.J.: Rutgers University Press, 1958), pp. 39–41.

3. Howard Levant, *The Novels of John Steinbeck: A Critical Study* (Columbia: University of Missouri Press, 1974), p. 27.

4. Joseph Fontenrose, *John Steinbeck: An Introduction and Interpretation* (New York: Holt, Rinehart and Winston, 1963), p. 15.

5. Lisca, *Wide World of Steinbeck,* pp. 42–43.

6. Sir James Frazer, *The Golden Bough: A Study in Magic and Religion,* 1 vol. abridged (New York: Macmillan, 1951), p. 538. Subsequent citations from this book refer to this edition and are identified by page number in the text.

7. Jessie L. Weston, *From Ritual to Romance* (Cambridge: Cambridge University Press, 1921; rpt. ed., New York: Doubleday, 1957), p. 36.

8. Astro, *Steinbeck and Ricketts,* p. 81.

9. Joseph Campbell, *The Hero with a Thousand Faces* (New York: Meridian Books, 1956), p. 41.

10. Richard Astro, "Phlebas Sails the Caribbean: Steinbeck, Hemingway, and the American Waste Land," in *The Twenties: Fiction, Poetry, Drama,* ed. Warren French (Deland, Fla.: Everett/Edwards, 1975), p. 231.

11. Robert DeMott, "Toward a Redefinition of *To a God Unknown,*" *University of Windsor Review* 8 (1975): 37.

12. Lisca, *Wide World of Steinbeck,* p. 47.

13. Fontenrose, *John Steinbeck: An Introduction and Interpretation,* p. 18.

14. Astro, *Steinbeck and Ricketts,* p. 94.

15. Levant, *The Novels of John Steinbeck,* pp. 24, 26.

16. Dan Vogel, "Steinbeck's 'Flight': The Myth of Manhood," *College English* 23 (December 1962): 225.

17. Chester F. Chapin, "Pepe Torres: A Steinbeck 'Natural,'" *College English* 23 (December 1962): 676.

18. John Antico, "A Reading of Steinbeck's 'Flight,'" *Modern Fiction Studies* 11 (1965): 45.

19. Warren French, *John Steinbeck,* 1st ed. (New York: Twayne, 1961), p. 81.

20. Fontenrose, *John Steinbeck: An Introduction and Interpretation,* p. 63.

21. John Ditsky, "Steinbeck's 'Flight': The Ambiguity of Manhood," *Steinbeck Quarterly* 5 (Summer–Fall 1972): 85.

22. Antico, "A Reading of Steinbeck's "Flight,'" p. 45; Ditsky, "Steinbeck's 'Flight,'" p. 83.

23. Ditsky, "Steinbeck's 'Flight,'" p. 82.

24. Lisca, *Wide World of Steinbeck*, p. 100.

25. Vogel, "Steinbeck's 'Flight,'" p. 226.

26. Chapin, "Pepe Torres," p. 676.

27. Ditsky, "Steinbeck's 'Flight,'" p. 84.

28. French, *John Steinbeck*, 1st ed., p. 137; Levant, *The Novels of John Steinbeck*, p. 197.

29. Sydney J. Krause, "*The Pearl* and 'Hadleyburg': From Desire to Renunciation," *Steinbeck Quarterly* 7 (Winter 1974): 4.

30. Ibid., p. 6.

31. Fontenrose, *John Steinbeck: An Introduction and Interpretation*, p. 114.

32. Ibid., p. 112.

33. Ibid., p. 114.

34. Ibid.

35. Levant, *The Novels of John Steinbeck*, pp. 191–92.

36. For a discussion of *The Pearl* and Twain's "The Man that Corrupted Hadleyburg," see Krause, "*The Pearl* and 'Hadleyburg.'" Krause places both works in the naturalistic vein of American literature.

37. French, *John Steinbeck*, 1st ed., p. 139; Levant, *The Novels of John Steinbeck*, pp. 204–5; Krause, "*The Pearl* and 'Hadleyburg,'" p. 14; Fontenrose, *John Steinbeck: An Introduction and Interpretation*, p. 114.

38. Steinbeck, "My Short Novels," *Wings*, October 1953, p. 4.

39. Arnold L. Goldsmith, "Thematic Rhythm in *The Red Pony*," in *Steinbeck: A Collection of Critical Essays*, ed. Robert Murray Davis (Englewood Cliffs, N.J.: Prentice-Hall, 1972), pp. 72, 70; Fontenrose, *John Steinbeck: An Introduction and Interpretation*, p. 64; Lisca, *Wide World of Steinbeck*, p. 10; Robert M. Benton, "Realism, Growth, and Contrast in 'The Gift,'" *Steinbeck Quarterly* 6 (Winter 1973): 3.

40. Richard F. Peterson, "The Grail Legend and Steinbeck's 'The Great Mountains,'" *Steinbeck Quarterly* 6 (Winter 1973): 9.

41. Ibid., pp. 12, 13.

42. Clifford Lawrence Lewis, "John Steinbeck: Architect of the Unconscious" (Ph.D. diss., University of Texas at Austin, 1972), p. 104; Peter Lisca, *John Steinbeck: Nature and Myth* (New York: Thomas Y. Crowell, 1975), p. 198.

43. Lisca, *Wide World of Steinbeck*, p. 103; Lewis, "John Steinbeck: Architect of the Unconscious," p. 106.

44. Robert DeMott cites Steinbeck's relationship with Campbell in

"Toward a Redefinition of *To a God Unknown*." For a discussion of Steinbeck's war dispatches, see my essay "The Threshold of War: Steinbeck's Quest in *Once There Was a War*," *Steinbeck Quarterly* 13, nos. 3–4 (1980): 80–86.

45. John Ditsky, "*The Wayward Bus*: Love and Time in America," *San Jose Studies* 1 (November 1975): 94.

46. Ibid., p. 97.

47. Ibid., p. 95.

48. Ibid., p. 93.

49. Levant, *The Novels of John Steinbeck*, pp. 224–25.

50. Lisca, *Wide World of Steinbeck*, p. 241; Antonia Seixas, quoted in Levant, *The Novels of John Steinbeck*, p. 214.

51. Ditsky, "*The Wayward Bus*: Love and Time in America," p. 100.

52. F. W. Watt, *Steinbeck* (Edinburgh and London: Oliver and Boyd, 1962), p. 88.

53. Quoted in Thomas Kiernan, *The Intricate Music: A Biography of John Steinbeck* (Boston: Little, Brown, 1979), p. 281.

Chapter Two: The Valleys

1. For a brief history of *The Pastures of Heaven*, see Astro, *Steinbeck and Ricketts*, pp. 95–96.

2. Lisca, *John Steinbeck: Nature and Myth*, p. 54; Lewis, "John Steinbeck: Architect of the Unconscious," p. 52; Slotkin, *Regeneration Through Violence*, p. 17.

3. Slotkin, *Regeneration Through Violence*, p. 22.

4. Lewis, "John Steinbeck: Architect of the Unconscious," p. 52; Lisca, *John Steinbeck: Nature and Myth*, p. 54; Fontenrose, *John Steinbeck: An Introduction and Interpretation*, p. 28; Levant, *The Novels of John Steinbeck*, p. 37; John Ditsky, "Faulkner Land and Steinbeck Country," in *Steinbeck: The Man and His Work*, ed. Richard Astro and Tetsumaro Hayashi (Corvallis: Oregon State University Press, 1971), p. 15.

5. Levant, *The Novels of John Steinbeck*, p. 36; Lisca, *John Steinbeck: Nature and Myth*, p. 48.

6. Steinbeck, quoted in Lewis, "John Steinbeck: Architect of the Unconscious," p. 51.

7. Ibid., p. 54.

8. Lisca, *John Steinbeck: Nature and Myth*, p. 50; Levant, *The Novels of John Steinbeck*, p. 40; Fontenrose, *John Steinbeck: An Introduction and Interpretation*, p. 26; Warren French, *John Steinbeck*, 2d ed., rev. (Boston: Twayne, 1975), p. 57.

9. Fontenrose, *John Steinbeck: An Introduction and Interpretation*, p. 28.

10. Lisca, *Wide World of Steinbeck*, pp. 64–65; Levant, *The Novels of John Steinbeck*, p. 43.

11. Levant, *The Novels of John Steinbeck*, p. 43.

12. Fontenrose, *John Steinbeck: An Introduction and Interpretation*, p. 24.

13. French, *John Steinbeck*, 2d ed., p. 61.

14. Astro, *Steinbeck and Ricketts*, p. 103.

15. Ibid., p. 97.

16. French, *John Steinbeck*, 2d ed., p. 76; Fontenrose, *John Steinbeck: An Introduction and Interpretation*, p. 43; Lisca, *John Steinbeck: Nature and Myth*, p. 68.

17. Fontenrose, *John Steinbeck: An Introduction and Interpretation*, pp. 44ff., 50; Lisca, *John Steinbeck: Nature and Myth*, p. 76.

18. An excellent study of Steinbeck's sources for *In Dubious Battle* is Jackson J. Benson and Anne Loftis, "John Steinbeck and Farm Labor Unionization: The Background of *In Dubious Battle*," *American Literature* 52 (May 1980): 194–223.

19. Levant, *The Novels of John Steinbeck*, p. 50.

20. Fontenrose, *John Steinbeck: An Introduction and Interpretation*, p. 58.

21. French, *John Steinbeck*, 2d ed., pp. 78, 79.

22. Astro, *Steinbeck and Ricketts*, pp. 122, 12–14; Lisca, *John Steinbeck: Nature and Myth*, pp. 65, 71.

23. For a discussion of Steinbeck's treatment of group-man and his biological thinking in relation to communist ideology in *In Dubious Battle*, see Sylvia Cook, "Steinbeck, the People, and the Party," *Steinbeck Quarterly* 15, nos. 1–2 (Winter–Spring 1982): 11–23.

24. Steinbeck, quoted in Lewis, "John Steinbeck: Architect of the Unconscious," p. 124.

25. Levant, *The Novels of John Steinbeck*, p. 55; Astro, *Steinbeck and Ricketts*, p. 126; Linda Ray Pratt, "In Defense of Mac's Dubious Battle," *Steinbeck Quarterly* 10 (Spring 1977): 42.

26. Pratt, "In Defense of Mac's Dubious Battle," pp. 37, 42.

27. Both quotations are in Lewis, "John Steinbeck: Architect of the Unconscious," p. 125.

28. Astro, *Steinbeck and Ricketts*, p. 128.

29. Fontenrose, *John Steinbeck: An Introduction and Interpretation*, p. 59; Lisca, *John Steinbeck: Nature and Myth*, p. 82; Donald Pizer, "John Steinbeck and American Naturalism," *Steinbeck Quarterly* 9 (Winter 1976): 13.

30. Fontenrose, *John Steinbeck: An Introduction and Interpretation*, p. 57; Levant, *The Novels of John Steinbeck*, p. 134.

31. Steinbeck is quoted in Fontenrose, *John Steinbeck: An Introduction and Interpretation*, p. 57.

32. Ibid., p. 59.

33. Astro, *Steinbeck and Ricketts*, p. 104.

34. Lisca, *John Steinbeck: Nature and Myth*, pp. 78–79.

35. John Ditsky, "Ritual Murder in Steinbeck's Dramas," *Steinbeck Quarterly* 11 (Summer–Fall 1978): 73; Joan Steele, "A Century of Idiots: *Barnaby Rudge* and *Of Mice and Men*," *Steinbeck Quarterly* 5 (Winter 1972): 16.

36. Fontenrose, *John Steinbeck: An Introduction and Interpretation*, p. 57; French, *John Steinbeck*, 2d ed., p. 91.

37. Astro, *Steinbeck and Ricketts*, p. 112.

38. For a study of this story, see Robert Benton, "Breakfast I and II," in *A Study Guide to Steinbeck's "The Long Valley,"* ed. Tetsumaro Hayashi (Ann Arbor, Mich.: Piernan Press, 1976), pp. 33–39.

39. French, *John Steinbeck*, 2d ed., p. 83; Fontenrose, *John Steinbeck: An Introduction and Interpretation*, pp. 63, 59; Reloy Garcia, "Steinbeck's 'The Snake': An Explication," in *A Study Guide to Steinbeck's "The Long Valley,"* ed. Hayashi, p. 26; Brian M. Barbour, "Steinbeck as a Short Story Writer," in *A Study Guide to Steinbeck's "The Long Valley,"* ed. Hayashi, p. 118.

40. Barbour, "Steinbeck as a Short Story Writer," p. 112; Mordecai Marcus, "The Lost Dream of Sex and Childbirth in 'The Chrysanthemums,'" *Modern Fiction Studies* 11 (Spring 1965): 54.

41. French, *John Steinbeck*, 1st ed., p. 83; Elizabeth E. McMahan, "'The Chrysanthemums': Study of a Woman's Sexuality," *Modern Fiction Studies* 14 (1968): 453–58; William V. Miller, "Sexual and Spiritual Ambiguity in 'The Chrysanthemums,'" in *A Study Guide to Steinbeck's "The Long Valley,"* ed. Hayashi; Roy S. Simmonds, "The Original

Manuscripts of Steinbeck's 'The Chrysanthemums,' " *Steinbeck Quarterly* 7 (Summer–Fall 1974): 107.

42. Marcus, "Lost Dream," p. 57; McMahan, " 'The Chrysanthemums,' " pp. 453–55; Miller, "Sexual and Spiritual Ambiguity," p. 72.

43. McMahan, " 'The Chrysanthemums,' " p. 458; Marcus, "Lost Dream," p. 57.

44. Simmonds, "Original Manuscripts," p. 108.

45. Fontenrose, *John Steinbeck: An Introduction and Interpretation*, p. 63.

46. French, *John Steinbeck*, 1st ed., p. 85; Fontenrose, *John Steinbeck: An Introduction and Interpretation*, p. 61; Arthur L. Simpson, Jr., " 'The White Quail': A Portrait of an Artist," in *A Study Guide to Steinbeck's "The Long Valley,"* ed. Hayashi, p. 77.

47. Fontenrose, *Steinbeck: An Introduction and Interpretation*, p. 63.

48. Barbour, "Steinbeck as a Short Story Writer," p. 118.

49. See "John Steinbeck's Acceptance Speech for the Nobel Prize for Literature in 1962," in *A Casebook on "The Grapes of Wrath,"* ed. Agnes McNeill Donohue (New York: Thomas Y. Crowell, 1968), pp. 293ff.

50. Barbour, "Steinbeck as a Short Story Writer," p. 117.

51. Clifford Lawrence Lewis provides convincing evidence that "The Harness" originally evolved as part of "The Chrysanthemums." See "John Steinbeck: Architect of the Unconscious," p. 117.

52. Fontenrose, " 'The Harness,' " in *A Study Guide to Steinbeck's "The Long Valley,"* ed. Hayashi, p. 49.

53. Warren French, " 'Johnny Bear'—Steinbeck's 'Yellow Peril' Story," in *A Study Guide to Steinbeck's "The Long Valley,"* ed. Hayashi, p. 57; Lisca, *Wide World of Steinbeck*, p. 96; Barbour, "Steinbeck as a Short Story Writer," p. 119.

54. Katherine M. Morseberger and Robert E. Morseberger, " 'The Murder'—Realism or Ritual?" in *A Study Guide to Steinbeck's "The Long Valley,"* ed. Hayashi, pp. 65, 66, 70; French, *John Steinbeck*, 1st ed., p. 86; Barbour, "Steinbeck as a Short Story Writer," p. 120.

55. Barbour, "Steinbeck as a Short Story Writer," p. 120; Morseberger and Morseberger, " 'The Murder'—Realism or Ritual?' " p. 70.

56. Roy S. Simmonds, "Steinbeck's 'The Murder': A Critical and Bibliographical Study," *Steinbeck Quarterly* 9 (Spring 1976): 46.

57. Morseberger and Morseberger, " 'The Murder'—Realism or Ritual?" p. 70.

58. Simmonds, "Steinbeck's 'The Murder,' " p. 47. In this essay Simmonds offers convincing evidence that "The Murder" may have been originally intended as one of the episodes in *The Pastures of Heaven*, a fact which Simmonds cites as a possible reason for the story's inconclusiveness.

59. Ibid., pp. 45, 47.

60. Edmund Wilson, "From Classics and Commercials," in *A Casebook on "The Grapes of Wrath,"* ed. Donohue, pp. 151–52.

61. Peter Lisca, " 'The Raid' and *In Dubious Battle*," in *A Study Guide to Steinbeck's "The Long Valley,"* ed. Hayashi, p. 41.

62. Malcolm Cowley, quoted in Lewis, "John Steinbeck: Architect of the Unconscious," p. 152.

63. Astro, *Steinbeck and Ricketts*, pp. 128ff.; Martin Shockley, "Christian Symbolism in *The Grapes of Wrath*," in *A Casebook on "The Grapes of Wrath,"* ed. Donohue, pp. 90–95.

64. Lester Marks, *Thematic Continuity in the Novels of John Steinbeck* (The Hague: Mouton, 1969), p. 79; Agnes McNeill Donohue, " 'The Endless Journey to No End': Journey and Eden Symbolism in Hawthorne and Steinbeck," in *A Casebook on "The Grapes of Wrath,"* ed. Donohue, p. 261.

65. Duane R. Carr, "Steinbeck's Blakean Vision in *The Grapes of Wrath*," *Steinbeck Quarterly* 8 (Summer–Fall 1975): 59.

66. Chester E. Eisenger, "Jeffersonian Agrarianism in *The Grapes of Wrath*," in *A Casebook on "The Grapes of Wrath,"* ed. Donohue, p. 147.

67. Donohue, "Endless Journey," p. 261.

68. Frederick Carpenter, "The Philosophical Joads," in *A Casebook on "The Grapes of Wrath,"* ed. Donohue, p. 89.

69. Warren French, "John Steinbeck and Modernism," in *Steinbeck's Prophetic Vision of America*, ed. Tetsumaro Hayashi and Kenneth D. Swan, Proceedings of the Bicentennial Steinbeck Seminar, 1 May 1976 (Upland, Ind.: Taylor University, 1976), p. 51.

70. Donohue, "Endless Journey," pp. 264–65.

71. Ditsky, "Faulkner Land and Steinbeck Country," p. 19. In more recent criticism, Patrick W. Shaw has defined Tom's journey as a "psychic journey from isolato to prophet." See "Tom's Other Trip: Psycho-Physical Questing in *The Grapes of Wrath*," *Steinbeck Quarterly* 16, nos. 1–2 (Winter–Spring 1983): 17–25.

72. Peter Lisca, "Escape and Commitment: Two Poles of the Stein-

beck Hero," in *Steinbeck: The Man and His Work,* ed. Astro and Hayashi, p. 83.

73. For a suggestion of antecedents in folklore and literature for this scene, see Celeste Wright's essay "Ancient Analogues of an Incident in John Steinbeck," in *A Casebook on "The Grapes of Wrath,"* ed. Donohue, pp. 159–61.

74. Donohue, "Endless Journey," p. 265.

75. Carr, "Steinbeck's Blakean Vision," p. 59.

76. Eric W. Carlson, "Symbolism in *The Grapes of Wrath,"* in *A Casebook on "The Grapes of Wrath,"* ed. Donohue, p. 100.

77. French, *John Steinbeck,* 2d ed., p. 141.

78. Steinbeck, quoted in Valjean, *John Steinbeck the Errant Knight,* p. 123.

79. Lisca, *John Steinbeck: Nature and Myth,* pp. 163–64.

80. John Ditsky, *Essays on "East of Eden,"* Steinbeck Monograph Series, no. 7 (Muncie, Ind.: Ball State University, 1977), p. 17.

81. French, *John Steinbeck,* 2d ed., p. 143.

82. Lisca, *John Steinbeck: Nature and Myth,* p. 163; French, *John Steinbeck,* 2d ed., p. 149; Levant, *The Novels of John Steinbeck,* p. 237; Ditsky, *Essays on "East of Eden,"* p. ix.

83. See my essay "The Threshold of War: Steinbeck's Quest in *Once There Was a War,"* *Steinbeck Quarterly* 13 (Summer–Fall 1980): 80–86.

84. French, *John Steinbeck,* 2d ed., pp. 149–50.

85. Clifford Lawrence Lewis, "John Steinbeck: Architect of the Unconscious," p. 261; R. W. B. Lewis, *The American Adam: Innocence, Tragedy, and Tradition in the Nineteenth Century* (Chicago: University of Chicago Press, 1955), p. 2.

86. Steinbeck, quoted in Lisca, *John Steinbeck: Nature and Myth,* p. 164.

87. Levant, *The Novels of John Steinbeck,* p. 242.

88. Ibid., p. 239.

89. Fontenrose, *John Steinbeck: An Introduction and Interpretation,* p. 126.

90. Steinbeck, quoted in Clifford Lawrence Lewis, "John Steinbeck: Architect of the Unconscious," p. 259.

91. R. W. B. Lewis, *The American Adam,* p. 1.

92. Steinbeck, quoted in Clifford Lawrence Lewis, "John Steinbeck: Architect of the Unconscious," p. 273.

93. Ditsky, *Essays on "East of Eden,"* p. 13.

94. Lisca, *John Steinbeck: Nature and Myth,* p. 169.

Chapter Three: The Sea

1. For information concerning the genesis of this volume, see Lisca, *Wide World of Steinbeck,* pp. 197–98.

2. For a discussion of Steinbeck's symbolism in *Once There Was a War,* see my essay "The Threshold of War."

3. Lisca, *Wide World of Steinbeck,* p. 197.

4. Garcia, "Steinbeck's 'The Snake,'" pp. 29–30; Charles E. May, "Myth and Mystery in Steinbeck's 'The Snake': A Jungian View," *Criticism* 15 (Fall 1973): 324–25.

5. For an account of the real experience, see *The Log from the Sea of Cortez,* pp. xxiii–xxiv.

6. J. E. Cirlot, *A Dictionary of Symbols,* trans. Jack Sage (London: Routledge and Kegan Paul, 1962), pp. 285–90.

7. May, "Myth and Mystery," p. 328.

8. Cirlot, *A Dictionary of Symbols,* p. 286.

9. May, "Myth and Mystery," p. 325.

10. Lisca, *Wide World of Steinbeck,* p. 78, and *John Steinbeck: Nature and Myth,* p. 61; French, *John Steinbeck,* 2d ed., pp. 57, 71; Arthur F. Kinney, "*Tortilla Flat* Re-Visited," in *Steinbeck and the Arthurian Theme,* ed. Tetsumaro Hayashi, Steinbeck Monograph Series, no. 5 (Muncie, Ind.: Ball State University, 1975), p. 18; Levant, *The Novels of John Steinbeck,* pp. 53–54.

11. Fontenrose, *John Steinbeck: An Introduction and Interpretation,* p. 36.

12. Arthur F. Kinney, "The Arthurian Cycle in *Tortilla Flat,*" in *Steinbeck: A Collection of Critical Essays,* ed. Robert M. Davis (Englewood Cliffs, N.J.: Prentice-Hall, 1972), p. 44.

13. Kinney, "*Tortilla Flat* Re-Visited," p. 19.

14. Steinbeck, quoted in Clifford Lawrence Lewis, "John Steinbeck: Architect of the Unconscious," p. 80.

15. Ballou, quoted in Lisca, *Wide World of Steinbeck,* p. 74.

16. Levant, *The Novels of John Steinbeck,* pp. 53, 63.

17. Kinney, "*Tortilla Flat* Re-Visited," p. 22.

18. For a discussion of the effects of the paisanos' Indian heritage,

see Clifford Lawrence Lewis, "John Steinbeck: Architect of the Unconscious," p. 81–82.

19. Both quotations are in French, *John Steinbeck*, 2d ed., p. 73.

20. For a brief summary of early criticism of this novel, see Lisca, *Wide World of Steinbeck*, pp. 197–98.

21. French, *John Steinbeck*, 2d ed., p. 124.

22. Steinbeck, quoted in Lisca, *Wide World of Steinbeck*, pp. 198–99, 208.

23. Stanley Alexander, "*Cannery Row:* Steinbeck's Pastoral Poem," in *Steinbeck: A Collection of Critical Essays*, ed. Davis, p. 136.

24. Ricketts, quoted in Lisca, *Wide World of Steinbeck*, p. 217.

25. Alexander, "*Cannery Row:* Steinbeck's Pastoral Poem," p. 136.

26. Lisca, *Wide World of Steinbeck*, p. 210.

27. Fontenrose, *John Steinbeck: An Introduction and Interpretation*, pp. 107–8; Lisca, *John Steinbeck: Nature and Myth*, p. 112.

28. Astro, *Steinbeck and Ricketts*, p. 159.

29. Lisca, *Wide World of Steinbeck*, p. 212.

30. Astro, *Steinbeck and Ricketts*, p. 161.

31. Lisca, *Wide World of Steinbeck*, p. 211.

32. French, *John Steinbeck*, 2d ed., p. 123.

33. Levant, *The Novels of John Steinbeck*, p. 178.

34. Astro, *Steinbeck and Ricketts*, p. 167.

35. Lisca, *Wide World of Steinbeck*, p. 215.

36. See Lisca, *Wide World of Steinbeck*, pp. 276–77.

37. Warren French, *John Steinbeck*, 1st ed., p. 156.

38. Ibid., p. 155.

Conclusion

1. Peter Lisca suggests that this shift in Steinbeck's approach begins to be evident as early as *Burning Bright* in 1950. See Lisca's "Steinbeck's Image of Man and His Decline as a Writer," *Modern Fiction Studies* 11, no. 1 (Spring 1965): 5.

2. Elaine Steinbeck apparently noted this problem in the manuscript stage, stating in retrospect: "It was awfully false and coy to me, but that was the one thing I couldn't say to John. I didn't like it at all." Quoted in Jackson J. Benson, *True Adventures of John Steinbeck, Writer* (New York: Viking Press, 1984), p. 872.

3. Warren French, "Steinbeck's Winter Tale," *Modern Fiction Studies* 11, no. 1 (Spring 1965): 67; Joseph Fontenrose, *John Steinbeck: An Introduction and Interpretation*, p. 137; Lisca, "Steinbeck's Image of Man," p. 10.

4. See Donald Stone's "Steinbeck, Jung, and *The Winter of Our Discontent*," *Steinbeck Quarterly* 11, nos. 3–4 (Summer–Fall 1978): 87–95; and Donna Gerstenberger's "Steinbeck's American Waste Land," *Modern Fiction Studies* 11, no. 1 (Spring 1965): 59–65. Still a third very perceptive reading of this novel is Charles T. Clancy's "Light in *The Winter of Our Discontent*," *Steinbeck Quarterly* 9, nos. 3–4 (Summer–Fall 1976): 91–101.

5. Steinbeck, quoted in Benson, *True Adventures*, p. 966.

6. Ibid., p. 858.

7. Lisca, "Steinbeck's Image of Man," p. 10.

8. Frazer, *The Golden Bough*, pp. 1ff.

9. Gerstenberger, "Steinbeck's American Waste Land," p. 12.

10. Weston, *From Ritual to Romance*, p. 115.

11. Ibid., p. 182.

12. Richard Cavendish, *King Arthur and the Grail* (New York: Taplinger, 1981), p. 71.

13. Ibid., p. 94.

14. Ibid., p. 170.

15. Steinbeck, quoted in Benson, *True Adventures*, p. 811.

16. Thomas Malory, *King Arthur and His Knights: Selected Tales*, ed. Eugene Vinaver (London: Oxford University Press, 1975), p. 109.

INDEX

223

Index